THE LIBERATED MAN

THE
LIBERATED
MAN

Beyond Masculinity:
Freeing Men and Their
Relationships with Women

Warren Farrell

RANDOM HOUSE NEW YORK

Library of Congress Cataloging in Publication Data
Farrell, Warren.
   The liberated man.
   Includes bibliographies.
   1. Men—Psychology. 2. Sex role. 3. Group rela-
tions training. I. Title.
HQ1067.F37   301.41'1   74–8045
ISBN 0–394–49024–X

Grateful acknowledgment is made to the following for permission to reprint previously published material:

William Morrow and Company, Inc.: For "Revolutionary Dreams" from *My House* by Nikki Giovanni. Copyright © 1972 by Nikki Giovanni.

Jules Feiffer: For the cartoon "In the beginning . . ." Copyright © 1972 by Jules Feiffer.

This book is dedicated to Ursie

eachother

Peace passing through the walls . . .
Hand passing through the hair . . .
Developing our sense of potential . . .
Knowing eachother is there . . .

Balancing security and freedom . . .
Growing each week, each day . . .
Seeing the one bud of love
Slowly become a bouquet.

Acknowledgments

My deepest acknowledgment and gratitude is to my immediate family: Ursie, Tom, Muriel, Lee, Gail and Wayne. Each has played an important role in this book by tes contribution to my identity, by bringing me up normally enough to experience the early upbringing of many boys and independently enough to question it. My gratitude to Jim Crown who saved me for the academic world by teaching me how to be human in it—teaching me not so much by what he said as by what he is. To Ted Becker, for restarting me by stopping me; to my men's consciousness-raising groups at Alternate U., at NOW and our joint group—all of whose names I must keep anonymous, but who have been, outside of my family, the most important people during my recent life—and the only ones to have shared almost every change in value and being. I acknowledge especially the exceptional dedication of Janet Burak Gordon, Deke Dusinberre, Karen Rosenblum-Cale, Phyllis Couvares, Nancy Kelton, Sue Shafer, Loraine Hutchins and Larry Zeller, each of whom assisted competently in the research of this book.

My appreciation goes to each of the following for unique contributions to the book: the staff of the Kinsey Institute for Sex Research; the Board of New York City NOW; the 240 men whom I interviewed and who completed the 217 variable questionnaire on women's liberation (and half of whom read 17 articles of women's liberation literature); Jacqui Ceballos; Ivy Bottini; Betty Freidan; Carol Tavris (for suggestions on the questionnaire); Kate Swift; Nina Finkelstein; Leonore Fleisher; Lynn Loraido; Evelyn Challis; Norman Mailer (for permission to print his letter); persons in the more than one hundred men's and joint consciousness-raising groups from which I received feedback as I worked with them.

Important contributions also came from Wilma Scott Heide, Elizabeth Duncan Koontz, Catherine East, the staff of the Women's Bureau, U.S. Dept. of Labor, Harriet Lyons, Gloria Steinem, Eleanor Freide, Joann and Bob Brannon, Dorothy Crouch, Elizabeth Janeway, Phil Donahue, Sidney Weinheimer, Bob Gould, Ann and Howie Rubin, Fred Hipp, Larry De Nardis, Mimi and John Lobell, Nancy Inglis, Toni Morrison, Bob Datilla, Martha Winston, Ned Foss, Bunny Sandler, Ilene Barth, Jane Sorenson, Edyth Cudlipp, Laureen Helen, Mary Jo Binder, Audrey Siess Wells, Joan Nicholson, Judith Hennessee, Lee Walker and hundreds of others whom space does not permit me to include.

Contents

Before The Liberated Man:
Questionnaire on Feelings toward Women and Masculinity

Instructions: Although this questionnaire is basically designed for men, women can take it by modifying some of the questions. Part I, attitudes toward women, is more amenable to this than Part II, which focuses on masculinity. While there is a scoring mechanism on page 367, in the final analysis being beyond masculinity includes an ability to use the questionnaire to rethink one's attitudes toward women and masculinity without worrying about "outscoring" someone else. Take the questionnaire *before* and *after* you read the book to see if you have modified any of your thinking.

PART I: ATTITUDES TOWARD WOMEN AND WOMEN'S LIBERATION

1. If the aims of the women's liberation movement are reached, how do you think they will affect men?
   _____ a) Men will gain much more than they lose.
   _____ b) Men will gain and lose about an equal amount.
   _____ c) Men will have to sacrifice more than they gain.
   _____ d) It will not really affect men.

Indicate the extent of your agreement or disagreement with each of the following questions:

	Strongly Agree	Agree	Disagree	Strongly Disagree
2. Children of working mothers tend to be *more* well-adjusted than children of unemployed women.	___	___	___	___
3. The natural childbearing function of women gives her a natural role as protector of the child and maintainer of the home.	___	___	___	___
4. Most of the women in women's liberation want to have their cake and eat it too; for example, they want				

xi

equal rights but are unwilling to be drafted, pay alimony or even light their own
cigarettes.   ____   ____   ____   ____

5. If your daughter was about to marry and asked your advice as to
   whether she should keep her maiden name in addition to her
   married name, what would you advise?
   ____ a) She should.
   ____ b) She probably should not.
   ____ c) She definitely should not.

6. If you were to choose an ideal attaché* or living friend, which
   would come closest to some of the characteristics you would like her
   to have?
   ____ a) Good cook, efficient homemaker, sexually attractive and a
           willing helper.
   ____ b) All of point a plus being intellectually your equal, ad-
           vising and correcting you as frequently as you advise
           and correct her.
   ____ c) All of point a plus being intellectually your superior,
           capable of holding a better position and making more
           money. Although her willingness is not less, her time
           to help you is less.
   ____ d) Intellectually your equal, but demanding her own career,
           a sharing of the housework and cooking and being
           about as capable at housework and cooking as you are.
   ____ e) Interesting person, intellectually capable, enthusiastic
           about life, willing to assume a responsible career,
           kind, thoughtful, poor housekeeper.

7. If you were to give your attaché a subscription to three magazines
   for her birthday, which three would you choose?

a. McCall's	e. Playboy	j. Ramparts
b. Better Homes & Gardens	f. Reader's Digest	k. Ms.
c. Ladies' Home Journal	g. Saturday Review	l. New Republic
d. Cosmopolitan	h. U.S. News & World Report	m. National Review
	i. Newsweek	n. Fortune
		o. Business Week

Choices are: 1. _____   2. _____   3. _____

Which three magazines would you choose for yourself?

1. _____   2. _____   3. _____

* See "Introducing Human Vocabulary."

8. Would you put your son in an adequately run child-care center while your attaché worked?

_____ yes   _____ no   _____ only part time

Your daughter?

_____ yes   _____ no   _____ only part time

Indicate your feelings about:	strongly favor	mod-erately favor	slightly favor	slightly oppose	mod-erately oppose	strongly oppose
9. Your own attaché having an abortion.	—	—	—	—	—	—
10. Child-rearing without regard for traditional sex-role stereotypes.	—	—	—	—	—	—
11. An end to sex-differentiated tracking in the educational system, e.g., so that women no longer are counseled into feminine careers.	—	—	—	—	—	—
12. An amendment to the U.S. Constitution to prohibit states and the federal government from passing laws which discriminate on the basis of sex.	—	—	—	—	—	—
13. Equal responsibility by man and woman for housekeeping.	—	—	—	—	—	—

14. Equal responsibility by man

and woman for
child-rearing
and child care
(including the
possibility the
man may take
off a year to
care for the
children) .   ___   ___   ___   ___   ___   ___

15. If you were in a hiring position would you hire a man with a family to support before a woman if the woman were only slightly better qualified?
___ a) yes   ___ b) no   ___ c) it would depend on (specify)

16. Do you think it is necessary for employers to be cautious about the hiring of women for career positions due to a tendency for women to leave too soon to get married, have children, or move with their attachés?
_____ a) Yes.
_____ b) Yes, unless there is evidence to the contrary.
_____ c) No.

17. The following include a few hypothetical situations. Please indicate how you feel about each of them.

A.) Your attaché suggests she is being discriminated against by society and that possibly even you are preventing her from developing herself. She wants to join an all-women group to discuss this every week. Do you:
_____ a) Strongly approve
_____ b) Moderately approve
_____ c) Feel uncertain, but that it is worth a try
_____ d) Moderately disapprove
_____ e) Strongly disapprove

B.) A man and woman come to your office to be hired as a secretary. The man is slightly more competent. Would you:
_____ a) Hire the man.
_____ b) Hire the woman.
_____ c) Hire the man unless there was a reason to believe he had homosexual tendencies.

C.) Miss D. is an attractive professional woman. She meets Mr. S. at a party and they are clearly attracted to each other. Before he can ask her to go to bed, she suggests that they spend the

night at her place. If you were Mr. S., how would you feel now?
(Neither Mr. S. or the woman is married.)

_____ a) Hesitant, but not sure why.

_____ b) Disappointed.

_____ c) That she has lost her femininity by initiating the encounter.

_____ d) Frightened at the aggressiveness of her approach.

_____ e) That she has become more provocative and interesting.

_____ f) Angry at her.

_____ g) My feelings would not change.

D.) If your attaché suggested that she would like to sleep with other men, how would you feel? (If she does, how do you feel?)

	Good	Not so good	Ugh!
On the intellectual level	_____	_____	_____
On the gut level	_____	_____	_____

18. For an attractive woman with whom you are well acquainted do you consider any of the following references to her offensive?

Yes	No		Yes	No	
_____	_____ a) Lady		_____	_____ d) Girl
_____	_____ b) Doll		_____	_____ e) Honey
_____	_____ c) Chick		_____	_____ f) Broad

19. When a pre-teenage girl says, "Daddy, I want to become a nurse," and a boy says, "I want to be an engineer," do you think these are examples of:

_____ a) the basic difference in direction that boys and girls pretty naturally take.

_____ b) a result of parental and peer-group influence (socialization).

_____ c) a combination of a and b.

_____ d) neither.

20. Would you consider the man-woman relationship that develops during the years of dating generally:

Yes	No	
_____	_____	1. Good for the maturity and independence of a woman?
_____	_____	2. Beneficial to the development of honesty in human relations?

21. Mr. and Ms. A. are both working in careers that provide much satisfaction and opportunity for personal growth. They are separately offered jobs in different cities that would greatly advance their careers. What is their best solution?

_____ a) Stay put.

_____ b) Mr. A. takes new job, attaché follows.

_____ c) Ms. A. takes new job, attaché follows.

_____ d) One partner takes the new job, decided by lot.

_____ e) Separate, each taking the job each wants, and see what happens.

22. Mr. and Ms. M share all household tasks and the care of their two small children. Both work half time, which reduces their income but allows them to maintain this family relationship. If you had just visited the M family and had an attaché, how would you feel about Mr. M?

_____ a) Worried, fearing my attaché might demand a similar arrangement.

_____ b) Think that M is probably somewhat weak and effeminate.

_____ c) Feel M is making a stupid decision since he is wasting his time and will never be successful.

_____ d) Think it is great that M has someone to share his economic responsibilities and permit him to spend more time with his family.

_____ e) Admire M but realize that I couldn't accept such an arrangement.

_____ f) Have no particular feelings one way or the other.

PART II. ATTITUDES TOWARD MEN AND MEN'S LIBERATION

1. If a man does something traditionally considered feminine, do you think he feels like less of a man?

_____ a) Always.

_____ b) Usually.

_____ c) Seldom.

_____ d) Never.

2. If *you* do something traditionally considered feminine, do you feel like less of a man?

_____ a) Always.

_____ b) Usually.

_____ c) Seldom.

_____ d) Never.

_____ e) I don't do traditionally feminine things.

3. Mention two significant ways in which you frequently reverse traditional roles with a woman (e.g., doing more than half of all the cooking):

_____ a)
_____ b)

4. You are asked to join a group of men to discuss your hangups about masculinity, and to develop a more liberated relationship with women. Would you join? (The group starts in a month.)
_____ a) Yes.
_____ b) I would probably give it a try.
_____ c) Probably not.
_____ d) No.

5. What do you feel most vulnerable about people discovering about you? (Write it out; be specific.) _____

_____
_____ a) I can't write it in the book where someone might see it.
_____ b) I can't think of anything I feel vulnerable about.
_____ c) I found myself making a joke out of this question.

6. Which areas do you feel vulnerable about revealing to a group of men friends who are your neighbors or colleagues at work?

	Very Vulnerable	Vulnerable	Feel Free
a) Your biggest failure that reflects negatively on your intelligence	_____	_____	_____
b) Impotence	_____	_____	_____
c) Sexual feelings toward other men	_____	_____	_____
d) Biggest problem in your relationship with your attaché	_____	_____	_____

7. With how many men friends have you recently discussed *two or more of these areas* in a way that applied to you?
_____ a) None
_____ b) One
_____ c) Two-three
_____ d) Four or more

8. You are at a high level meeting at work. A topic is on the agenda for which you have a reputation for being opposed to. You have to

make a new presentation of your point of view. In the meantime a convincing presentation is made by another person which invalidates your premise. What are you likely to do?

_____ a) Avoid the invalidation and try to focus on some of my strongest points.

_____ b) Admit to everyone, "I was wrong."

_____ c) I would have been too busy preparing my presentation to have heard it.

9. How would you feel about putting on your resumé "1972–74 I took care of my children."

_____ a) Never happen—irrelevant.

_____ b) Embarrassed—I'd have to explain what else I was doing that year.

_____ c) Good.

10. A) How do you feel about actually taking off from work for a year to take care of the children?

_____ a) Not so good.

_____ b) In theory great, but it's impractical in my case.

_____ c) Hesitant, but willing to try to work it out.

_____ d) Good idea—want to do it.

_____ e) I'm already doing it.

B) If you do not object, have children, but only your attaché has taken a year or more off, why is that? _____

11. During the past week, how many hours of sports events did you watch on TV?

_____ a) None

_____ b) 1–3

_____ c) 4–7

_____ d) eight or more

12. How many more hours per week do you think you could beneficially spend communicating with your attaché and/or child?

_____ a) None

_____ b) 1–3

_____ c) 4–7

_____ d) eight or more

13. Think of the name of the car you own (e.g., Ford Mustang, Dodge Charger). If your car were called Ford Pansy or Dodge Daisy how would you feel about owning it?

_____ a) The same as I feel now—no more or less embarrassed to pick up my boss or buddies in it.

_____ b) A bit more embarrassed than now.

_____ c) I probably would have chosen another car.

_____ d) I definitely would have chosen another car.

14. The last two times you and your attaché went to a social event together, who drove the car?

_____ a) me both times

_____ b) once each

_____ c) her both times

15. Have you ever smoked an Eve cigarette in public? (If you don't smoke, would you ever smoke one in public?)

_____ yes   _____ no

16. It is your son's sixth birthday. How do you feel about giving him a doll?

	Good	Not So Good	Ugh!
On the intellectual level	_____	_____	_____
On the gut level	_____	_____	_____

17. You are attending a joint consciousness-raising group (men and women) with a group of women you have never met. You are particularly attracted to one. You are to do a group experiment of touching toes while sitting in a circle. You situate yourself across from the woman you like. The lights are turned off and you and she start touching. You get turned on. The lights are turned on and you realize you and she are *NOT* touching each other—that you have been caressing another *man's* foot. How do you feel?

_____ a) Repulsed

_____ b) Turned off, but not repulsed

_____ c) Turned on at the recognition I could get turned on to another man

_____ d) Recognize that I was only turned on because I fantasized a woman

_____ e) I would not have done the experiment to begin with.

18. You are just arriving at a party. Four or five men are gathered in one corner and four or five women are gathered in another. Toward which group are you most likely to drift?

_____ a) Men

_____ b) Women

19. You read in the morning news that tests on vasectomies show they are now completely reversible. Do you think you will get one? (Assume you do not want children for two years or longer.)

_____ a) Definitely—no fears

_____ b) Definitely, although I would need to talk out my fears

_____ c) Probably
_____ d) Unlikely
_____ e) No
_____ f) Already have a vasectomy

20. I think I develop sexual relationships with women faster than most men.
_____ a) True
_____ b) False

21. You are at the office. Your boss tells you that you will not get a raise due to your inadequate work and calls you in for an interview with his boss. On the way in you get a telegram that a loved one has died. What are the chances of your crying during the interview?
_____ a) None
_____ b) Unlikely
_____ c) Good
_____ d) Definitely

	Past month	Past year	Past 3 years	Can't recall (or over 3 years)
22. When was the last time you cried?	_____	_____	_____	_____
23. When was the last time you cried in public?	_____	_____	_____	_____

24. Your attaché proposes that since she has taken on your family name for the past few years, that just for this next year you should assume her original family name. Write it out (e.g., Ms. Linda Lovelace's attaché might become Larry Lovelace) : _____.
How do you feel about adopting that name (your attaché's) for a year or more?
_____ a) No way!
_____ b) Don't like the idea, but if it was really important to her, I'd consider it.
_____ c) Like the idea—seriously consider it.
_____ d) I'm already doing it!

25. When you first heard of men's liberation, was your reaction closer to:
_____ a) "I think I could learn something from that" or
_____ b) "I don't think I need liberating."

26. Would you have taken this questionnaire if there were no way of scoring it?

_____ a) Yes

_____ b) No

_____ c) Uncertain

27. *Essay question* (Unscorable)

If you could do anything you wanted to do *outside* of your present area of interest, what would you choose? What barriers prevent you? Jot down some alternative ways of overcoming those barriers.

A Personal Introduction . . .

Writing this book has changed my life. The achievements that preceded this change and some that followed are mentioned in the "Note on the Author." That description is the me without doubts, uncertainties, insecurities, faults. For years, the attempt to make that description impressive discouraged me from personalizing—or even considering writing a personal introduction—lest I reveal my weaknesses and limitations. Lest I lose my mystique. It discouraged me from concentrating on internal rewards such as warmth, openness and listening. No one introduced me as "Warren, a human being who listens." So I did not introduce myself to the world in those terms.

When I began *The Liberated Man* in 1969 I was three years into an "ideal" traditional marriage. Ursie, my attaché, worked, but at the outset did so primarily to put me through my Ph.D.—until I got my J.O.B. She ironed my shirts, cooked our meals, washed the dishes. I "helped," with no concept of the difference between helping and sharing the responsibility. Basically, she played Superwoman, while I played Superman. Superwoman then meant husband, home and career, but we expected that would change to Supermother—children, husband, home and "career-if-convenient." With the consciousness of the women's movement in 1969 we began questioning those priorities.

The women's movement meant a lot to me from the beginning. I had experienced my mother going into and out of depression as she went into and out of jobs. Yet she did not feel she should leave the children for a permanent job, although we were all in school. When I began seeing the pattern in neighbors and friends' parents I realized it was more than my mother's problem. But it took the women's movement to get me to see the pattern.

Perhaps the experience of this cycle encouraged me to devote psychological support to Ursie's job. But it is only in the past year that I have come to recognize that it wasn't my words of encouragement that encouraged Ursie, it was that I *needed* her to work. And on her job she felt needed. She was *experiencing* growth rather than my telling her she had the potential for growth. Simultaneously, I experienced my first major failure—failing a section of my Ph.D. exams in an attempt to rush through my degree and assume my primary breadwinning role. But my failure only added to Ursie's feeling of being needed, of taking herself seriously. And her seriousness took the pressure off of me. I could rethink my upwardly mobile pattern. It was my first insight into the connection between women's liberation and my own freedom.

What was wrong with my upwardly mobile pattern? After all, it was promising me $10,000 worth of scholarship money

and staff assistance (before the dollar was devalued!), access
to resource materials to complete my dissertation in a year,
the promise of a high-paying prestigious job when I came
out and a published dissertation. There was one catch. I
would, of course, do the dissertation in that field of political
science where the grant money was available. So I began to
specialize, taking courses I knew would help me in that position rather than courses that fit other areas of my interest.
I considered this specialization "maturity" (a woman could
"dabble," but I must prepare for a serious occupation). *It
was assumed the focus of my life could be bought by offering me money, power, prestige and publication—in essence,
male bribes.* And I almost took them. Gladly.

A turning point came when I saw some of my teachers
spending years of their life researching areas in which they
had lost interest but needed to continue for "just another
year" so they could publish the results. When they got
published they found themselves starting a new project in the
same sub-subfield. Why? Now they had a reputation, an investment in that area. Opportunities were "coming to *them.*"
They would be "silly to pursue new interests just now." This
was their chance to publish in the top journals, teach in the
top schools, and prove to themselves and their friends they
were competent men. That was my first insight into the
shortcomings of my upward mobility. But it took my failure
and Ursie's seriousness before I could reexamine myself.

Ursie's and my relationship was also beginning to change
as we both joined consciousness-raising groups. As she went
from "*helping* with the breadwinning" to "sharing the responsibility" for it, I went from "helping with the housework" to "sharing the responsibility" for it. In one men's
group we fantasized what this meant to our own freedom.
We found ourselves able to ask, "*First, what do I really want
to do, and second, how do I make a living doing it?*" When
we were asking "First, how do I make a living?" we tended to

limit ourselves to traditional fields that produced high income. When we asked first "What do I really want to do?" without considering income, more alternatives came to mind. And *then* we started working on the alternative ways of making a living doing it. We've found that we don't have to make a living all the time, a revelation that has given us the freedom to fail. It has been important for me, though, to make a living enough of the time so Ursie does not become the sole breadwinner, or the surrogate male subject to the male bribes.

My first attempt to apply this portion of liberation was a half success. I was interested in the politics of education. I heard of an opportunity to be an assistant grants director. I took it. But *I* still had not made the choice. I took what was there. I was not asking "What is the most interesting thing I could do in the politics of education?" and then trying to *create* a job doing it—or coming as close to doing it as my experience allowed. When I reasked the question that way the answer was "president of a university." I finally got up the courage to approach the president of New York University (N.Y.U.), explain that I wanted to do something with him that would help me learn whether being a university president was really my choice, or whether the *image* was my choice; that I did not want to spend my life finding out. We worked out an arrangement that was mutually beneficial: a half-year paid assistantship.

Something was happening as I was "becoming" an administrator. N.Y.U. was making a "man" out of me. Just prior to my first faculty senate meeting at N.Y.U., an administrator and I were discussing the doubts he had about a proposal he was preparing to present to the faculty senate. He spoke to me in a shaky voice, somewhat high-pitched, in confiding whispers of uncertainty. Then we walked into the meeting. He made his presentation. He spoke in a deep voice —steady and rational-logical. He revealed none of his doubts.

The first three faculty members supported his plan, the fourth called the question and it passed. The next day he explained to me how he had asked some of his "allies" to speak immediately following his presentation and asked another to call the question right after the supporters spoke. As an "up-and-coming young administrator" I was to be grateful for this "slice of reality." And I was. Until I looked at it a different way.

As I was grooving on this "games*man*ship" I understood his goal, like mine, was to get as high up as he could at N.Y.U. (or a similar institution). He knew intuitively that he had to appear confident and decisive, and speak in strong, deep, unemotional tones. That appearance became his personality. He had to gather allies. These became his friends. By trying to "psych out" in the institution, he was developing an institutional psychology that was hurting the decision-making process of the institution (the best decision might have evolved from a discussion of some of the weak areas of his plan). He was becoming a prisoner of the institution. I later connected this with our men's group. We had all fantasized being independent of an institution and spending our lives on more human goals. But we were all becoming less human and less independent of our institutions as we started climbing toward the top. Even a truckdriver in the group found himself working overtime until he hardly knew his children—but "it would be an insult to have the old lady go to work."

All of this created a crisis for me. I was beginning to see one connection after another between the problems of masculinity and women's liberation. But I was also in the middle of my research for a dissertation in political science. Yet wasn't this just the male dilemma—trying to get beyond being tied to my investments? For weeks I worked on alternatives—until I got my department to agree on a dissertation on sex roles and politics (summarized in the highlights chapter).

"This won't help your political science career," I was told. It
didn't. It just helped me.

I soon found that few of the creative thoughts coming
from my dissertation research could go in a dissertation. The
only outlet was a book, but that would postpone my finishing
the dissertation. And that would certainly not help my political science career! Liberating myself to write the book even
though it would postpone the dissertation was the first step
to *The Liberated Man* (formerly *Beyond Masculinity*—a
title I preferred).

From that point on each new experience seemed to add a
new perspective to the meaning of liberation. When I received a position teaching urban politics at Rutgers I found
myself questioning at faculty meetings without worrying
whose side I was on—a freedom that came only when I
stopped worrying about how far I would get.

Then came the ultimate test. Ursie applied to become a
White House Fellow (assistant to a Cabinet member). If she
got it, it would mean leaving Rutgers and moving to Washington. I went through a long supportive process despite
visions of her working—from my perspective—on the highest
level of corruption. She became a "Fellow." And me? "The
wife of a Fellow." I left my post at Rutgers in what appeared
a move for women's liberation. But it was also the biggest
step in my own freedom—freedom to switch fields, at least
temporarily, to teach the politics of sex roles, freedom to
teach part-time (at American University), to write and speak.
In essence, freedom to make a living doing what I had come
to love. But it wasn't as easy in the gut: being introduced as
"Ursie's husband," explaining why *I* was not the Fellow;
explaining to White House Fellows and spouses—predominantly high achievers and their supportive wives—why I was
teaching part-time. It was hardly a receptive audience for my
interests in changing sex roles. I had left my support groups
in New York and was experiencing the difficulties of moving

to a spouse's turf. To become myself I first had to unbecome
—unbecome the wife of a Fellow. I'm still working on it.

I have written this introduction personally because it represents the most difficult change for me—changing on the personal level. Different chapters in this book have meant the
most to me at different stages in that change process. Since
my first insights into my problems of masculinity were
through women's liberation, Chapter 10, on the examples of
women's liberation as men's liberation, meant the most to
me then—along with "Factual and Self-Fulfilling Myths."
Perhaps a person who feels te* is at that stage might wish
to start with those chapters and then return to Chapter 1.

Although Chapter 1 is a beginning chapter, which persons
into a human liberation view of women's and men's liberation will find quick reading, Chapter 2, "The Masculine
Value System," is one of the most difficult in the book. I
think it will be the most misinterpreted chapter, the most
oversimplified, but in the long run, the most important. It
needed five rewritings and is hopefully worth one rereading.

The remainder of Part I has received very positive reactions (based on early readings) from women who have done
a lot of thinking about sex roles and from men who have
not tried to seek "the exception to the rule." For the fault-
finding personality who hates a generality because te is sure
te does not fit it, I would suggest starting with Part III,
on consciousness-raising. Those chapters are the specific, personal experiences of two groups—a men's and joint (men
with women) consciousness-raising group. Ironically, while
the more general statements in the first chapters are based on
general patterns evolving from experience with over a hundred men's and joint consciousness-raising groups, many
readers relate more easily to one personal example. Men

---

* Te = he or she; tes = his or her, tir = him or her. See "Introducing Human
  Vocabulary."

especially feel less defensive about identifying with a portion of the problems of another person than with perhaps a more technically accurate picture which suggests the problem may be them.

My experience is that men—no matter what age or class background—will often respond, "I'm different," or "That's relevant to older (or younger) men, but not me." They play *"man the fault-finder,"* looking for what does not apply, rather than what does, hoping to dismiss the whole chapter by finding an irrelevant example. They lecture the "irrelevant" portion to their attaché, rather than *asking,* "Do you think any of this applies to me in a way I might be overlooking?" In coed college courses with equal numbers of men and women, the male denial usually predominates, inhibiting the woman from saying why the observation might match her experience. In women's groups these observations come out. The one consolation is that, for all the denial, many men remember the generality they are incensed by and will sometimes see it in themselves a few days later. (If you reacted defensively to these general patterns, it might be best to start with the consciousness-raising section.)

On a daily basis, some of the most defensive reactions by men come with attempts to change vocabulary. "Why," a man asks, "must I say 'salesperson'? Salesman is generic, as is mankind. My actions count, not the rhetoric." Yet no one says "the secretary, he" and claims it is generic (unless they mean the Secretary of State) . I have been finding that in the case of vocabulary, words are a type of action—an action in raising consciousness. When someone does say "he or she" in referring to a secretary, even if the person is standing before a typing pool of all women, the rhetoric does make us wonder why someone in that typing pool is not a man.

I have outlined below some human vocabulary. Most problems with vocabulary I will not deal with (e.g., the masculine words included in almost every human or feminine word—

wo*man,* per*son,* hu*man,* s*he,* *man*kind, *he*r, and so forth).
Many vocabulary coincidences are just that—*his*tory does not
seem to have any masculine etymological derivation. Yet
others words, like "lib," are found to mean "castrate" when
looked up in the Webster's Unabridged Dictionary. Coincidence. If vocabulary is really unimportant, it will bother
no one when you use a more human vocabulary.

Summer, 1974
Sociology Department
Brooklyn College, C.U.N.Y.

PART I

Beyond Masculinity

Introducing Human Vocabulary*

Attaché: (at'ə•shā'; pronounced like attaché case; spelled the same in masculine or feminine form) *An attaché is a person with whom one has a deep emotional attachment.* The purpose of the word is to describe this attachment without branding the relationship either as monogamous or open to other relationships. The attaché may be a man or woman, so that a person saying "my attaché" may be involved in a homosexual, heterosexual, bisexual or asexual relationship. An attaché may be a person to whom one is married or with whom one is living, or neither; the deep emotional relationship is its only distinguishing quality. One may have one,

---

* The author asks that articles written about this book use this vocabulary accompanied by the definitions in italics.

two or more attachés. It may be used instead of girl friend, boyfriend, husband, wife or lover.

Living Friend: *A person with whom one is living; used when one does not wish to categorize the relationship as sexual or deeply emotional.* For example, communal partners, elderly persons who cohabit to save money, college roommates, or persons sharing an apartment may or may not be sharing sexual or deep emotional relationships. They are living friends.

The Human Pronoun*:   *Te* (pronounced like *tea*) = *he* or *she* (nominative)
Tes = *his* or *her* (possessive)
Tir (rhymes with *her*) = *him* or *her* (objective)

The human pronouns are only used in place of a pronoun that could be referring to either a man *or* woman. ("A *person* gets what *he* deserves" becomes "A person gets what *te* deserves") . But a reference to a specific man or the male gender stays the same (e.g., "A liberated man is secure within *him-self*" would not change) .

Each of the human pronouns consist of a *t* plus one letter from both the masculine and feminine gender of the old pronouns. *Te* takes the *e* from *he* and *she; tes* takes the *e* from *hers* and the *s* from *his; tir* takes the *i* from *him* and the *r* from *her.*

All words are pretested for easy readability and pronunciation.

---

* The inspiration for the use of *t* as the first letter comes from Kate Swift.

One

Women's Liberation and the Masculine Mystique: The Neglected Connection

In the United States, when the roles of men and women are questioned, it is usually within the context of the women's liberation movement. We make little effort to examine directly the problems resulting from the normal upbringing of a man. If men's liberation is mentioned, it is at best passed over with a rhetorical "I've always said women's liberation means men's liberation." But there is little understanding of how men change or why they might want to, the barriers involved in bringing about the change in everyday life, concrete alternatives to overcome these barriers, or the way to use tools such as consciousness-raising to apply general alternatives to the unique circumstances of an individual's life.

The evolution of a women's liberation movement isolated from men is a phenomenon almost unique to America. In

Sweden, where women's liberation has made the most progress, the movement is not called "women's liberation," but a
"sex-role debate." It is therefore not perceived so exclusively
as a woman's problem in which men might "help," but as a
two-sex problem, in which women and men can learn from
each other. Reports from Western European groups reveal
that they possess "a far deeper drive to 'liberate' men as well
as women from their traditional role as workers and competi-
tors, enabling men to play an active, more satisfying role
within the family."[1]

The isolation of the women's movement in America feeds
the male tendency to avoid introspection. The white middle-
class American male likes to think that everything is always
someone else's problem. He can see that blacks have a problem, that women have a problem, that chicanos have a
problem, but not that he has a problem—that his own socialized masculinity might be confining or worth reexamining.

A new movement is evolving which is beginning such
introspection. It might be called men's liberation (in alliance
with women's liberation), a human liberation movement or
a human alternatives movement. Each term holds importance but none is complete. "Liberation" is important because it connotes a psychological freedom; "human alternatives" is important because it suggests that the purpose of the
psychological freedom is to allow a choice among the human
range of alternatives rather than imposing a new dogma.
Retaining the sex distinction between men's and women's liberation—rather than combining them into human liberation
—is important in the first stages because it highlights the need
for liberation from the stereotypes of masculinity and feminity. Right now the term "human liberation" is too vague.*
People agree to it, yawn and never really think about it.

* Human liberation in its fullest sense also requires "generation liberation."
One can envision consciousness-raising groups of children, parents and
grandparents, with the parents liberating themselves from being protective

SEPARATE BUT EQUAL?

Some women are vehemently opposed to the alliance of men with women's liberation or any interaction between the two groups during the process of liberation. The vehemence of these "separatists" is not without justification. When men attend women's liberation meetings they tend to stand up and give speeches; they dominate small discussion groups; they expect women to operate in the system of power, money and organization established by men; they solve problems rather than ask questions, and continue to assume the masculine roles which have simultaneously limited men and established barriers for women's self-development.

Some women have openly declared men the enemy,[2] saying that the need for total separatism is analogous to the black movement's need to discover a black consciousness. There is considerable validity to this analogy, particularly at the beginning stages. But the analogy breaks down on many levels. A white person and a black person can go through their entire lives quite separately, in terms of intimate emotional contact. But the intimate association that almost every woman has with a man—father, brother, friend, husband—makes the sacrifice which comes with a segregated women's movement much greater. *This is the only revolution in which the so-called oppressed is allegedly in love with and sharing the children of the oppressor.* The constant contact between women and men on every level and at every stage of their development makes it much more possible for the growth of one person to benefit the other.

The ubiquitous contact between men and women, and the unconscious patterns that result, is also the strongest argu-

---

role models and puritans devoid of sexual fantasies; the children feeling free to deviate from their parents' guidance without betraying the sense of identity offered by parental ties. The subtleties of generation liberation are worth a good book.

ment for men and women communicating in separate groups —called consciousness-raising groups. (These are groups of about eight to ten persons who meet regularly for the purpose of questioning every aspect of their life which might be being dictated by stereotyped expectations of themselves or their attachés.*) These separate groups are particularly effective for about three months, *after* which it is usually helpful to *alternate* meeting *separately one week* and bringing the men's and women's groups together for a *joint meeting the next week*.† The following incident is an all-too-graphic example of the need for separate groups to be followed by joint groups and a movement directed at both sexes.

Sandra, a woman from a New York suburb who saw a news article about our men's group, contacted me to ask if I would speak to her husband about joining. She had been attending a woman's consciousness-raising group for six months, and her husband considered her involvement a disease which made her neglect their three children and her wifely duties. Her husband, Tony, a mechanic of traditional immigrant background, refused to talk to anyone in the group.

Over the period of the next six months, Sandra and Tony fought bitterly. Their oldest daughter came home crying from school after a particularly bad fight, and Tony repeatedly threw this in Sandra's face. *The more support Sandra received from the woman's group, the more conflict she incurred at home.* For the first time in eight years of marriage they were swinging at each other. At one point he took a knife out of the closet, chased her out of the house, and repeatedly threatened to kill her, the children and himself. Sandra called me after a third incident of a similar nature, asking if she could talk to our group about sending a few men down to talk with Tony. Eventually a couple of us

---

* Attaché: A person with whom one has a deep emotional relationship (see frontispiece) .

† See the final chapters for details of running consciousness-raising groups.

spoke to him, but a few weeks later she wrote me a note about her trip to the city that evening to see our group:

I stood on the platform of the subway station, wavering between running back to Tony and asking his forgiveness for my selfishness and running away from him forever. The children kept flashing through my mind. Moments in which Tony had been so kind (and he can be kind) alternated with the picture of his fierce red eyes—ready to push a knife through my throat. What had I started? Why couldn't I accept what other women want? I looked down the tracks and saw the light at the end of the tunnel flickering closer and closer. I looked at the tracks and the train and the tracks again and finally made a decision—I would throw myself in front of it. The train was about twenty feet in front of me. I could even see the driver's face. I stepped out off the platform with one foot and for some reason reached my arm out. I felt my hand hit the iron pole on the platform. I don't know why I held on but I caught my balance and wavered back. Warren, I still don't know whether that pole was a blessing or not. I really still don't know.

Tony and Sandra are still together. Why? "It isn't easy, Warren, when you have three children, when every time you think of leaving you look at them and wonder how they'll suffer. And I quit college for Tony, too—so how can I get myself a job, an education, and take care of the kids at the same time? Why do I have to make a *choice* between me—my real self—and my husband and children? The more I grow, the further apart we get. He's not an evil man—if he'd only listen, we could really grow together." Tony and Sandra have reconciled the worst of their conflicts through marriage counseling, although one of the counseling recommendations was that Sandra become more fulfilled as a "wife." And in spite of the counseling, Tony is still overly job-oriented. His image of "fem lib" as something he was opposed to never allowed him to become involved in consciousness-raising. He still keeps

thinking of women's liberation as "her problem." When
Sandra goes to a meeting, she is responsible for the baby-
sitter; she is neglecting him and the children; it is "her night
out." Our encouragement for him to join a men's group
could not quite counter his image that men don't join groups
to discuss personal doubts. The popularization of women's
liberation had encouraged Sandra to start growing, but our
encouragement for Tony came in a vacuum.

For many women, ignoring the simultaneous resocializa-
tion of men means closet liberation. Or it can mean drastic
conflict. It can be lonely living one's life on principle
and waking up alone every morning. The radical approach
that "all women can change best without men" makes men
the enemy of change. It prolongs the agony by making every
attempt at change a fight, producing guilt and the fear of
being abnormal. Continual fighting with men wastes the
energy necessary for additional progress.

Men's attitudes and behavior are often blamed for holding
women back, and correctly so; but then to deny that men's attitudes are important or that a man with positive attitudes can
have a positive influence is to blame men where blame is due
without giving credit where it is due. *This concern with
men's attitudes is not to be confused with dependency on
men's attitudes. The concern is to develop in men enough
internal security so that both women and men can attain the
psychological freedom to control their own lives.*

Bella Abzug openly states that her decision to run for the
House of Representatives would not have been made without
Mr. Abzug's "full approval." She said of Mr. Abzug: "Of his
qualities, the biggest is maturity . . . He's responsible, he's
got a lot of gentility. No man will ever feel threatened as long
as he's mature."

THE MASCULINE CONNECTION

Men's involvement in breaking out of the strait jacket of sex roles is essential because of the way it confines men at the same time as it confines women. As soon as men define themselves as the only ones capable of handling certain situations, of being aggressive, of earning the most money, then a woman who is equally capable in these areas becomes a threat to his very self-definition. He defines himself as *having* to earn the most money, and that definition still further defines him as a person who cannot afford too much time with his attaché, housework, his children or their routine discipline.

But men are limited in much more subtle ways—in almost every interaction of our most important relationships. We learn to articulate, to pick out the flaw in someone's statement or to come up with the exception to the rule in a generality, but in the process we forget how to listen and *seek out the nugget of truth* in what someone is saying. When we do listen, *our training to be logical often preoccupies us with the logical formula and formal structure of a thought rather than understanding its emotional impact.*

I have found in my work with men that at first these concerns appear trivial to most men. They would rather hear a good sociological argument. But the more I become involved with seeing men change and resist change the more I find that the men who most limit themselves have one thing in common—they cannot listen. These are also the men who limit their relationships with their attachés, since the growth of any deep emotional relationship hinges on the sense of self that develops by knowing your opinion is being carefully heeded.

Some men respond that "women have just as much trouble listening as men do." When women are speaking with other women, this is often true. But when women and men are talking together, and the conversation strays from light social discussion, then the men dominate. If the reader is doubtful of tes* own involvement in this pattern, try these experiments when there are about six to ten men and women involved in a serious conversation:

Experiments

Dominance Timing. Use a watch with a second hand to simply time the amount the men speak as opposed to the women. (A woman who is without a watch with a second hand might ask why!) Usually the men will speak two to ten times as frequently as the women, particularly if the conversation is considered *serious* and is not personal.

Topic Security. The men will sometimes justify their dominance by suggesting they "just happen to know more about this particular topic." This is usually true, but the unresolved question is how the conversation first got on to a topic about which the men knew the most. To determine whether the conversation is dealing about equally with topics of interest to both the men and women, make a list of the interests of each person in the group. (If the men have more "serious" interests, that alone is worth a consciousness-raising session.) Then observe whether the conversation has moved to an area in which the women or men have the most interest. Most of the time the topic will revolve around the men's areas of expertise or topic security. Once this occurs, the dominance appears justified. The man is hurt by the process because he misses out on entire areas of conversation into which he does not feel comfortable delving. The woman is hurt by not having a chance to develop the sense of identity that comes from interest expressed in her endeavors.

Man the Problem-solver. Both the men and women are involved in moving the topic to the man's area of topic

* *Te* = he or she; *tes* = his or her; *tir* = him or her.

security. The woman does it by her tendency to ask questions (even if she already knows the answer to the questions) with her eye contact directed at a man. This forces him into a problem-solver role; he feels he must answer the question even if he doesn't know the answer. Once the man has developed this habit, he tends to lecture condescendingly even when his thinking is tentative. His appearance of certainty cuts off the verbalization of doubts that others might possess. This can be measured by counting the number of questions as opposed to statements asked by both the men and women. Also note the tone of voice (certainty, or softness with hesitation) and ask whether the men are making statements to the group at large, while the women are asking questions with their eye contact on the men. The man's strait jacket is being unable to ask questions (except rhetorically) because it makes him appear weak in front of the women.

Man the Fault Finder. Count the number of "buts" used by the men and women, and the number of "ands" used by both sexes. Often men will find fault while women "add a thought." Even when the contributions are identical, the first is inhibiting while the second encourages the continued contribution of others.

Self-listening. Self-listening is a process in which the man (and sometimes the woman) will listen to the first sentence or two that a person makes, assume he knows what is to follow, and start forming his own story related to his own accomplishments (or ego) while the other person is still talking. One can almost see the man forming the story in his mind by watching his eye movements and his head nodding in "yes, but" agreement with whatever is being said, and then, at the first pause, jumping in with his own already-prepared story. While both sexes do this, when a man does it, he generally drops in a credential and ends his story by a reference to himself, which encourages the group to focus on something *he* brought up rather than returning to the talker. Also, when a man does this, the remainder of the group (both women and men) usually cooperates in transferring the focus to him. This transfer of focus is what completes the process as *self*-listening.

This style prevents the people who are really listening from speaking up since they must first think through what is being said and then prepare their own thoughts. By that time the self-listeners are already speaking. If a woman has been self-listening all along as well and is also ready to interject at the first pause she can generally do so only if a man is not competing with her, since a man's deeper and louder voice will usually capture the group's attention. The problem with a conversation that keeps moving at that pace and level is that there is no way a woman can enter it without adopting the male way of talking. In the meantime the group misses any contribution that a soft-spoken person might make.

To measure whether this is being done more by men or women, count interruptions, giving twice as much credit if the interruption actually transfers the focus to the interrupter. If two or more people interrupt simultaneously, note to whom the attention of the group finally goes.

Men's involvement in breaking out of the strait jacket of sex roles is important because children see their fathers as role models for all the behaviors mentioned above. Studies show that fathers get even more upset than mothers when their children deviate from "proper" sex-role behavior—especially boys.[3] In my own research, I found men totally unwilling to give their sons dolls, with no thought that this might help them become better fathers.

Men who have not changed their attitudes toward their "proper" role are also unlikely to be found sharing full responsibility for child-raising. When their children greet only their father returning from the office while their mother has been caring for them they don't tend to picture themselves working out an equal sharing of the child care should they have their own children. Equal responsibility for child care is now seen only as a women's liberation goal, but it is impossible to achieve unless men view the responsibility as part of their freedom to be less job-oriented and more child-oriented.

Men's attitudes toward the woman as inevitable child-bearer limit women's alternatives in the business world. Jane Evans, at twenty-six president of a Genesco subsidiary, attributed her appointment to the positive attitude toward women in management held by the chairman of the board of Genesco, Maxey Jarman. She explained that Jarman's "positive attitudes toward women in business have pervaded the entire corporation."[5] The fact that she was not just an exception was evidenced by the fact that two women preceded her as president. A less enlightened chairperson of the board would have considered Evans still in "the childbearing stage" and would have argued that "I could lose her at any minute," without recognizing that he could lose any man at any minute to another corporation or that a woman with such responsibility is highly likely to make arrangements for child care which will enable her to continue in her position.

Men's attitudes limit women's alternatives in the business world by suggesting that women cannot advance in their jobs because of premenstrual tension symptoms such as anxiety, irritability, headaches and depression. Premenstrual tension symptoms, though, are not purely biological phenomena. An attitudinal study by Morris J. Paulson indicates that these symptoms are correlated with dissatisfaction and conflict in a woman over her proper sex role.[4] If this conflict is intensified by a man who is making a woman's every step to realize herself a choice between liberation and her family, the premenstrual tension symptoms will tend to increase, and solidify the man's belief that the woman is limited by her biology (to say nothing of the woman's doubts about herself). By contrast, the man who is sharing the responsibility for housework and child-raising tends to find an *improvement* in the marriage and a reduction of most tensions, including his wife's premenstrual tensions.

Most importantly, changing men is connected to women's real liberation as a result of the ability men have to prevent women from seeking a whole range of alternatives *unless* women play the game by men's rules or value system. Men's ability to do this is apparent: They control the hiring and firing, have the upper hand in choosing a woman, a career, the time and place of sexual relations, when and where to move for job purposes; they make laws concerning abortion, divorce, property settlements, child custody, birth control, the definition of normal and legal sexual relations, marriage, annulment, child adoption, estates and wills, artificial insemination, sterilization and medical care. In essence, they control a woman's freedom in relation to society and make laws regarding even her most personal possession, her body. Men control this system so completely that women who enter find it easier to adopt the masculine values and admit other women on the same terms. Both men and corporations forfeit any of the human qualities women might otherwise have integrated into the masculine value system.

Two

The Masculine Value System:
Men Defining Reality

Guys still have it in their heads that a revolutionary is a murderer. Uh-uh. A revolutionary is a changer, a teacher. Somebody who hangs in and keeps at it, and keeps loving people, until they change their heads.

—Kate Millett

i used to dream militant
dreams of taking
over america to show
these white folks how it should be
done
i used to dream radical dreams
of blowing everyone away with my perceptive powers
of correct analysis
i even used to think i'd be the one
to stop the riot and negotiate the peace
then i awoke and dug
that if i dreamed natural
dreams of being a natural
woman doing what a woman
does when she's natural
i would have a revolution
                —Nikki Giovanni

The masculine value system is a series of characteristics and behaviors which men more than women in our society are *socialized* to adopt, especially outside of the home environment. Men are not born with masculine values. They are taught them by both men and women. But one lesson derived from the teaching is that it is more permissible for a man to lead and dominate than a woman. Since the dominant group in a society generally has its values adopted by the majority, masculine values have become the society's values in the public sphere. As they become society's most rewarded values, it is easy for both men and women to assume that masculine values (and therefore most men) are superior to traditionally feminine values (and therefore most women). Many women, therefore, who seek equality seek it on men's terms, or by adopting masculine values, such as by becoming an aggressive salesman. The woman questions neither the function of aggression nor the assumption that she is a sales-*man*. (Our language is just one example of society's taking the dominant value system for granted to such a degree that our everyday references are cast only in those terms. To counter this bias this book has adopted human language and created new human pronouns.*)

ASSUMPTIONS OF SUPERIORITY

What are some of these masculine (now societal) values which we assume to be superior to traditional feminine values?

- a good talker and articulator *rather than a good listener*
- logic *as opposed to emotion*
- visible conflict and adventure *rather than behind-the-scenes incremental growth*

* *Te* = he or she; *tes* = his or her; *tir* = him or her.

- self-confidence *in place of humility*
- quick decision-making *rather than thoughtful pondering*
- charisma and dynamism *more than long-term credibility*
- an active striving for power *rather than a general desire to achieve even if power does not accompany the achievement*
- politics or business as an end in itself *rather than a human concern as an end*
- a hard, tough and aggressive approach *instead of a soft, persuasive approach*
- a responsiveness to concrete results and to external and tangible rewards (money, trophies, votes) *rather than less concrete, more internal satisfactions, as the rewards of learning, of communicating, or of a good family life*
- sexuality *rather than sensuality*

There are some characteristics associated with men, such as sexual conquest and stoicism, which are not considered superior to feminine characteristics, but are still developed by men as a consequence of the other expectations of masculinity dealt with in the next two chapters. The masculine characteristics above are valued by both men and women as most worthy of adoption in the "real world"—defined by society as the world outside the home. Women might display these characteristics, such as quick decision-making, in the world inside the home, but it is seldom assumed they can transfer them to the "real world."

The assumption that the masculine values are superior encourages the liberation of women to be narrowly interpreted as women coming "up to" masculine values. Women, for example, can put "Dr." on their résumé and gain society's respect; men cannot put "1972-74 I took care of children" and earn respect. (When I asked a group of employers how they would react to a man with such a résumé, the first response was, "Oh, he must be a fag!") Despite the assumption of the superiority of the masculine value system, in almost all cases some balance between or combination of the masculine and feminine value systems is usually most desirable.

The responsiveness to external rewards such as titles, power and status are perhaps most apparent in the obsessive use of the business card by men or women adopting the masculine value system. The business card is a "masculinity card." Through it a man (generally) can tell the world whether he is a Ph.D., vice-president of ———, director of ———, or a campus minister—in essence, an indication of how well he has performed the male breadwinning role. (A woman does not hand out cards saying "vice-president of the family" or "mother, M.A. in psychology.") Theoretically, the man offers his "masculinity card" as a quick way of transmitting his affiliation, phone number and address. Yet I knew one man who changed his card three times despite the fact that his affiliation, phone number and address had remained the same. Only his title had changed. The masculinity card is the grown-up man's equivalent of the growing boy's mark on the wall as he "progresses" toward manhood. It is the middle-class man's equivalent of the working-class man's tattoo.

In the real world, a man's world, the best of the feminine values, which are more humane values, are considered nice but unrealistic. Many of the traditional female values, though, are just the qualities politics and management are now discovering are missing. Politicians and business people have learned to talk their way in and out of anything, but thousands of companies are discovering that some of the salespersons who do best are the ones who listen. A customer will often have a need for something in the back of tes mind, but it is not drawn out by the aggressive man in sales who is too ready just to sell his preplanned package. Research by Wyer, Weatherly and Terrell indicates that while aggressiveness is considered an important quality in the hiring of salespersons, when actual performance is measured, equally successful results are frequently achieved by persons of directly *opposite* personality traits.[1]

Once we are trained to look for one characteristic it takes considerable awareness to prevent ignoring others. Sheila Tobias, who heads the Women's Studies Program at formerly all-male Wesleyan University, says, "I never cease to be astounded at how readily male students will talk in class and how long it takes women students to respond . . . A woman's questions are more subtle, her appreciations more complex. She digests a lecture slowly, referring to it or the reading weeks later." If Ms. Tobias had just assumed that those who responded immediately were her sharpest students (and many women who adopt the male or societal values make this assumption as readily as men), she would be discounting perceptive students and missing important contributions. The quick response of the men is rewarded over slow deliberation: an aggressive approach is praised more than a considered approach which seeks out subtleties.

MASCULINE VALUES AS REALITY: THE "NEWS"

If Ms. Tobias gives her aggressive talker a higher grade and if the employer does hire a salesperson on the basis of aggressiveness, then the male system of values becomes the masculine system of realities. In almost every occupation realism is used as an excuse to fulfill masculine values. News reporting in the papers and on TV and radio is a prime example. News reporters contend they must report crimes to the extent they do because "crime is reality—to ignore it would be unrealistic." Yet reality is ignored all the time—the reality of *growth,* constructive and incremental growth. In education, for example, reporting reality would be reporting how students best learn or how effective teachers teach, not just how a few male union leaders conduct a strike once every two years. Yet the latter makes the front pages more than all the former put together. The strike is conflict and combat. Normal education is growth. The strike is male-conducted. Normal education is female-conducted.*

News reporters do not report reality because it is uneventful and doesn't sell papers to men or women. The public and the news reporters, both operating within the masculine value system, assume reality is found in the conflict that surfaces rather than within the events and nonevents beneath the surface. "Stories" mean conflict, and conflict gets "covered." *Good news is no news. So we hear more about Watts during the few days it burst into flames than in the fifty years preceding this and the nine years since.* The masculine value system in news coverage reinforces the male socialization to create conflict by making it the only way to capture the attention necessary to create change. It also forces women who want change into the masculine value system. The Equal Rights Amendment, for example, sat in a House Committee for almost fifty years with millions of quiet supporters, but it took a women's liberation movement, with its concomitant sit-ins and demonstrations, to provide the atmosphere for its increased coverage. Careful arguments documenting injustices did not warrant coverage until the conflict atmosphere preceded it.

The masculine value system also limits news reporting by its focus on active decision-making, rather than the decisions which grow incrementally, that may in fact never be consciously made. For example, fascinating and crucial news such as how our everyday investments in Latin America force the U.S. government to support dictators are seldom reported

---

* Education becomes less female-conducted the more the status and income increases. Status and income are external rewards which men have learned to associate with their masculine role as breadwinner.

until a situation erupts into conflict. The conflict can be tossed off as the product of rebels because the background events are seldom reported. The masculine value system, then, focuses on the biases which erupt into conflict, but rarely on the biases clouded in consensus or incremental growth.

Female-conducted conflict, the crises of romance magazines and soap operas, are not considered "news" worthy of coverage on the front pages of newspapers or by the Cronkites and Grimsbys of the media world. In fact, they are not worthy of front-page coverage. But neither is most of the male-conducted conflict which receives the coverage.

Journalists balk at the suggestion that crimes be listed in small type, as are obituaries; that an obituary page and a crime page be at the back of the paper. The protest goes "but obituaries do make the front page when an outstanding person dies." Crimes, though, make the front page when *any* person commits them, as long as the adventure, violence and blood are outstanding. The inherent value of crime is that very conflict and violence. With white-collar crimes, the participants must be important or the conflict value great before it is covered extensively. Watergate possessed both important participants and conflict value and was therefore covered extensively. With crimes of violence, though, the participants can be insignificant. Men's upbringing treats conflict and combat as the all-important processes of life. This is their reality. Women's upbringing treats growth as all-important. The humane value is clearly growth.

MASCULINE VALUES AS REALITY: BUSINESS

In business, men's attitudes and values force women to play the game by men's rules—unless they are willing to take "women's jobs." The woman is forced to take on a double load of the masculine value of aggressiveness to overcome the special barriers to success which are placed in her way. She then fulfills the male prophecy that "those women who make it are worse bitches than the men—what they really need is a good roll in the hay." If she continues to act aggressively, she provokes fear; if she returns to feminine values, she provokes laughter. She finds herself saddled with a burden of "proving herself" which is worse than any man's. In the meantime, the corporation and the men in it forfeit any of the human qualities women might otherwise have brought into the system.

When women do employ some of men's tactics, in addition to their "own," their effectiveness is often overlooked. For example, the direct power which men exert in business situations blinds them to the contributions of indirect power which women have traditionally made. In an article in the *Harvard Business Review,* Orth and Jacobs estimate that "in almost every company there is an informal power group of women that everyone knows about but no one overtly recognizes. The president's secretary eats lunch each day with a group of other senior women, and as a result, the group knows more about what is really happening in the company than do most of the senior officers."[2]

In my interviews with employers, I found many managers readily admitting, "I could not do my job without my secretary. She's invaluable, and actually, I'll tell you, she's highly competent." The "I'll tell you" is often said with an inclination of the head and a quick glance with the eyes to make sure no one is looking; and in a confiding manner which signals a "Now, don't tell anyone." Ironically, no one does tell anyone, and as Orth and Jacobs point out, even those women who do recognize their own competence and resent its lack of formal recognition hide their resentment and continue to channel their competence toward making the men feel good. While the managers are benefiting from their secretaries' luncheon discussions, they will often gaze benignly at the secretaries gathered at a table and consider their discussion "gossip." Their own gossip, though, is considered "realistic," "a broadening of my information base" or "a deepening of the understanding of the way the company really works—its corporate politics."

Women operating in a masculine value system are often overlooked for their effectiveness because their effectiveness just piles up credit for the men they are supporting. The indirect power of women has another limitation—its minimal scope. The woman is usually limited to influencing one man. She must choose to influence in the areas which he chooses to have influence, according to his timetable (or that of more influential men), his priorities, but most importantly, his talents—meaning that her talents seldom get recognized in their most unique form. (Gloria Steinem might have been a talented assistant to a president, but not until she defined her own talents as editor, speaker and writer did she stand out in a way she could not have by doing someone else's bidding.) In business and in marriage the man recognizes "the invaluble help" he receives. Her true effectiveness, though, can never blossom as long as the focus is on his career and his ideas. On the job, in the home and in the bed she helps *him*. She is like a jockstrap—always supporting but never seen.

The validity of the argument that woman's focus is on the man should not cloud the lack of freedom which confronts the man. He also has little choice in the decisions he makes. He is caged by limitations imposed by his position within the corporation or factory and by the limited focus of the corporation itself. Yet the threatened man often complains about "those women's lib ladies," instead of looking to the source of his own unhappiness—male-imposed corporate goals and bureaucratic power-seeking. Nor does he see how, when his own attaché is sharing the responsibility for breadwinning, he becomes freer to question these goals, since if his questioning results in his being fired, his attaché provides a cushion of financial support, offering him the freedom to seek another position without panicking.

MASCULINE VALUES AS REALITY: POLITICS

In politics the integration of the more human-oriented of the traditional female values is most effectively repressed. Internal approval, satisfaction with one's self, and self-improvement for its own sake are sacrificed in politics for the masculine values of external approval and success depending upon another's failure. The politician's very existence is dependent on external approval. This is almost the definition of electoral politics. Internal satisfaction with seeking the truth is irrelevant unless it can be translated into external approval terms, and as most politicians know all too well, "The truth never catches up with the lie (during the campaign)." Success for the politician is dependent on the *failure* of everyone else. The politician cannot win unless all tes opponents lose. The politician cannot succeed unless everyone else fails *if* the politician defines success as obtaining office. The masculine value system has defined success that way; many women politicians also define success that way. Few seek the internal satisfactions of communicating or the rewards of the learning experience, or are satisfied with alternative paths of influence or the influence involved in the campaigning process itself.* It is not that winning office is inherently wrong. It is that society gives so much positive feedback for concrete success—and so little for a person losing with 49 percent of the vote—that only an exceptionally strong person can count the blessings of a loss.

* Two exceptions are Shirley Chisholm and Harold Hughes.

The need to win is reinforced by the American winner-take-all political system, in which there is only one winner—the one with the most votes. This contrasts with the political system of many of the countries of Western Europe—the proportional representation system, in which, say, ten delegates will represent a larger area, with a party that receives only 20 percent of the vote still sending two of the ten delegates to represent that party in office. In addition, the fact that the focus is on the *party's* percentage of the total votes, rather than the individual's, means there is less personal ego at stake from an electoral loss. It means as well that the internal value of seeking the truth as one sees it, although it may only be convincing to 20 percent of the electorate, is still rewarded externally, thereby making the seeking of internal rewards a more realistic goal.*

The masculine value system of success in politics is reinforced by the definition of success in capitalism. The competitiveness of business tends to make the electorate itself not only insensitive to the development of internal values but disdainful of them as not pragmatic in the "real world." The real world of the capitalist does conflict with the development of an inward-turning personality. The success of the salesperson (the backbone of business), like the success of the politician, is dependent on external rewards—the very definition of commission. External rewards such as money, power, votes and titles are the essence of business and politics. Most persons unconsciously evaluate themselves on the basis of their ability to outdo others in the accumulation of these rewards. Competition for success is so important that I have witnessed persons who, upon hearing of a friend's failure, react with a suppressed smile.

---

* The proportional representation system has many more advantages and disadvantages, but the purpose here is only to illustrate how the U.S. system reinforces the male value system.

MASCULINE VALUES AS REALITY: THE BEDROOM

Playgirl is perhaps the perfect example of masculine values defining women's reality in bed.[3] It is produced by a man who views the bedroom as the domain of sexuality rather than sensuality. So *Playgirl* pictures a male nude—women "coming up to" men's standards of *sexuality*. If an attempt had been made to appreciate the feminine value system, the editors would have seen the focus in "women's magazines" on the senses—the smells of body oils and perfumes, the tastes of foods and spices, the touch of embroidered materials and fabrics. They might have translated this into close-ups of men's lips, earlobes, body hair; toe-touching, tongue-caressing, or men and women eating foods together in novel and sensuous ways. Of the Best Films of the New York Erotic Film Festival only one was made by a woman. It was an incredibly erotic film of the sectioning and peeling, the touching and eating, the squeezing, tormenting and fingering of an *orange*—done photographically so close up that it appeared as if it were the most intimate body part.

Men's magazines, though, view the bedroom as almost entirely sex-oriented and woman-oriented. If men are pictured, it is never being sensuous. The exceptions are so few they stand out. For example, the wrestling scene between two men in the film version of D. H. Lawrence's *Women in Love* was portrayed with great sensitivity. But it still contained all the male symbols of dark wood, trophies, thick red velvet, deep fireplaces and, of course, the wrestling.

The advertisements in men's magazines also deal with the power and status symbols associated with sex—sleek sports and racing cars, the Marlboro Man on horseback, ties, and gadgets from digital clocks to stereo systems.

Men learn to be more "thing"-oriented—be it a gadget or a penis; women more total body- and sense-oriented. When men deal in senses—the taste of wine, Scotch, beer or gin—it's always surrounded in status. Finding the "right wine," a status Scotch, a man's beer, an extra-dry martini. In the masculine value system, sensuality is distorted with the reinforcement of men's insecurities about their sexuality.

The assumption in the producing of *Playgirl* is that women will come up to men's concern with power, status and things —that they will be concerned with *sex* and *men* rather than sensual experiences with men, women, themselves or nature.

HER PLACE FOR HER VALUES

The masculine value system is like an exclusive WASP Wall Street brokerage firm which, upon admitting its first Jew, examines tir microscopically for any unrefined sign of greed. The masculine value system does this with women who attempt entry. The slightest lack of refinement brings accusations of "karate types" or "Lesbians"; women are accused of flaunting their nudity as a way of showing their liberation. As one writer points out, "It was all right when the girl in the *Playboy* centerfold was photographed naked, since that event was *arranged by and for men*. But let a woman initiate nudity, especially if it is for her own pleasure, and immediately men see the apocalypse upon us."[4]

The masculine value system has another dimension—the assumption that certain general values, like creativity, are applied by men in ways that count, but are applied by women only in roles assigned to them. For example, men will compliment a woman for being creative in decorating, but will stop short of imagining how that creativity could also work in an employment situation. They will give a woman credit for being a disciplined student, but will never offer her the chance to apply this discipline in a bureaucratic setting, where constant distractions require such discipline. They praise women for their patience with children, but do not realize that the same patience could be applied gainfully to adults. Appreciation is shown for women's human concern as teachers, mothers and social workers, without recognizing that the same ability could be effective with customers.

If women were to twist their value system to eliminate men from certain areas, their argument might look like this:

Why We Oppose Votes for Men

1. Because man's place is in the army.
2. Because no really manly man wants to settle any question otherwise than by fighting about it.
3. Because if men should adopt peaceable methods women will no longer look up to them.
4. Because men will lose their charm if they step out of their natural sphere and interest themselves in other matters than feats of arms, uniforms, and drums.
5. Because men are too emotional to vote. Their conduct at baseball games and political conventions shows this, while their innate tendency to appeal to force renders them particularly unfit for the task of government.

—Alice Duer Miller, 1915

Liberation will mean little for men or women if women enter men's world on men's terms. Yet there is plenty of evidence to indicate that any real liberation will be threatened by this likelihood. The threat is illustrated by the ease of women's absorption into the Air Force R.O.T.C. since it began opening its doors to women in 1970 on a selective experimental basis.[5] Within the first year, over 500 women enrolled and the experiment succeeded so well that all coed institutions offering R.O.T.C. were permitted to enroll female candidates. Only 9 out of 136 institutions rejected the move. Within one year many of the women were doing "at least as well as the men, probably a little better," according to Major Arthur Hall of the University of Miami. Not one woman backed out of even the toughest part of the program,

FEIFFER
by JULES FEIFFER

IN THE BEGINNING THERE WAS OPPRESSION.

OPPRESSION BEGAT CONSCIOUSNESS.

CONSCIOUSNESS BEGAT RAGE..

RAGE BEGAT REBELLION.

REBELLION BEGAT THEORY.

THEORY BEGAT HOKUM.

IN THE END IT WAS JUST LIKE THE BEGINNING.

Publishers-Hall Syndicate

the outdoor survival and parachute jumps. This acceptance
by women of men's values, on men's terms, is one of the
strongest threats to the possibility of women's liberation
making a contribution to society's values. Perhaps the car-
toonist Jules Feiffer illustrates this most succinctly.

Three

The Development
of Masculinity

UNDEFINING MASCULINITY AND FEMININITY

It is useless in this book to give my own definition of masculinity and femininity, since the purpose of the book is to overcome the way society has defined male and female humans, and by so defining, limited them. When I refer to something as "masculine" or "feminine," I am referring to the socialization of men or women as it exists, which is impossible to outline here. At an early age boys see models of men who seek material success, physical and psychological strength, leadership, invulnerability; who suppress their fear, control their emotions; who are pragmatic, know all the answers, never seek help, are tough and independent; who have a substantial degree of power, ambition, and physical and sexual aggression; who have control in sexual relations and in all relations, initiate sexual relations, make decisions, can get what they want when they want it; who generally want to be on top, be a protector, earn more than ——— and in general be better than ——— (preferably a man; if not, then a woman). If John Wayne—the Moses of masculinity—were to hand down "The Ten Commandments of Masculinity," they might look like this:

Ten Commandments of Masculinity

1. Thou shalt not cry or expose other feelings of emotion, fear, weakness, sympathy, empathy or involvement before thy neighbor.
2. Thou shalt not be vulnerable, but honor and respect the "logical," "practical" or "intellectual"—as thou defines them.
3. Thou shalt not listen, except to find fault.
4. Thou shalt condescend to women in the smallest and biggest of ways.
5. Thou shalt control thy wife's body, and all its relations, occasionally permitting it on top.
6. Thou shalt have no other egos before thee.
7. Thou shalt have no other breadwinners before thee.
8. Thou shalt not be responsible for housework—before anybody.
9. Thou shalt honor and obey the straight and narrow pathway to success: job specialization.
10. Thou shalt have an answer to all problems at all times.

And above all: Thou shalt not read *The Liberated Man* or commit other forms of introspection.

The woman's socialization encourages domesticity, nurturance, dependency, modesty, coyness, deviousness, warmth, emotionality, illogicality, the ability to be sensually and sexually arousing (while simultaneously properly inhibited and submissive), fearfulness, the need for protection, tenderness, fragility, displays of affection and "sugar and spice and everything nice" (meaning: something extra to be added to the real substance). These traits are off-limits for the male.

Perhaps Dan Wakefield best describes at least a few of the characteristics of masculinity in his novel *Going All the Way*. "You had to have some quality that was hard to pin down, a certain kind of confidence, a little swagger but not in a boastful way, an easiness, a style, an air of casual good nature, of leadership that wasn't sought but seemed to come natural. You couldn't pin it down but you could see it in a person."[1]

GROWING UP A STEREOTYPE . . . FROM BIRTH

The stereotype of masculinity that a given culture accepts is imposed upon a boy from the day he is born. Goldberg and Lewis, who conducted one of the very few studies of six-month-old infants, found that infant girls are touched by their mothers much more than infant boys.[2] Mothers breast-fed girls significantly more than boys* and vocalized to girls significantly more than boys.[3]

The importance of these findings can be seen just seven months later. Goldberg and Lewis found that "the more physical contact the mother made with a boy at six months, the more he touched the mother at 13 months."[4] In a similar vein, "when the children were six months old, mothers touched, talked to, and handled their daughters more than their sons, and when they were 13 months old, girls touched and talked to their mothers more than boys did."[5] *Boys are unconsciously taught to be emotionally constipated.* The self-fulfilling prophecy of stereotyped masculinity is flourishing by the time a child is thirteen months old. The image of masculinity is so all-pervasive and so much more important than any possible initial tendency of a man toward aggression or passivity that the California Gender Identity Center has discovered that *it is easier to use surgery to change the sex of an adolescent male who has been brought up as a female than*

---

* Breast-feeding is important not for its own sake, but as a form of intimacy, as is any warm human contact important to a child.

*to undo the social and cultural conditioning that has led him
to behave like a woman.* Similar research by Money, Hampson and Hampson concludes that gender role is entirely a
learning process which is quite independent of chromosomal,
gonadal or hormonal genders.[6]

While the Goldberg studies are enlightening on this level,
they share a shortcoming of almost all studies in this area—
they *only deal with the behavior of mothers.* Therein lies
one of the fundamental fallacies of the research on "parenthood": It is research on motherhood. By definition, these
studies cannot conclude anything about the effects of fatherhood. The result is that millions of mothers reading popularized versions of these studies develop a guilt complex if
they work, while fathers can get away with giving lip service
to a desire to spend more time with their children. Only recently has similar research been done on fatherhood, leading
to the discovery that a father's presence was as important, and
in some cases more important, to the child as the presence of
the mother.* The lack of attention to this research has hurt
the father, making him feel like "half a man," should he cut
back his career to spend more time with his child.

GROWING UP: THE ESCAPE FROM FEMININITY

The second stage in the development of masculinity, apparent in the preschool and early school-age educational process,†
may cause even greater damage than the neglect of the boy
described by Goldberg and Lewis.

*The one common element between both high-achieving
and highly creative boys and girls is that neither adopts tradi-*

---

* Absentee-father studies are examined in the chapter on the family.
† The school system's encouragement of discipline and sitting still and listening does not encourage traditional male values directly. Only the slow
build-up of the contempt for femininity encourages the rebellion against
the feminized educational system in the early years as a proof of manhood.

tional sex roles.[7] Kagan and Moss find that academically high-achieving girls remain tomboys the longest—they are "fearless, independent, and competitive. Girls who were bold and daring from ages 10–14 became the most intellectual women as adults."[8]

The damage of stereotyping is even more irreparable for the boy than for the girl. *When boys learn stereotyped male behavior there is a 20 percent better chance that it will stay with them for life than when girls learn stereotyped behavior.*[9] This implies an even greater need to think through the results of a stereotypic upbringing for boys than for girls.

Despite the damage of stereotyping, many parts of the education process, including children's books, give every boy very clear messages as to what it takes to be a boy—as *opposed* to a girl. In NOW's study of 2,760 stories in 134 children's books by fourteen major publishers, boys' and girls' roles are clearly differentiated in a substantial proportion of the more than two thousand stories. While NOW concluded that the image of women in these stories was so bad as to make this a major women's liberation issue, it largely ignored the implications of this as a men's liberation issue.

Part of what is presented as the boy's role is not objectionable—the wide range of career options, the inventiveness and the self-confidence (if possessed in moderation). But *in order to be a real boy, a boy must not be caught being at all like a girl. A fundamental disrespect for everything associated with a girl permeates the school readers.* A fear can develop in some boys as to what will happen to them if they are at all like "those girls." These boys may feel they have to live up to all those characteristics the books say a boy is supposed to have. *In this drive to escape from resembling a girl even those masculine traits that could be positive, like self-confidence, become false and obsessive.* As a boy gets somewhat older (late grammar school and junior high), his fear of appearing "like a girl" increases.

The extent to which these images become part of a boy's
early concept of what a girl is and what a boy ought to avoid
being can be most graphically observed by a brief examination of this image as presented in the children's books. The
NOW study found that "there were 67 stories in which one
sex demeaned the other; *65 of these were directed against
girls, only two against boys* (italics mine).[10] The study
continues:

Girls are attacked as a class. The negative behavior always goes
unpunished and is never commented upon as such. The way to
gain a sense of superiority, albeit a highly immature one, is to
make someone else seem unimportant. Possibly this is a mis-
guided attempt on the part of the readers to butter up the boys,
since they have more difficulty learning to read.[11]

Pretending boys are superior in order to mask an underlying
deficiency (a reading difficulty) is the beginning of the
building of the false male ego structure—something a secure
man does not need. Yet the reading difficulty itself is perpetuated by the fear of studying, and the insecurity by the
fear of appearing like a girl. The basis for the ego-building is
so weak that it is no wonder a man's ego becomes, as Marya
Mannes puts it, his second most fragile instrument.

The girls, though, learn that their role is to contribute to a
man's false ego by self-mockery. The girl characters in the
stories consistently demean other girls and themselves with
comments like "It's easy. Even I can do it. And you know
how stupid I am."[12]

In these stories there are innumerable examples of the
mockery of girls; these ultimately feed boys' fear of being like
girls. In one story a character says, "But who wants to eat
dinner with a lot of girls anyway?" and "Women sure are
funny."[13] Another story includes this line: "Jerry always ran
away when his friends walked with girls."[14] In another series
a character comments, "Women's advice is never worth two

pennies. Yours isn't worth even a penny."[15] Yet another series mentions that "when you mix the clay [to make a woman], mix in guile and cunning, a shameless mind, a deceitful nature."[16]

No children's book in current use (almost all of these are as of 1973) would claim that a black boy's advice isn't worth two pennies or that he is made up of a shameless mind and a deceitful nature or that "blacks sure are funny" or even "but who wants to eat dinner with a lot of blacks anyway?" Consistent comments such as these seen in almost every book can make the fear of femininity a potent force for society to use against boys.

The stereotypes in children's stories even foster biological explanations of male-female differences. For example, Mr. Applegate offers Judy a possible explanation of why she got a nosebleed on Rocky Mountain: "Perhaps, because you are a little girl, your skin is thinner than ours, and so it isn't quite as strong as ours."[17]

The themes continue in this direction as the children receive readers in later grades. The stories picture men in 166 occupations, but women in only 25. In over 2,700 stories there is not one girl who becomes a doctor, lawyer, professor, astronaut, engineer or even a computer operator or a salesperson. Among the twenty-five options for girls, however, are witch, cleaning lady, baby-sitter, queen and fat lady in the circus.

It is no wonder boys run away from femininity, and tomboys are among the most intelligent girls.[18] These stereotyped images are not only related to, but are absorbed by, children, even children whose own parents are working. Numerous studies on children's concepts of male and female roles, such as those by Hartley, demonstrate an overwhelming propensity for children to accept the role divisions society puts before them. When 157 girls and boys (half with working mothers) listed 640 items to describe all aspects of women, "64.5% [of the items] were in the traditional domestic activities having to do with household care and management, child care, and relations with husbands."[19] These are reinforced every day in school, even in the rhymes girls sing as they jump rope. They sing about the men they will marry: "Rich man, poor man, beggar man, thief; doctor, lawyer, Indian chief." Boys don't sing: "Actress, heiress, social worker; nurse; Marry a woman with money in her purse."

The contempt for women extends far beyond the children's books, as a quick glance at the clichés about women reveal*: dumb broad; dumb blonde; chick; pussy; ski bunny; hen-pecking; slut; tramp; sexpot; loose woman; spinster; old maid; old bag; little old lady; little woman; my little lady; my little princess; woman driver; feminine wiles; gal friday; castrating bitch; ballbuster, and so on.

To grow up a boy is to be able to say something condescending *about* women (they're "sugar and spice and everything nice") , or something contemptuous about women ("find 'em, feel 'em, fuck 'em, forget 'em"—the four F's") or something condescending *to* women ("don't worry your pretty little head") . As a boy becomes an adolescent he wonders if she "goes all the way," or "does she or doesn't she"; after he gets married he "admires" the Playmate of the Month, or "what a pair of legs," or "what a piece of ass." To his own daughter he preaches "that's not ladylike" or brags about "mommy's little helper." If she develops her own identity, he marvels at her accomplishments "for a woman." In the meantime, he worries about his own success, never forgetting, should he "make it," his wife's role: *"behind* every great man there's a woman." No wonder a man is afraid to come into contact with the feminine parts of his personality. He can only rejoice, as in the Jewish Orthodox prayer, "Thank God I'm not a woman."

Children have already picked up their dislike for the

* Clichés compiled by Lois Bass.

woman's role by the age of four.[20] By kindergarten about
half the girls prefer the father's role and about a quarter of
the boys prefer the mother's role.[21] By the sixth and seventh
grades girls who act like boys are much more socially accepted than boys who act like girls.[22] Among adults, 20 to 31
percent of women prefer the male social role while only 2½
to 4 percent of men prefer the woman's role.[23] It is apparent
that each sex gradually accepts its stereotype, but that men
almost unanimously recognize the relative advantages of
their role.* These sex-typed traits are normally accepted even
more by lower-class than by middle-class boys.[24]

The fear of femininity is only a first step in the race to
build masculinity. The second step is an easy corollary: boys
must take on what girls are allegedly afraid to do—actions
such as killing. For example, from a 1970 Lippincott Basic
Reader: "Mrs. Allen shuddered. To think that her boy had
killed such a creature made her a bit proud, but also just a
little bit faint."[25] This was just one of close to a hundred
stories that condoned meanness and cruelty as part of the
story line.

From the 143 examples of strength, bravery and heroism
for boys (as opposed to 36 for girls) came consistent examples of the burden placed on the boy to be an undaunted
hero. From the legend of "Jack and the Beanstalk": " 'Do not
be afraid, Mother,' said Jack. 'I will do what I can.' . . .
'Mother,' he called, 'get me my ax!' "[26]

Pressure to make the boy perform becomes almost as much
the girl's role as performance is the boy's: "It was dark, the
water swirled angrily beneath them, but her faith in Pedro
was unwavering."[27] If a boy does not have outlandish expectations of what it takes to prove himself a boy, he may never

---

* The probability that the male role does have more advantages than the
female role does not, of course, deny the possibility of improving the male
role, by integrating the best of both roles and eliminating the neuroticism
of dichotomized roles.

be insecure about it. Most boys, however, build expectations that are higher than their achievements. This produces anxiety and a need to constantly prove one's masculinity. Gray's study, for example, finds that *boys who score high in sex-appropriate behavior (possessing masculine outlook and behavior) were also the ones who scored highest in anxiety.* Gray speculated that "striving to maintain a masculine role is for the boy of this age group stressful enough to be associated with manifest anxiety."[28]

THE STRIVERS: CORE OF THE MASCULINE MYSTIQUE

Most boys recognize they cannot prove themselves on all levels. This alleviates some anxiety. But they must still choose between two basic images of what a man is and can be—images which are apparent from both the children's books and numerous other sources. One image is the "physical-striving" man, and the other the "job-striving" man. The job-striving man is often a leadership striver when in school and not infrequently a student striver after elementary school.

The physical-striving man is often the image choice of the boy who is not getting rewards from the classroom. This is not always the less intelligent boy. It can also be the boy whose environment places little emphasis on education or a high emphasis on sports. The boy for whom making the Little League and later being on some high school athletic team are all-important has much of his self-concept wrapped up in such an achievement. If he fails, he must quickly find a new achievement. Two failures in succession in a physical area can produce numerous attempts to seek compensatory challenges—such as ripping off the guarded jewelry counter in a local department store. (There are more "masculinity points" involved in ripping off something at a guarded counter than an unguarded box of candy from a supermarket—"Any jerk can do that.")

Jokes reveal a lot about people's underlying feelings. One can listen to boys "mock each other out": "How did you lose to so-and-so, he's a weakling!" A bigger insult—"even Mary almost beat him last week"—reveals a disrespect for weakness and girls which can be so deep that while tolerance for girls is possible, this tolerance is accompanied by an assumption that they have their place.

The physical-striving boy's major rewards stem from his peers. The job-striving boy is at this stage usually a student striver or class-leadership striver. His major rewards stem from his teachers. However, the student striver is still concerned about what his peers think of him; the physical striver considers it masculine not to care about what his teachers think. "How much you can get away with" is far more masculine than an enthusiastic "Look how much I learned!"[29] The physical striver is not required to do well in even one subject. *The irony is that the school's own children's books have reinforced in the boy a need to be masculine, which leads to a rebellion against the school, a rebellion against femininity and an association of the school with femininity.*

While leadership and job striving are more male problems, the problem of the student strivers is endemic to both men and women until women reach the last year or two of college, when they often begin to substitute husband striving. As a woman learns that grades in college will not determine the *essence* of her future, she becomes less a prisoner of the striving system. She will still achieve, but not at the expense of almost all other values. Yet as she gives up the need to be a winner, she substitutes the need to have a winner. The man's side of the coin is "living it and winning it"; the woman's side is "living it vicariously and winning it vicariously." The entire coin is tarnished.

The student strivers write exams according to the teacher's biases. They are manipulated by the system through their own striving to manipulate the system. Rather than choosing

to write and analyze the way they want to, they confine them-
selves by "psyching out" someone else's wishes. Eventually
their own psychology *is* someone else's. They often choose
colleges on the basis of what others will think of them
should they obtain a degree from that college. Once in
college, the student strivers confine themselves to easy
teachers or name teachers. In essence, they choose someone
who will give them the grades they believe someone else will
want them to have. They are the early pleasers. They perform in whatever way demanded for the currency of a grade.
They are the adult prostitute in stage one.

The student-striving male uses the questioning process to
prove his prowess in the way that the physical-striving male
uses sports. Both try to appear verbally self-confident and
invulnerable. The poorly educated physical striver makes
absolute statements often bordering on the authoritarian. In
this way he feels no one dares challenge him. The more
educated student striver learns to articulate and hedge his
statements so carefully as to never be vulnerable. He doesn't
mind being challenged because this gives him the opportunity to articulate further, to explain how he already thought
of that question. In fact, the more he is challenged, the more
attention he gets and the more people can admire his ability
to respond. He stops short of asking questions to which he
does not already know the answer. The fundamental similarity is that *both strivers are concerned with proving them-*
selves right rather than discovering what is right. In the
process, the original purpose of questioning—to learn and
develop a critical but open mind—is lost.

It is not a long jump from the person searching for the
teacher with the easiest grade or most prestige to the person
searching for a job offering the most status. Again the need to
climb breeds caution. A man cannot question on a job unless
he feels the questioning will please. If the questioning is

encouraged, he then becomes a questioner; if discouraged, he shuts up. In his need to hold a higher position in his male role as breadwinner, he allows society to manipulate him. As one psychologist observed: "He may have been a hero in high school—president of the student body or a star athlete, that sort of thing. But then he gets out into the world, and he becomes a cog in the organization, and he comes home feeling defeated."[30]

While striving on the inside, the student and leadership striver must not appear to care too much; it's respectable enough to have intelligence, but not respectable to "plug" and "sit down and always be studying like Carol." He must remain aloof from his work and have it "just come naturally." To prove that he's not this type of "sissy boy" he'd better have at least one sport in which he can do well. No parallel requirement is made by the student striver that the physical striver succeed academically.

The physical striver proves his success by muscle-building, the job striver by leadership building. Leadership and articulateness are the educated man's proof of muscle. His self-worth is dependent on his leadership of a campus radical contingent, a student government or a literary journal. He is the class's Abbie Hoffman, Eldridge Cleaver, Richard Nixon, William Buckley or Norman Mailer. *Whatever his ideology, he must stand out. The leadership striver has got to have the solution to all problems.* He is the one who stands up at NOW meetings and tells "the girls" the best way to dress for a demonstration.

If the leadership striver is a radical he is quick to espouse the latest line with the greatest fervor. He is able to change, but only by making speeches proclaiming, "I *used* to believe that way, too, until I realized . . .," with a new self-righteousness based on an "I've been through it all" (often reminiscent of the father he may have rebelled against) . If he is a student-government type much of his interest in people becomes a "What can they do for me?" interest. He loses the ability to know them except insofar as they relate to his election or organization. The radical leadership striver confines his friendships to adherents and loses the ability to be friends with a nonideologue unless te is a member of the working class with potential for conversion.

Of all the strivers, the physical striver appears to suffer the most from the masculine values the older he gets. With the exception of the few who play sports professionally, the student and leadership strivers become the most successful job strivers. Once high school is over most rewards come from this source. The physical striver somehow senses this throughout grammar and high school. Many of his put-downs of the "teacher's pet" can be mere covers for his insecurity. John Canaday, a renowned art and literary critic, describes this phenomenon in recalling some of the roughest boys in his neighorhood, who on the surface cared not the least about intelligence:

One day when I couldn't get my arithmetic problem and knew I was going to cry, I left the room and sat on the steps outside. In a few minutes one of the big, Italian boys, sent by Miss Clark, I suppose, came out and sat beside me and asked what was the matter. When I told him, he said there was nothing to cry about, he never could get his arithmetic and he didn't cry about it. Whatever else he said, he made it clear that although I was skinny and pale and scared of everything, he'd like to be as bright as I was.[31]

If this sensing of the future makes the physical striver insecure, the fear of disapproval from peers makes the male student striver just as insecure. Both of these insecurities could be lessened if the pressure for a male to achieve and prove that he is not like a girl were lessened.

THE ARMY

The physical striver's three major ingredients—physical strength, insecurity and an unquestioning mind—find their most appropriate outlet in the armed services. While the student striver is chasing grades and "tail" in college, the physical striver might be serving his apprenticeship in Southeast Asia. The process of building the male image by creating contempt for a woman is especially clear in the Army. A look at a Vietnam war veteran's experiences in basic training illustrates this:

> You want to run but where can you go. This [basic training] is where the Army breaks you down. Most break easily, but some of us were stubborn. . . . They have ways of dealing with rebels. First they try verbal assault. "What is *wrong* with you? You a *pussy* or something?" If this fails there is always the time honored institution of the "Blanket Party" to make you a man. You are suddenly awakened in the middle of the night. It is dark and five to ten people are carrying you into the shower room. You don't know who it is because you are kept under the blanket. Next they proceed to kick the shit out of you. It isn't worth the effort to scream for help. Nobody ever hears. Yes, they will make a man out of you if it kills you.
>
> Once the men are broken, it is time to rebuild them in the Army image. Your life is still hell, working 18 hours a day at backbreaking shitwork, but now you are offered glimpses of what it will be like when you reach the Army paradise, Asia. You hear war stories of hunting and killing "Gooks." And best of all, there are the Gook Chicks.
>
> "There's a lot of loose Ass over there, men, and they just love GI dick." The pride starts growing . . . the spirit reaches a peak and it is time for the unit cheer, "Who are you, Fuckers? What do you got?—Balls! What you gonna do with them?—Kill Charlie Cong; What's that again?—Kill Charlie Cong." The spirit soars and the team marches on.[32]

The veteran then describes how the soldiers learn about

their two weapons—the rifle and the penis. They are told to kill gooks with the first and screw gooks with the second. A man's penis is called his "gun." Marines learn the distinction between a gun (the penis) and a rifle by chanting, "This is my rifle, this is my gun; the first is for business, the second for fun." With this racist and sexist basic training the men proceed to the more advanced military schools:

At school, you also learn more of the promised land. The War stories come very thick now. My Lai was child's play compared to some of the stories that are told in schools. Being out in the field is compared to a big game hunt. But the hunting is even better back in the base camps. The Chicks are thick and they are cheap, too. And best of all, they are only Gooks, so if you get tired of them, you can cram a grenade up their cunt and "waste" them.[33]

Dr. Robert M. Liebert, the drafter of the overview to a major government inquiry on violence, concludes unambiguously that violence in American society is taught, learned and acted upon.[34] Six volumes of studies document his conclusions. Is violence not taught as much to girls as to boys? Very simply, no. Boys are actually encouraged to be aggressive by parents while girls are not.[35] Additionally, almost all the models on television which encourage aggression are men, thereby encouraging boys to *continue* the aggression they learn from their parental role models. In fact, this is just what happens in boys: childhood aggression predictably results in continued undisguised aggression when the boys become men.[36] In girls this is not true.

DIMENSIONS OF CONTEMPT I: THE SEX-OBJECT TRAP

Men often ask "What's wrong with appreciating a woman who's physically attractive? After all, that's the first thing you see, isn't it?" In context, nothing is wrong, but as Lewis, a man in one of my consciousness-raising groups, discovered, "the first thing you see" led him into what might be called a sex-object trap:

"I got to the party after not having sex for weeks. My girl and I broke up two weeks before. So I looked over all the girls at the party. One was really a turn-on, but I didn't think she would be attracted to me. Besides, this lawyer fellow seemed to be putting the make on her. I didn't want to hack the competition. But there was another chick, er, girl, who was almost as attractive, so I decided to see if I could get her —I mean, have a relationship—ya know what I mean.

"Well, I got up the nerve to approach her—see if she wanted a drink, or something. I spent most of the evening on her—er, with her. When it got later, she made up some excuse about having to get to bed early because she had to get up early—but I wasn't included in her bedroom plans that night. It took another couple of outings.

"The problem is, I like her physically and all, and she's interested in what I have to say, but I always find I'm having to bring her up to my intellectual level—I kind of like that for an evening, but I want a more liberated long-term relationship. I've really been looking, but it's a problem. I guess I'll break up with her if she doesn't change. But it's always a hassle to have to go back out and find someone else. I've sort of got an investment in her now, you know?"

Lewis chose a woman primarily on the basis of physical appearance and expected mental compatibility. While he would not have pursued a relationship with a "dumb broad," he would have found it much easier to find someone compatible in terms of mental vibrations and warmth had his focus been on that from the outset and on appearance secondarily. By focusing on the physical the rest only came by coincidence. We eventually started referring to this as the first stage of "the sex-object trap." The subsequent stages are more subtle. We found that often our assumptions that we were bringing the woman up to our level only meant that we were evaluating her from our area of topic security—bringing her to our functions with our friends discussing topics with which we were familiar.

The sex-object trap becomes greater if a man's investment in a woman is greater and if she finds him attractive. Then he really feels trapped, looking for a graceful way to back out. His resentment increases the longer he plays the game, eventually becoming very deep; at that point he usually gets out, but not without a mark on him and his feelings toward women. He is determined not to make the same mistake again, but he doesn't know how he made the mistake. Now he knows only that the last weeks of the relationship were without sex. He's hungry for sex. So once again he looks for a beautiful woman. He goes to a party, sees one who's a turn-on, and it starts all over again.

While the resentment occurring from finding oneself trapped with an incompatible woman may lead to contempt if his "investment" in her is great, a small investment can lead to a different type of contempt. A woman (a "chick") who does initiate physical contact or goes to bed the first night still has unspoken (or spoken) aspersions cast upon her. She is suspected of being just a sloppy two-bit whore, an oversexed, insatiable bitch, a nymphomaniac. She is the subject of myths such as "a woman who goes to bed a lot gets a big sloppy cunt." As Germaine Greer put it, "The best thing a cunt can be is small and unobtrusive; the anxiety about the bigness of the penis is only equaled by anxiety about the smallness of the cunt."[37] The trapped man's contempt for women increases, no matter what his investment, and the woman denies her sexuality, risks being termed "a cunt," objectifies the man for his investment capabilities, or finds herself in all three traps.

The negative connotations in calling a woman "a cunt"

also stand in marked contrast to the positive connotations of terming a male a "man with balls"—a man who stands up for his rights. If a guy is "hairy," he's smart and conniving, and "Man, what a fucker!" is even more a phrase of inspiration than the military slogan "He came, he saw, he conquered" (unless inverted: "he saw, he conquered, he came").

At first it may appear that the compulsion a woman feels to keep slim, dye her hair, make weekly trips to a beauty parlor, use a feminine-hygiene deodorant, apply make-up, and shave her legs and underarms is just a way of keeping herself properly maintained. However, this same woman is often expected to accept a beer-bellied man who, in Germaine Greer's words, sports "bad breath, farting, a stubble, baldness, and other ugliness without complaint. Man demands in his arrogance to be loved as he is."[38] The difference is not absolute—everyone likes everyone to look nice—but a matter of degree. The degree to which slimness and shaved legs and underarms is presumed *necessary* for a woman and the degree to which it is of little importance to a man is evidence of how little consequence anything other than the way a woman looks is to a man. Women's own self-doubt reinforces this. She, who has spent all her life learning the importance of a man in her life, dares not challenge him to "Accept me as I am" or she believes she may find herself rejected. It may not be an exaggeration to claim that a person who feels te may be rejected if tes looks are not maintained may be the object of underlying contempt.

DIMENSIONS OF CONTEMPT II: HUSBAND AND BREADWINNER-PROTECTOR

It is occasionally argued that the husband's image in cartoons and on television commercials is almost as poor as the woman's image. Brenton points to a series of downgrading commercials about married men.[39] However, the men are pictured as "gushing-housewife types," often doing chores such as the family wash. *This mockery of men is often of men doing women's work (which is really a mockery of women). It is invariably of married men, of men who allow themselves to be controlled by women (as he would be mocked if he were controlled by his children, his maid or some other "inferior"). All of this increases the contempt for women.* A married man is subject to mockery because he has allowed himself to be trapped by "them." The single man is portrayed as individualistic and rugged, able to attract the *sex* provided by women ("With a little bit of luck . . . you can have it all and not get hooked") while not getting caught by an individual woman. A Temple University professor, analyzing comic book characters, also finds that it is the married man who is the subject of mockery.[40]

The breadwinner role creates one of the strongest pressures on men. By linking the male role to breadwinning we are indirectly saying, "The higher your achievement in that role the more masculine you are." Like most pressures on men to achieve this pressure also creates a simultaneous disrespect for women who do not achieve. When Gary Wills pointed out in *Nixon Agonistes* that "the mystique of earning has inflicted a crippling sense of inferiority on our nation's nonearners," he was speaking of the nation's welfare poor.[41] He should also have been speaking of the nation's women, the majority of whom are nonearners despite the fact that they *do* work, and some of whom receive money from their husbands as if it were welfare. The masculine mystique of earning has also inflicted a "crippling sense of inferiority" on our nation's women. *Men usually think of their wage earning as part of their protective function, but the power to pro-*

tect implies the power to leave unprotected. The protector, on a personal level or a national level, can always be found striving to prove itself an adequate protector (for example, the arms race between the United States and the U.S.S.R.). The protector almost always looks down on those it is protecting (the "underdeveloped" nations). Men find themselves in the same dilemma—pressured to prove themselves adequate protectors while simultaneously condescending (in the biggest and smallest of ways) to those they protect.

Two possible solutions to this problem are sharing of both the breadwinning and child-care roles or homemaker payment—payment of half of the income of the household to the person staying in the home. Both of these are discussed in detail in the chapter on concrete alternatives. Neither will be put into practice without overcoming substantial barriers. For example, in my survey of male employers I frequently found that when I asked the employer if he would ever consider taking a year off to care for children, he would consistently reply something like: "Personally I would like to do it, but I could really endanger myself here at work—imagine telling my boss I'm going to be a mother for a year!" If I agreed that might be impractical and asked, "Would you actively support a child-care center here in your company?" a not atypical reaction was: "If I keep pushing for things like that, I'll end up Vice-President in Charge of Girls (laughter)." Over and over, *the employers seemed scared, even to the point of sweating, to be a part of anything out of the ordinary, particularly if it associated them with something "weaker," like women, or showed what our society considers "weakness," like self-examination.* They never perceived the corporation as controlling their lives but were petrified to do anything that would deviate from its norms—especially if they could be laughed at.

DIMENSIONS OF CONTEMPT III: THE SEX STRIVER

The physical, student, leadership and job strivers have in
common another major area which simultaneously limits
them and hurts women: These men are usually sex strivers.
Women become objects not only of the male sex drive but of
a man's need to use women to prove himself a man to other
men. As Wakefield puts it in a description of his two main
characters' "ass-chasing": "What the hell would Gunner think
of him if he couldn't produce a girl he could lay." However,
*the more a man has to "produce pussy" the more he molds
himself into the object he thinks will attract the woman.* As
Wakefield's character Sonny points out, "That was the most
important thing of all, that aura of success: the cunts could
smell it on you. They could sniff a loser from here to South
Bend. With their eyes closed."[42] *A woman becomes a sex
object as a man becomes a success object.*

The pressures, still common in high school, to "score" with
girls, to "make" as many as possible, to "see how far you can
get" and a myriad of other pressures do little to encourage a
young man to feel free to concentrate on the sincerity and
intellectual and human qualities of a woman. Rather, her
body becomes a physical adventure. He may be taught to be
careful in his *strategy* for *disrespecting* her "territorial integrity," but he is not encouraged to respect her total integrity
or even to look for her mental integrity.

When a man measures his manhood by his ability to lay a
woman who doesn't normally "fuck around," he makes sex
into a challenge. But he also defines a "desirable woman" as
one who is sexually elusive, one who, in essence, *denies her
sexuality.* In addition, when the challenge becomes the whole
meaning of sex, after the challenge is over, then sex itself has
lost its meaning. As one of Wakefield's characters observes:
"He knew he could do what he wanted with her, which

maybe was why he didn't want to do it anymore." In essence, his masculinity is being measured by the degree to which he robs women of both their humanity and their sexuality and robs himself of the ability to be human.

Many a college man is quick to claim he is liberated from all this, but his every motion betrays dominance. Even in college it is still the man who develops a fragile ego by always placing it on the line. He may not call it "dating" but he still initiates "getting together" whenever sexual overtones are involved. Even on a casual stroll with a woman he will lead to make a turn. He will still drive unless the woman asks. He will still "suggest" what they might consider going to—while letting her know why his interests might be best, although "I'll do anything she wants." He still initiates the first physical contact in each area—from hand-holding to genitalia-caressing. At a dance, college men still ask women to dance more than the reverse. If payment is involved, the woman may volunteer to pay for her share, but she, unlike the man, never *starts out* assuming she might pay for both, unless special circumstances require a *deviation*. In all of these instances a woman is in the position of reacting or falling back on coyness and coquetry to initiate interest; this co-quetry in turn reinforces men's contempt for her, the male performance ethic and the fragile male ego. Most importantly, it forces the man to always be the aggressor—to plan, calculate and fantasize his sexual advances. We assume this behavior is more subdued as a man outgrows adolescence, and we seldom associate it with professionals. But when male professionals get together (as in the U.S. Senate or the Supreme Court), we find many of the same attitudes expressed in a more sophisticated manner. Perhaps best illustrating this is an excerpt from the graffiti on the bathroom stall of the New York University School of Law during the spring of 1973:

A Growing Body of Law:
The Mona Goldman — Elaine Haberfeld controversy
WHO HAS BIGGER TITS?

Is this a justiciable question? No, but I've had jurisdiction

Judge Younger is going to take
judicial Notice of Mona's dimensions
Label them exhibits 1 + 2 for identification
          Enough procedure! Let's get on with the
          adjudication of the issue: WHO'S BIGGER?
We must stop this senseless writing on the walls!!!!

I move to appoint myself special master
to decide the issue of fact on the basis of
feeling, tasting, measuring, etc.
                                  What about size?
—GRANTED—
Interim findings **suggest** that the WEIGHT of the evidence is in
Motion for summary judgment.
                                  Mona's favor
—GRANTED

    Doesn't Elaine appeal?

NOT TO ME!

New test granted on the grounds that the verdict
was not supported by substantial evidence—
on the face of the verdict for Elaine "Boobs" Haberfeld

Haberfeld should lay. However, we are reversing and remanding for a new trial de novo (have fun — now I know why they call you the lower court and us the court of "appeals")."

Bulletin — the Supreme Court just noted Pendente Jurisdiction —
(Too bad Douglas isn't around — he would have liked to settle the issue)

This wall is a good example of male chauvinist infantilism! — So?

Sour Grapes

He's probably a root

Go back across the hall (women's room) where you belong!
men's Room: Love it or leave it!

Right On!

This Wall is great! It proves you learned something in Law School
—Dean McKay

Sometimes the graffiti loses its sophistication:

Karen Wasserman sucks big cocks
She wouldn't settle for less
Are you boasting or complaining?

Complimenting both her and me, but also
Complaining because although she can
accommodate big cocks in her big fat mouth.
She can't do more than flap her lips
In the breeze — I came, but with
little thanks to her.

The more sophisticated graffiti of the lawyers and law students in what is acknowledged to be one of the best law schools in the country still contain the same contempt for women, the same use of humor as an escape mechanism from serious male-female relations, and the same focus on women as sex objects. The one male who attempted to deviate has aspersions cast on his masculinity by every other contributor. The development of masculinity dictates the atmosphere which develops our laws.

Four

The Confines of Masculinity

One of the ironic limitations of masculinity is an inability to enjoy the sex for which the "masculine" man has allegedly been clamoring. The psychology of many women has changed so that sexual enjoyment is now possible—as far as *she* is concerned. Dr. Herbert A. Otto, chairperson of the National Center for the Exploration of Human Potential, explains that the women who have changed are discovering that for all the men's talk, many men become impotent the moment women show any overt desire for sex. He observes that men are beginning to perceive women as "sexually demanding and possibly insatiable, since the fear of pregnancy which has acted as a deterrent to her sexual appetite has been removed."[1]

What causes this impotence? According to Dr. B. Lyman

Stewart, president of the American Urological Association's western section, one cause is an unconscious hostility many men feel toward women.[2] We have discussed many of the dimensions of this hostility, but at least one is connected directly to the challenge associated with the male role of initiating sex with a female playing sexually elusive.

After the challenge part of sex has worn off, after the object has been conquered and the woman has become liberated enough to stop denying her sexuality, then the first major possibility of impotence sets in. His penis was used to rising to the excitement of the challenge of conquering. Now that the challenge is over, the penis has no reason to rise—*unless* a new challenge can replace the old. The pseudo-liberated man controls a woman by playing teacher and excites himself by exciting her with his ability to introduce new sexual techniques, thereby presenting a new challenge: the persuader, always the teacher, usually the winner in the end (she learns "his" techniques). The woman may be pleased with each form of experimentation, but he is restricting himself by the one element common to both situations that excites him and keeps his penis hard—control. *The moment the woman begins to assume control he finds he doesn't know how to be dependent on a woman.* He has never thought of her that way, so fear sets in. He cannot become excited from her excitement unless it is controlled by him; his penis becomes soft. He fears her and fears his supposed loss of masculinity. He does not recognize that all his life he has never concentrated on developing resources to get excited by learning from a woman. In that position he is insecure and afraid, and his penis cowers.

A man's penis turns soft when he cannot control a woman, but it also turns soft when he worries about it being hard. Man's sexuality is still penis-centered. It is, in fact, a narcissism of the penis. He is haunted by the possibility of not getting his penis hard. Once he "fails," his self-consciousness keeps it soft. His impotence is compounded by the fear of impotence. His penis-centeredness blinds him to the sensuality of sex not connected to the penis. A hard penis is not necessary for sexual enjoyment. Some cultures have, in fact, developed a rich and varied sex life for large groups within it without even having intercourse.[3] Germaine Greer puts the problems of penis-centeredness succinctly:

The man who is expected to have a rigid penis at all times is not any freer than the woman whose vagina is supposed to explode with the first thrust of such a penis. Men are as brainwashed as women into supposing that their sexual organs are capable of anatomical impossibilities . . . women must humanize the penis, take the steel out of it and make it flesh again. What most "liberated" women do is taunt the penis for its misrepresentation of itself, mock men for their overestimation of their virility, instead of seeing how the mistake originated and what effects it has had upon themselves. Men are tired of having all the responsibility for sex; it is time they were relieved of it . . . the emphasis should be taken off male genitality and replaced upon human sexuality.[4]

It is obvious men must take the bulk of the responsibility to "humanize the penis" or, as I prefer, to integrate the penis into sensuality rather than integrate sexuality into the penis. One of the pleasures of some of the men in the consciousness-raising groups who have worked on this is an ability to enjoy sex after orgasm, something they formerly believed only women could do. I now feel a man can develop this ability concurrently with that of being able to share emotions. When an emotional flow is added to semen flow, the woman gradually becomes less of a semen receptacle to be discarded after use, since the emotions are still with him when the semen is with her.

Greer addresses this problem from the parallel perspective of the clitoris:

Women's continued high enjoyment of sex, which continues
after orgasm, observed by men with wonder, is not based on the
clitoris, which does not respond particularly well to continued
stimulus, but in a general sensual response. If we localize female
response in the clitoris we impose upon women the same limitation of sex which has stunted the male's response.[5]

Psychological changes in sex require a man to listen for
feedback in order to know what excites a woman the most.
He can get excited, not by knowing how to overcome her, but
by knowing how to help her come, by being part of creating
feelings in a body that shivers and vibrates with excitement.

There can be considerable reward for a man in knowing
he's not being made a fool of by a woman who is feigning
excitement; not more than a few seconds need be spent on
love-making ineffectually. At the same time her increased
enjoyment makes arousing her a part of his pleasure. For a
man to know that a woman wants his body is stimulating,
even more ego-gratifying than feeling that she's touching him
out of an obligation that it is part of love. Only sadomasochism can thrive when the man gains enjoyment while the
woman resists and protests until she convinces herself that she
has no sexual desires of her own. Sadomasochism can produce
a type of enjoyment if it is what both people want, but love
should not obligate a woman to be masochist, to undermine
her own sensuality—a fact which some women have discovered.

Effecting the change in penis-centeredness requires a drastic downplaying of impotency centeredness. Whether impotency is defined as premature ejaculation or as a soft penis,
impotency centeredness puts a premium on performance. The
tendency to call a man "impotent" the moment he "can't get
it up" only reinforces his need to perform, which in turn
leads to nervousness which in turn fulfills his fears about his
impotency. A new word, *readiness,* should replace "impotence," unless the lack of readiness becomes the rule rather

than the exception. The sexually liberated woman is not nearly as vulnerable to charges of frigidity as the man, since a lack of readiness on her part is not as easily observable, except in the extreme. Her comparative lack of vulnerability in this area gives her a psychological freedom not available to the man. She feels much less pressured to perform than the man does; he can ignore or overcome this pressure only if his penis is not considered essential to love-making and if its softness is considered just a sign of lack of readiness for intercourse per se. Most men feel free to say "I'd really like to lay her" but do not feel free to say "I'd really like to lay *by* her." We become "pressure-cooker lovers." When the pressure is off the hard penis the focus on the rest of the body—on caressing, on sensual games like toe-touching under water or finger-sucking—tends to be greater. Redefining impotency, then, means eliminating the pressure on the penis to be upwardly mobile.

THE CLOCKWORK EXECUTIVE: HIGH-LEVEL MEDIOCRE

A man's need for an upwardly mobile penis is only outpaced by the pressure to be upwardly mobile in his career. *The pressure on the man to appear successful compels him to make others appear unsuccessful.* An otherwise honest man is pressured into small dishonesties, and small dishonesties are requisite for a trap called "gamesmanship." The rules of the game are the hierarchy, the roles and the goals. Men find themselves, therefore, playing these roles and not questioning the goals in order to win the game of upward mobility through the hierarchy.

What is wrong with upward mobility? First, the usual pattern of upward mobility is to specialize in an area and then move up to managing a group of specialists by defending their specialty. As we accept the goal of reaching the top it tends to inhibit basic questioning about the goals determined by the top. Second, past a certain point *this special-ization inhibits expansion as a person.* And yet it is difficult for us not to specialize. Almost all of us who are men have confused love with respect—we have sought to gain love by gaining respect. We feel we will be more respected as a school superintendent than as an elementary school teacher; as a corporation president than as an honest salesman; as a professor at Harvard rather than at a junior college. We feel the twinkle in a woman's eyes as she introduces us with our newest title. We are almost oblivious to the ways that twinkle is a pressure. It makes us forget to ask the basic question: *Is our particular specialization reaching past the point of diminishing returns for our own personal growth?*

"Liberated" women may eventually feel similar pressure if they adopt the masculine value system in the name of liberation. But it will be a long time before a high position makes us look at a woman as more feminine in the way that a high position makes us look at a man as having made it "as a man."

Does all of this mean a deemphasis on achievement? And if it does, will that mean a weakening of the country, or even of us as people? For the most part it means the opposite. It is not to give up achievement, but to avoid being locked into one type of achievement. To perform without choosing the way one performs is to become, in Anthony Burgess's terms, a "clockwork orange." An orange develops reflexively through each stage, and according to a certain schedule, or "clockwork," it grows from an orange seed to an orange blossom and then an orange. Some oranges may be bigger than others, some may get there faster and some types may be more valued than others, but the orange itself has little choice. This is what the average man is doing in his striving for a higher level. He is making himself "big" by being a bigger orange, but not by questioning the type of orange he wants to be or whether or not he wants to be an orange to begin with. Not only does he respond reflexively to *having* to achieve, he does little questioning of his *need* to achieve. The criterion for success is established by someone else, according to someone else's clockwork. He is a clockwork executive.

To overcome the pressure to perform is not to return to mediocrity, it is to gain the freedom to escape mediocrity. Kafka portrayed the ordinary man as tepid, narrow and distinguished only by his mediocrity—a man who wanted merely to "do his job" or "get through the day." *Men today who believe they are not mediocre because they have achieved are often merely "high-level mediocrities."* Society suggests that men "achieve" by being productive in certain areas and by achieving certain positions; they have gone scampering in just those directions. *To be secure, men have to be in the right position when they produce and in the right position when they reproduce.* The woman's attempt to "complement my husband" keeps him in his place. Her inability to change places makes it impossible for him to change, even if he were secure enough to try.

Becoming a liberated man, then, is not stopping the pursuit of excellence, but rather discovering the ways excellence has become distorted into pursuing mediocrity in the name of excellence. If one were to draw up a contrast to Vince Lombardi's pursuit of excellence, the comparison might look like this:

> Winning is not a sometime thing.
> It is an all time thing.
> You don't win once in a while,
> You don't do things right once
>   in a while,
> You do them right all the time.
> There is no room for second
>   place.
> There is only one place and that's
>   first place.
>   Vince Lombardi

Liberating Excellence

The pursuit of excellence is the pursuit of balanced person-hood, a free body, an open mind. It is being able to contribute my all to my work by causing it to contribute to me. It is bringing about that contribution by listening. By learning. By admitting error. By trying the uncertain. It is drawing out the potential in others so that their potential becomes my experience. It is realizing that time away from work improves the person who comes to work. It is first choosing one's love as one's goal and *then* seeking a way to make a living through that love. It is forgetting the "How can I fulfill society's expectations of me" and asking "How can it fulfill my expectations of me?" It is recognizing that being practical is working on the ideal at present rather than making the ideal an ideal.

If the status game preserved men's health or happiness, it might be worth the deception, but even the market analysts recognize it is the man on the way up who needs status symbols and hard liquor to prove to himself that he is successful; a Johnny Walker Black Label ad, for example, assures "a taste of success" on the way to the top. He disguises his increasing nervousness by drinking more and his increasing insecurity by switching to Chivas Regal.

The relationship of drinking to status and masculinity first struck me when on a plane trip I sat next to a top-level executive who described in quasi-inebriated fashion his weekend spent repairing his yacht, and boasted about his birdie on the sixteenth hole and the new room he was adding to his Cape Cod home. Yet he could not make it through the trip without drinking two dry Beefeater martinis. Beefeaters "extra dry" may seem unrelated to masculinity until we try to imagine an executive asking for a whiskey sour, extra sweet, or a daiquiri in front of another man and a stewardess. The need to increase liquor status with job status may seem trivial until its connection to the status of his ulcers is understood.

What discouraged me most was that this executive was continuing in this style despite his recognition of the consequences. When I politely confronted him he replied, "Yeah, now I can afford the best liquors—but get ulcers when I drink them. I'm a member of a racquet club, but I'm afraid of a heart attack every time I play. I know I'm nervous, and a few of my friends have had cancer—and doctors are beginning to link that to nervousness and anxiety too. I don't know. I've spent all my life getting here. What can I do?" (No wonder a major Connecticut life insurance company has instituted its own in-hour Alcoholics Anonymous aimed at top executives.)

The need to continue despite the consequences is perpetuated by an image of the male executive as independent, assertive and creative. Brenton explains the fallacy of this:

A considerable number of men in the larger corporations seem to be more assertive in their jobs than they really are. Fence-sitting is often developed into a specialty that sees a man through many long years of steady advancement. Decision-making by committee or computer or both can take the edge off individual responsibility . . . The corporation man sometimes emerges as much less than heroic to the one person in a real position to know—his secretary, on whom he often becomes markedly dependent. He may rely on her completely. She stalls people he doesn't want to see. She fields for him when his superiors are pressing him for a decision he'd rather avoid making. She buys his wife's birthday or wedding anniversary gift for him. In extreme cases she presses his clothes in the office and makes sure that his tie is on straight.[6]

Men's liberation means breaking down stereotyped roles so that men can gain the freedom to change places with women, or switch jobs or even just resist on their jobs without risking the entire family income. The ability to resist can be an important part of creating a sense of self. For me, resisting traditional ways of teaching at Rutgers University was an important part of helping me discover my own creativity. Psychologically, though, I found myself freer to resist (and therefore be creative) the more losing my job did not mean losing the entire family income. This meant devoting supportive hours to my attaché's career. Ironically, that supportiveness of *her* freed me to develop a sense of myself.

Erving Goffman discusses this in his book *Asylums:*

Our sense of being a person can come from being drawn into a wider social unit; our sense of selfhood can arise from the little ways in which we resist the pull. Our status is backed by the solid buildings of the world, while our sense of identity often resides in the cracks.[7]

THOU SHALT NOT BE VULNERABLE . . .
THOU SHALT SPECIALIZE

This "sense of selfhood" is difficult for men to discover. It will remain difficult as long as men are not free to be vulnerable or to admit they are wrong without thinking less of themselves. The fears of self-examination and vulnerability are limitations of masculinity which are exacerbated by the job striver's concern for external rather than internal rewards. These fears are characteristic of men in all classes and are an essential part of the striving male.

Norman Mailer expressed this fear in a painfully honest manner. In a discussion with him he agreed to join a men's consciousness-raising group. When I followed up our talk with a written invitation, I received the following response:

November 5, 1971

Dear Mr. Farrell:

. . . Frankly a men's consciousness-raising session does not interest me much. I'm leery of that and sex discussions and panels and all such apparatus, if you will, for I think it's a way of digging too close to the source of one's work. Obviously I would rather write a good book than go around raising my consciousness. If you think the two go together, I'm not at all certain I agree. Man is verily a bag and when he blows out in one place, caves in at the other.

But cheers,
Norman Mailer

One implication of what Mailer is saying is that *when a man spends his life building an expertise, he cannot afford to reexamine his consciousness in a light which may prove him wrong.* One cannot dig "too close to the source of one's work." In a culture where men are supposed to be the experts, men also have the most at stake when their expertise is invalidated.

If this is not a problem of all males or only males, it is a problem emanating from the masculine system of values, which places success above vulnerability.* For example, most top-level bureaucrats are men—men highly protective of their expertise, men insecure about someone coming too close to the "source of one's work" lest their function be eliminated. A highway commissioner is not likely to support an investigation which might conclude that mass transportation is more important and valuable than highways. Each bureaucrat builds a constituency without which he would have no position. In this atmosphere, honesty is secondary to leaving undisturbed the constituency so carefully acquired. It can become a lock step into which a top executive or writer can force himself to march.

The problem becomes clearer when we examine other men at the top of their fields. Can William Buckley really open his mind to a liberal position, now that his whole life and constituency is based on his conservatism? Could Abbie Hoff-

---

* To the extent that women adopt this system, everything mentioned about masculinity (except comments about the penis) can be applied to women.

man or Eldridge Cleaver concede even one point to William Buckley and accept the loss in their constituency? If Richard Nixon's trip to China persuaded him that communism is really superior to capitalism, could he make a reversal while President? Why were Clark Clifford and Dean Rusk unable to act on their feelings about the war in Southeast Asia? These are all men operating in environments that discourage too close an examination of one's consciousness, men afraid that man is verily a bag and if he blows out in one place, he will cave in at the other.

The bureaucratic specialist is further discouraged from questioning his own conclusions because his expertise discourages others from questioning him ("He must know; he's the expert"). To maintain that aura, he must never admit weakness or fault, never submit to emotional outbursts, always maintain a "cool hand on the switch." These demands are especially clear in the political world.

What do George Romney, Edmund Muskie and Thomas Eagleton have in common? Each had a political career severely damaged or totally ruined after an admission of weakness. George Romney admitted to being brainwashed; Edmund Muskie allowed tears to escape his eyes; Thomas Eagleton admitted to having had electric shock treatments. American society responded to each confession of vulnerability as its own shock treatment, thoroughly willing to castrate each of them. In the 1968 primary campaign Romney's admission that he was brainwashed by White House briefings about the war in Vietnam supposedly made him "unfit for the Presidency," where presumably he could be brainwashed by anybody. The public's reaction was not "Here is a man big enough to recognize when he is wrong and admit it in the middle of a primary," not "Too bad Lyndon Johnson, Dean Rusk, and Clark Clifford could not admit their mistakes while they were in office." Instead, it was a nationwide torrent of criticism exacerbated by the press, which forced

Romney to withdraw from the primary race against a man less willing to admit vulnerability, Richard Nixon.*

In the next primary campaign it happened again. During his 1972 campaigning in New Hampshire Edmund Muskie learned the price of crying when he broke into tears while countering a slur on his wife. The crying generated much speculation about Muskie's emotional stability, not only in New Hampshire but throughout the country. *The New York Times* reported that Muskie "showed himself here, in the view of many politicians, to be a man who tires easily and tends toward emotional outbursts under pressure."[8] There were no headlines saying "Muskie not emotionally constipated."

If the cases of Romney and Muskie are important, the disaster befalling Thomas Eagleton is the perfect example of the male eunuch. Eagleton, the first vice-presidential candidate in the history of the United States who was forced to resign, admitted he had received shock treatments, the last of which were six years prior to his candidacy. Despite no recent evidence of depression, his admission of vulnerability, *of seeking help to solve a problem* (rather than projecting his problems into public policy), indicted him to a much greater extent than if he had refused to admit that he had suffered through periods of depression or had sought help. To internalize weakness—to keep it to oneself and consequently to allow it to remain within oneself—is the American public's method of castrating its leaders and itself; the weakness that remains within the leader is his ultimate defeat and often the nation's defeat as well.

The masculine mystique in all of us prevents us from electing leaders who can admit to being brainwashed or ad-

* In late 1972, as a Secretary of Housing and Urban Development, Romney became one of the rare American politicians to suggest that the programs over which he presided were largely unsuccessful, request their dismantling and withdraw from his post.

mit fault in Vietnam. It is that mystique which allows us to accept a Watergate—even after the wire-tappers are found guilty and directly connected to the Office of the President. Nixon's genius politically was recognizing that the American people would accept erased tapes, ignored subpoenas and a blaming of the incidents on Haldemans—but not an admission he was wrong or brainwashed. Rather than cry, he "toughed it out," "kept a stiff upper lip," associated the pressure for him to quit with a national weakness, saying "we are not a nation of quitters." He not only refused to examine himself but refused to give others the tools for that examination. He knew the American people well enough to know that wrongdoing clothed in weakness would be met with rejection, but that mistakes clothed in strength would be met with cynical acceptance ("that's just politics"). We can accept scandal with cynicism—cynicism is an emotion we know how to express. No wonder Watergate is virtually a male soap opera. The masculine mystique is the masculine mistake.

Working-class men are also afraid of self-examination[9] and the vulnerability it breeds. Police departments, for example, are strongly opposed to real self-examination or even civilian review boards. Although its job is to pry into the affairs of others, its members do not want to expose themselves to examination by others. The police are also conservative as a group,[10] a fact which is highly correlated with authoritarianism[11] and with opposition to women's liberation,[12] all characteristics of the "masculine" man.

MASCULINITY AS EMOTIONAL CONSTIPATION

Males in bureaucracies reinforce each other's tendency toward specialization and protect each other's safe bastion of expertise. As they specialize and protect, their personalities adapt. Max Weber's description of the development of bureaucracy is striking for its similarity to the male personality: "Its specific nature . . . develops the more perfectly the more bureaucracy is 'dehumanized,' the more completely it succeeds in eliminating from official business, love, hatred, and all purely personal, unrational and emotional elements which escape calculation."[13] In this atmosphere, men cannot help but be either emotionally incompetent (unable to handle emotions expressed by others) or emotionally constipated (unable to express their own emotions) or both.[14] His emotional constipation leaves no outlet for his stomach but ulcers. One wonders if there is such a thing as a liberated top executive, or does the trip through the bureaucracy maim them all?

When a man does question the criteria for success or the reflexive need for a schedule of achievement, he often does it in the form of a socially accepted cocktail cynicism: "Anyone who wants my job can have it!" Cynicism is a man's emotional diarrhea. Real emotions are stuck in his system. He does not have the strength to carry out the logical conclusion of his cynicism—open protest. His defense is the same as an unliberated woman's—"the risks are too great." They are both insecure.

If the emotionally constipated man acknowledges that he has emotions, he certainly cannot *show* them. A cardinal tenet of the masculine mystique is that a man must not cry. When confronted with this edict, many men say, "If a man wants to express himself crying or what have you, no one's stopping him." It is not easy to find a man who has tested this proposition in public. The overt liberalism expressed toward crying is like the overt liberalism once expressed by northern whites toward integration: People were free to do it until they did it.

A friend explained to me that he broke down and cried in front of a colleague at the office after some personal tragedies and office frustrations. He explained, "The news of my crying

was all over the office in an hour. At first no one said anything. They just sort of looked. They couldn't handle the
situation by talking about it. Before this only girls had cried.
One of the guys did joke, 'Hear you and Sally been crying
lately, eh?' I guess that was a jibe at my masculinity, but the
'knowing silence' of the others indicated the same doubts.
What really hurt was that two years later, when I was doing
very well and being considered for a promotion, it was
brought up again. My manager was looking over my evalua-
tions, read a paragraph to himself and said, 'What do you
think about that crying incident?' You can bet that was the
last time I let myself cry."

One of the conditions men will gain from breaking down
sex roles is not only the freedom to cry, but ultimately a
change in the environment which will encourage men to cry
when they feel the need. One of the incidents revealed in a
consciousness-raising group was related by a man who had
recently had a highway accident. The man, Larry, and his
friend, Joyce, were in Larry's car which Joyce was driving.
She wasn't used to the steering mechanism and the car
swerved into the onrushing traffic in the opposite direction.
A number of cars swerved around them and a Trailways bus
skidded to a stop a few inches before their car. After a
moment, the people in the bus piled out to help them. The
women went up to Joyce. They took her aside, asked her if
she was upset, and created the conditions which encouraged
her to cry and obtain the needed relief by crying. The men
approached Larry, who was also totally shaken, and said,
"Wow, that was a close one, man—are you sure you're okay?
How's the car?" For the next five minutes they discussed the
problems with the steering mechanism and its possible connection to other mechanical difficulties. When Larry and
Joyce returned to the car, they were both aware of the
tremendous tension Larry still had pent up within him, as
well as the relief from the tension which Joyce felt. Yet on

the surface, Joyce had been the one who appeared to be emotionally upset. By allowing Joyce to appear weak, society allowed her to gain internal strength, while Larry suffered the consequences of surface strength.

DEPENDENCY CONSTIPATION

A man's emotional constipation is supplemented by his dependence constipation. The job and leadership striver thinks of himself as independent, but the very characteristics which make him appear independent—his success, money and status among peers—are the things on which he is dependent: success, money and peer-group approval. His dependence on success may lead to assertiveness at work, but it saps his energy to the point of his being passive with his family. He refuses to admit his dependence because his identity is attached to everything on which he is dependent. The vicious cycle makes dependency constipation an important topic for consciousness-raising groups.

While dependency constipation is less acute among men in consciousness groups than among men in general, because entering a consciousness group in itself is a sign of willingness to ask for help and engage in introspection, examples of dependency constipation still occur at almost every meeting. Some men cannot let their attachés drive without feeling uncomfortable; others have difficulty even asking for driving directions until it is absolutely proved they are lost. Still others will avoid doctors until it is proved they are sick. Psychotherapy provokes the worst cases of dependency constipation. To see a psychiatrist is to admit not only weakness, but mental weakness, the kind unrecognized by "real men." To enter a consciousness-raising group is even harder for some men, since it entails a trusting of equals, a partial dependency on and opening up before the type of men before whom one is normally especially closed. For this reason consciousness-raising and psychotherapy are usually good preparation for each other. It is this freedom to change and to examine oneself, growing out of a willingness to be vulnerable on a number of levels, that is an important dimension of the liberated man.

Denial of dependency and emotions leads to silence and the creation of a male mystique. Silence seems to contradict the description of the male as a striver and dominant interrupter, but men employ silence in special situations—those requiring the expression of emotional and dependency needs. Silence is an obvious by-product of the striver's need to maintain an image of success, omniscience and invulnerability. This silence can also affect women, as Nicholas von Hoffman, an insightful male journalist, notes:

We master women by exuding a male knowableness. Men yuk about women being mysterious, but it's usually the other way around. Women lay themselves open to men who stay silent: many, many women build their lives around their men, derive their identity from them. They often sacrifice their friendship with other women in doing so, while the men hide large patches of their lives and living processes. Such an imbalance gives men great power over women, and we use it.[15]

Men can use this mystique of silence about their fears and emotions to inhibit women. They know that women will try to understand a man's unverbalized fears and not trample on them. Steinmann and Fox find that 66 percent of women believe men will not like it if they are promoted to a better job than their husbands. Only 29 percent of the women, however, felt the men would express these feelings. They felt, in fact, that the men would verbalize surface approval of their promotion while thinking negatively about it. More than a third (38 percent) of the women believed that holding a better job would pose a threat to the husband's masculinity; but only 4 percent thought their husbands would say so. The men did not agree that their masculinity would be threatened, but they agreed a man would not admit it if it were.[16]

Women appear to be either more aware of men's ego problems than men are aware of their own, or they are projecting problems on the men which men do not have. Both possibilities have implications for women's and men's consciousness-raising groups. The separate women's groups can often bring a woman's fears about her husband's ego problems out in the open; the separate men's groups can provide an atmosphere in which a man might express his fears—such as his attaché having a higher status job. When the separate groups combine, the conflict can be observed more easily, since if the woman then shies away from mentioning what she feels is the gap between her husband's surface and underlying feelings, five or six other women can encourage her to have the confidence to speak up. The man benefits from the situation by being encouraged to face his own problems of masculinity, enabling him to gain the freedom of being comfortable with and even proud of his attaché's success.

A liberated woman can help a man out of his masculine mystique of silence about emotions, not by protecting him but by confronting him directly. She can also be an important factor in helping him overcome his imprisonment to his job. For example, a man in a consciousness-raising group formed after a speech in Iowa explained he had received a promotion to move to the New York branch of his company. For the first moments of his discussion he was boasting how grateful he was that his wife—unlike some of the "liberated types"—would move wherever he wanted, and was even encouraging him to make the move. "She knows it's important to me and the family, and that's the type of freedom a guy should have." A friend of his said "Yeah, but I'll miss you, Jack, and so will a lot of the people in town. And

your son is going to have to leave school and the Little
League where he is supposed to be the star pitcher this year.
Don't any of the friendships you've made mean anything?"

Jack looked a bit stunned. "Yeah. They mean a lot. But
suppose I lose the promotion—what will my wife think, and
the guys?" The supposed freedom Jack had from his "encouraging" wife was at second glance a pressure to keep
defining himself in terms of his job, to forget considerations
of friends and children. Had his wife confronted him with
these considerations it would, in fact, have left Jack with
more of a choice. Also, we never did find out whether his wife
really did want to move. When women were asked by Steinmann and Fox whether they thought a wife would want to
move they said she would not, but that she would not say
anything. This willingness on the part of women to keep their
desires to themselves may be part of the reason they believe
men do not say what they think. Most psychological tests do
conclude that men display hostility more overtly and women
more covertly.[17] Again, a function of consciousness groups is
to encourage the woman to voice her hostility directly, to
make the man aware of the freedom he loses by thinking only
of his career, and to raise the possibility that he is projecting
when he claims that "my wife wants me to take the promotion even though we'll have to move." He will no longer
have to hide from himself behind his wife.

THE REAL "FEMININE" MALE: CONFORMIST

The "masculine" male will vehemently deny that he is at all
like a woman, but many of his character traits are similar.
Women are often stereotyped as conformists as well as being
dependent, and yet men are not liberated from dependency
on an institution or conformity to its norms. The conformity
of men striving to advance in a bureaucratic setting is unsur-

passable. Clothing and hair styles are part of a conforming subculture to such an extent that observers can often differentiate between men working for a university or government agency (in his sports jacket), IBM (in his blue suit and striped tie), Grumman Aircraft, Bell Labs and dozens of others. Even in the relatively liberal New York City Police Department as of 1973, beards, long sideburns, long mustaches and long hair (to the collar) are prohibited.[18] The U.S. Air Force discharged best-selling author Richard Bach (author of *Jonathan Livingston Seagull*) for refusing to cut his hair at a waste to taxpayers of hundreds of thousands of dollars worth of jet-pilot training. Stereotyped sex-role behavior is a part of maintaining the corporate sales image or government authority image. Both sexes are limited by the stereotyping and the masculine values of success.

THE REAL "FEMININE" MALE: "MOTHERING INSTINCT"

It can also be claimed that men have their own version of the "mothering instinct," revealed in their constant need to protect women. An overprotecting mother finds that her children never grow up. Yet the men who most protect their wives are often the ones to wonder why their wives are not growing. Most parents cannot understand their teenager's rebellion when they first get a taste of freedom; most men cannot understand their wives' rebellion when they have discovered the confining nature of their husband's "protection." Men "mother" in their own way.

This male mothering has implications which extend beyond the family. This type of man wants to be the one to assume all the responsibilities for protecting "virtue" ("We must be the protector or policemen of the 'free world' "). He always needs to protect while romping over the territory of smaller, unarmed countries—claiming all along that the victim "really likes it" and would "much rather have me there than somebody else." His might is always right for himself and other people. The psychology of arming a country and teaching men to fight, of giving certain countries the role of protector and teaching others that they need not arm because they will be protected, establishes the basis of a competition for spheres of influence under the guise of protectiveness and chivalry. Rival "protectors" compete and teach the next generation the necessity of arming for the purpose of protecting. The very concept of arming and protecting becomes a lifelong self-proclaimed vocation which in practice translates into "conquering."

THE REAL "FEMININE" MALE: LIVING VICARIOUSLY

The success syndrome produces another allegedly female problem which is also a male problem—living vicariously. While a woman lives through her husband and children, a man lives vicariously through other things. Some are minor, like a stock, a horse in the Kentucky Derby, a baseball or football team. However, a man also lives vicariously through what he considers major things—his job title, the deed to his house, a status car, or the ways in which his wife or children reflect his success. A wife shows that a man is "being a good enough provider to let her remain at home." She must clothe herself handsomely, keep herself young and raise the children in their value system. Ironically, the more successfully she clothes herself and the more completely she keeps herself at home, the greater the burden is on him. Her need for his success keeps the pressure on him to keep living through his job. The tension mounts, and if success is escaping his grasp in a major area, he will often turn to a minor area for gratification, such as gambling or the stock market. She becomes bored and disrespectful, especially of his minor preoccupations. The boredom and disrespect create more tension. The unliberated woman, who has internalized her need to live through her children and her husband, has unwittingly contributed her half to the strength of the cage the man has built around himself. The man contributes the other half. Living vicariously has become a two-sex problem.

THE REAL "FEMININE" MALE: NARCISSIST

Both sexes have developed different but harmful versions of another allegedly feminine trait—narcissism or vanity. The leadership striver watches and admires his words with the critical vanity of a "feminine" girl applying make-up. The physical striver watches his muscles, develops them and tests them relentlessly. His muscle size is as important as the "feminine" girl's breast size, except he can do something about it. Push-ups, pull-ups, weight-lifting and wrestling ready his body for its daily display. His stomach muscles are subject to constant tests of muscle tone, his chest to constant tests of chest size, and his neck under constant scrutiny for strength. He measures his penis and keeps an eye on his ejaculations as an extension of what his penis can produce in the "circle jerk." Narcissism, like all forms of masculinity, breeds insecurity. Measuring and testing means worrying whether one measures up. An excerpt of a conversation from the joint consciousness-raising group illustrates the connection between measuring, narcissism and insecurity. The women had asked the men to discuss "our first memories of masculinity."

One of us responded: "The circle jerk—that's one of my first memories. We all stood around in a circle, told stories about girls or rubbed our penises until we got hard-ons. Then we ejaculated. The purpose was to see who could ejaculate the farthest. The guy whose sperm went the farthest was

'the biggest man.' He was the one who could really 'give it to
some chick.' The guy who couldn't produce or who had a
dinky little ejaculation—well, we sort of laughed at him.
There was even an element of pity in it."

"That's incredible. In other words, your penises were the
measure of what you were?" one of the women asked.

"Oh, yeah," I offered, "even literally speaking. I can remember at Boy Scout camp every year the jokes centering
around 'this guy with a ten-inch dick'—how he was really able
to satisfy a girl. You began to feel inferior if you had a penis
that was shorter than your foot! I can remember one of my
first childhood impressions of black men being positive because they were supposed to have 'larger pricks.' "

Another woman raised both eyebrows. "Did you *actually*
measure your penises?"

"Sure, we'd use the area of our fingers between the knuckles
—which was supposed to be an inch—and see how many
inches our penis was. Of course we tried to do as much overlapping as possible so we could get it to eight or nine inches.
And then the big guys would say they had more space
between their knuckles so they should really get some extra
inches counted on for that. That would make the little guys
feel even worse."

While penis-measuring can be understood as a form of
narcissism bordering on self-homosexuality, it is not a big
step to understand how the boy so concerned about the size
and performance of his penis will engage in heterosexual
activities for the purpose of proving to himself that his penis
really does "measure up."

The narcissism associated with masculinity can also be seen
in the Latin American counterpart of masculinity—*machismo*.
The matador and male flamenco dancer are often used to
illustrate the epitome of masculinity. Kate Simon, a Mexican
specialist, links the two. "Maschismo is the defiance and
narcissism of the bullfight, the torero, a flash of lustrous

splendor; arched like a jeweled saber, dancing a pavana with the dark bulk of death." Her description of the male flamenco dancer suggests that "his tight suit is outer skin for the taut, vain body, tensed like a bow; his face is distant and noble, distorted in a very private pain." The distant face of masculinity in the male flamenco dancer is not dissimilar to the distant face of the cowboy in the Marlboro ad. This same distance is found in the masculinity of men who are also fathers—which contributes to the son's difficulty in successfully identifying with his Dad.[19]

MASCULINITY UNCONFINED AND UNCONSTIPATED

It will take a new social pressure to define masculinity as seeking internal self-improvement goals with the freedom to express dependency and emotions, and the development of a broader sense of sexuality. But it is only that attitude which will allow for a balancing of financial success and human success. Men's liberation, however, will meet some of the same resistance which greeted women's liberation at the beginning and which women's liberation is still facing. The persons who need it the most have most internalized their role and are most afraid to question it.

Some men use women as an excuse not to change—"My wife likes me the way I am." Women who place all the blame for their not growing on men are guilty of the same escape mechanism, but the excuse is not nearly as valid for men. Women's liberation has advanced far beyond men's liberation. Liberated women who have questioned their own limited roles invariably find it easier to question the limited roles of men. Even the traditional woman has a much more open view of what she would like men to be than men have of women. Studies of the ideal wife a man would choose indicate that only 31 percent desire women who are courageous, forceful, independent, deliberate, daring, rugged and sharp-witted.[20] The woman's image of the ideal man, though, is one who should have many "feminine" as well as "masculine" qualities.[21] In the mixed consciousness groups it often comes as a surprise to men to find the women willing to forgo many of his stereotyped masculine qualities for some of the more human of the so-called feminine qualities.

When a discussion of men's and women's liberation starts questioning one stereotype after another, men usually get frustrated: "Won't there be any differences left? Is everyone going to be alike—unisex, uni-everything?" The answer is exactly the opposite: people will develop as individuals rather than mold themselves into a sexual stereotype. Men still ask, "What will happen to the chemistry between the sexes?" The potential for chemistry among individuals whose attitudes and behavior cannot be predicted is much greater than it is between two persons who are largely two stereotypes. There is no chemistry in confinement. The person searching for a stereotyped self is escaping from the freedom to develop a true self. A man reaching toward an image of masculinity, seeking the vicarious excitement of football and the symbols of nationalism as his security blanket, has little chemistry of his own when his personhood is uncovered.

Five

Super Bowl: Sexism, Patriotism, Religion, Gangs and Warfare

There is nothing wrong with watching a football game. There is something suspect when a man gives lip service to "I wish I could spend more time with my wife and children" and then watches three football games in a weekend. There might be something suspect in football being held in such priority that sixty-five million people can arrange their day to allow a three-hour bloc of time for one event—the annual Super Bowl.[1] Sixty-five million persons is between one third and one quarter of the American population, the very great majority of whom are men[2]—doubtless more than half the men and boys who are old enough to watch TV in the United States.

Sixty-five million (as opposed to, say, one million) American (as opposed to non-American) males[3] (as opposed to

females) have chosen one activity above thousands of alternatives. This alone makes the phenomenon worthy of analysis.
What are all these millions attracted to? When one adds to
this the fact that this may involve persuading their attachés
or living friends to rearrange schedules to allow the men to
do this and then *serve* them beer and chips during the game,
some attention might profitably be paid to the needs served
and both the conscious and unconscious ways in which football makes its appeal to American men. A systematic analysis
of every part of the Super Bowl (the pregame and half-time
activities, the game, and the commercials) provides some
fascinating answers.

The Super Bowl's first appeal to the viewers is patriotism
and power. If we follow almost any Super Bowl from beginning to end we can see it first in the pregame activities. In
the 1972 Super Bowl alone, for example, patriotism is represented in the pregame activities by the U.S. Air Force, which
uniformly and with precision discipline marches onto the
field. They are immediately followed by four flights of Phantom jets—the Tactical Fighter Wing of the U.S. Air Force—
which thunder overhead, again with precision and discipline.
Power and patriotism are linked. Speed and display of force
are inseparable from patriotism. The Phantom jets are just
leaving the viewer's field of vision when the male announcer
invokes in a deep voice (with background noise fading to
silence) a plea to "remember *our* veterans in your *prayers*."
Religion is now linked to power—but American power. There
is no question that a God exists and that this God approves of
power only as displayed by brave Americans.

The announcer's invocation needs a visual focus now that
the jets are gone. The camera zooms in on the American flag.
Patriotism is reinforced by music. The U.S. Air Force band
plays "The Star-Spangled Banner." Feeling is running high—
our jets, our Air Force, our flag, our anthem, and finally, our
boys. The unquestioned power of our country is associated

with the discipline and uniformity of every Air Force jet and
Air Force marching-band member. *No deviance is tolerated*
in this display. Freedom of choice seems to be *every* man
choosing short hair since there was no man in the pregame
activities without it. The power of "The Star-Spangled Banner" reached enormous heights, but it is followed by a final
call to patriotism—the U.S. Marine Corps's silent drill team
marching in quiet but precise step. This is the silence following the climax. Now the American male may watch the game.

Football, like war, is a scientific and brutal game; even the
vocabulary of football is similar to that of war. A "bomb" is
something thrown which destroys the opposite side. To bomb
effectively is to "score." There is always an us and a them.
There are commands to take the offensive and to prepare
one's defenses. Both football and war feature spying and
scouting, and special units for extra degrees of violence.
(When the vocabulary is not interchangeable with that of
war, it is with that of sex: "getting into the hole," "thrusting," and the announcer's admiration for each man successful at "deep penetration.")

The special team employed during every kickoff or punt is
called the suicide squad. The comparison to war is made by
Rich Saul, a lineman for the Los Angeles Rams who is
notorious for his play on suicide squads. "If you compare
football to war, then the special teams are the marines or the
infantry. We're the first ones to get into the game, we initiate
the hitting, we determine where the battle is going to be
fought and on whose grounds."[4] Saul, who says he enjoys his
job, "slams into ball carriers with such intensity that he
mangled five steel face masks on the front of his helmet."[5]
John Bramlett, a thirty-year-old veteran, says, "I just think
about hurting the other person because every time you get
kicked senseless, you can count on knocking two or three
other people senseless. That's a pretty good feeling."[6] Fans
made a legend out of Gil Mains of Detroit almost ten years

ago. His fame was based on his willingness to launch himself feet first at the heart of an offensive wedge (a group of about four especially tough and quick men who block for the ball carrier). His attacking position is commonly called a "head-hunter" (his primary aim is to get the ball-carrier's head). On the special teams the injury rate is eight times greater than for any other position.[7]

The dependence on approval is so great that players continue to play with injuries no matter how painful they are. The men entering the suicide squads are tough men who use their strength as a way of compensating for their insecurity about making it on the club in any other way. These men are "mostly tough rookies and second year men" who "realize that their survival on the club—and the road to a starting job—is directly related to their ferocity and fearlessness."[8]

On the field a series of rituals are taking place which are designed to reinforce and provoke the utmost aggressiveness of which each man is capable. The pep talk is one ritual. The boy is manipulated by a number of reinforcing loyalties—the loyalty to his school, the coach, his team and team pride, and his own personal pride. In the game itself the loyalty to family and neighbors is added. Prior to the game the team captain yells, "Okay, let's go get them!" and the team screams, "Yeah!" repeatedly. A third ritual, described by Dave Meggyesy, formerly of the St. Louis Cardinals, as part of his high school team's preparation, is a special church service by a minister (a former college athlete), who gives an inspirational talk.[9] Almost every type of tactic is permitted when the boys go all out for victory. The side with which one identifies is seen as all good and the other as all bad.

If the effect of professional football is not clear by the end of the first half of the game, it becomes clear at half time. The first event is the introduction of young male children who will competitively vie with each other for honors such as the best passer. Seven-year-old boys test their strength before

sixty-five million people, and the young boy at home sees
already that he is not quite the man some of his peers are.
Furthermore, the other person with whom he identifies is
sitting an arm's length away, glued to the TV set. Both the
football game and the presence of his father increase the boy's
sense of identity with both, but somehow he often feels he is
not yet worthy of being a part of what is on the field or
deserving of the full attention of his father. If the father is a
rabid football fan and the boy a fair-to-middling athlete, the
father's presence reinforces the son's *need* to identify without
enabling him to get the feedback to fulfill that need. There is
no consistent transmittal of that warm feeling which tells the
son he is accepted. Such a boy will either try to prove himself
on various playing fields or will live vicariously through men
who can.

No sooner do the boys clear off the field than women
(called "girls") come onto the field. They are scantily clad,
swinging their hips in unison, with outfits cut to reveal their
buttocks and bosoms. As the cameras zero in on the former
their legs slowly withdraw in a coy but obvious "see if you
can get me."

The "girls" are not only selling the importance of slim,
sexually coy bodies. They are selling the importance of *white*
bodies (not a brown or black face was among the hundreds
onto which the camera focused). But the sexism of selling
bodies and the racism of uniform whiteness was not enough.
These women were used to sell American patriotism. The
scanty outfits were red, white, and blue "Aunt Sam" outfits, and in case the point was missed, each girl had a
plastic American flag molded into an umbrella. As the distorted flag umbrellas were opened and closed the announcer
explained the theme—"remembering the birth of America."

While sex is selling patriotism on the ground, power is
used to sell it from the air. U.S. Air Force jets fly overhead,
dropping dozens of American flags amid a cloud of smoke and

a huge burst of firecrackers. The flags are distorted so as to fit into a parachute. The camera now returns us to the ground and the girls, where we witness hundreds of plastic flags laid on the ground and being danced around by "the girls."

The next group of ladies appears in frilly red tights cut similarly to those of the last group. These women sing "Hello, Dolly" and literally lay around in a circle on the field and spread their legs, lift them up and spread them again. Carol Channing also sings "Hello, Dolly" but in front of a fifteen-foot football. The U.S. Air Force Academy Choir replies to Ms. Channing by singing "Hello, Dolly." Suddenly dozens of dollies appear—it's the women in the red tights who now promenade off the field by passing the men. The camera zooms in to pick up the eye contact between the men and the women, the essence of the half-time game. The proper distance is always maintained. The men have made their eyes while maintaining their stiff all-male ensemble, and the women have made their appeal without physically being "had." The half time ends. The women who are on the field because of their bodies leave the field to make way for the men who will come on the field because of their bodies.

The viewer has now come through half a game and the half time. On the conscious level the man's power has been supported by his identification with the football players and his fantasizing an "I'd like to get her" relationship with one of "the girls" the camera brought into his living room. In fact, during the Cornell at Dartmouth game the ABC cameras picked out individual women in the stands and *rated them*. The evaluation (by males) were literally placed on the TV screen as "not too bad," "terrific," and other more condescending phrases. An ABC-TV spokesman indicated in a telephone interview that this was used on four broadcasts.[10] It was not an isolated incident and the pressure brought to bear on the network was obviously not great enough to make them discontinue its use (the spokesman said he "did not remember any reactions to this").

The armchair viewers of the Super Bowl meanwhile have been treated to a spectacle which the crowd at the stadium has missed—the commercials. The theme of all but two of the commercials was muscle, strength, power and speed (no different from the football game). The first of the two exceptions featured five women in sexy outfits attempting to gain the favor of one man by being chosen to serve him a Dutch Masters cigar. The man, literally on a throne, acts unaffected and coolly discriminating as the five women move their bodies caressingly toward him in repeated attempts to be recognized. The smoke from the cigars creates a fantasy atmosphere of clouds as the commercial ends, along with the fantasy of millions of men.

The second exception is the only advertisement which deals even remotely with emotions or with a father's relationship with his children. Four-fifths of the commercial is an incredibly good portrait of a close and warm father-child relationship. Then the father is told he might die. It is implied that if he loves his children he will buy insurance. His love has been exploited and twisted into fear for the purpose of selling him insurance. Now the father has a way of showing his love for his children: He can spend money. He alone is responsible for their support, if he's living or if he's dead.

A beer advertisement first prepares us for the introduction of the beer. We see a rowing team of all men. The camera focuses on their muscles—the strength and power of the men become clear, but they all take directions perfectly from their leader. The importance of strict obedience is coupled with victory, and victory coupled with being a man. The beer is introduced as the well-earned reward, with the concluding comment, "It's sort of good to be with men who won't settle for second best."

The razor-blade ad follows a similar pattern. The blades are tungsten, but they are not introduced until they are associated with a powerful steelworker drilling through tough tungsten steel. His shirt sleeve is cut short (and ragged) to reveal his muscles. Sparks bounce off his helmet. He balances himself above the city drilling the steel that makes the city (a far cry from "softer hands with Dove"). Now the tungsten blades can be introduced. They are blades "as tough as steel, for men with tough beards."

The marketing researchers know where it's at. Most of the ads were car ads—cars with "wide-grip tires" (not "pretty white walls"), with tremendous speed, and generally from the sports-car lines of whatever company is advertising. Men want adventure, freedom, a feeling of power, strength and status. They think that they are untouchable and unemotional, and are unaware that they are totally psychologically dependent on an authority figure. But marketing researchers are reinforcing this dilemma even more adeptly in the 1973–1974 football season. The new theme is selling products through the *fear* of becoming *effeminate* (as opposed to the *aspiration* of becoming *masculine*). Perhaps a New York Life Insurance ad illustrates this best:

A bespectacled, effeminately portrayed man in a white shirt and tie is pictured in the middle of a football field surrounded by eleven muscular football players—in uniform. By mistake the ball lands in his hands. By mistake he trips his way toward the goal line, stumbling haphazardly past each player. His wife is shouting from the stands, "Come on, Hubby, make it for the mortgage"; his daughter is shouting, "Come on, Daddy, make it for my college education"; the dog is almost pissing on the bleachers at the shock of seeing his effeminate master reaching his goal. Daddy trips and stumbles past another, then still another astonished "real" football player. With a look of happy bewilderment he finds he has made a touchdown. His wife, daughter and dog run from the stands—kissing, hugging and praising their hero. Daddy is stunned.

The male voice-over announcer is not stunned. He has the answer: Daddy is being protected by New York Life Insurance Company to make it to his goals. N.Y. Life Insurance Company has spent the entire commercial showing millions of men a symbol of a daddy who fears not being able to make it to his goal of bringing the bacon (represented by the football) home (represented by the goal line); who fears he is surrounded by barriers of invulnerable managers and executives (represented by the football players) through whom he will only be able to "muddle through"—at best; *who thinks he is being supported by the cheers of his family from the stands, but somehow recognizes that every cheer is a pressure.* Every cheer is a pressure to make it: it is the woman saying "I don't have any control over the mortage. I have to cheer you on to do something about it. I have to make a man of you." It is the daughter saying "I don't have any control over my college education, but I can cheer, 'I love you, Daddy, if only you'll make it.' " In tes own own way the dog cheers too, and in tes own way the dog is still another pressure.

In a world where men's cheerleaders are men's pressures, who supports the man? New York Life Insurance is there in case we don't make it. It too is a pressure which twists us into understanding our burden just enough to seek their protection, but not enough to seek the protection of having it shared with our attaché. The motto of New York Life is "We guarantee tomorrow today." New York Life understands. It does not run these ads during soap operas. *Its* phallic symbols are rising.

The game draws to a close. The winning coach is Tom Landry, "the man they say is unemotional." The winning team is the Dallas Cowboys, "the team they say is unemotional." But the victory is tremendous, a clear-cut triumph: 24 to 3. The cameras pick the victorious coach out of the crowd.

He barely cracks a smile. The time for emotions is certainly here, and a few of the football players do express happiness, but the game ends on a note of patriotism, not emotionalism. The *National* Football League champions are repeatedly referred to as the *world* champions. There are no boundaries to male power and no limits on male fantasies—except emotional limits.

SUPER-SPORTS . . .

If this relationship between masculinity, sexism, patriotism and violence stopped with professional football, there would be enough need for concern. However, the relationship can be seen in almost every sport. With some exceptions the more violent the game or match, the larger the crowd it draws. The emphasis on violence is not unrelated to what is making ice hockey grow. The television advertisements for ice hockey stress quite clearly the blocking, hard-hitting and violent aspects of the sport. Soccer is the most popular sport in the world but has barely caught on in the United States. Persons who have lived in the United States and other countries observe that even when soccer is played here, the emphasis on body contact is great—a phenomenon peculiar to this country.

On almost all the levels on which sports are played, sexism is a fundamental part. What high school basketball game is without cheerleaders to support the men's efforts? In many schools cheerleaders even support grammar school teams, and for a girl, "making it" as a cheerleader is as important a step in her view of herself as feminine as making the team is in the man's view of himself as masculine. Cheerleaders are still essential in college football, high school football and college basketball. The New York *Post* captured the identity problem of the woman cheerleader most graphically in a picture of a crying cheerleader slumped on the floor after Fordham lost in the 1972 N.I.T. play-offs. Obviously, the more the cheerleader supports, the more pressure is on the man to perform.

The woman, of course, can not usually influence the outcome of the game by *playing in it.* If participation of both sexes is permitted, the spotlight still shines on the masculine contest.

An interview with Phil and Marge Donahue[11] about their children's involvement in skating illustrates this point. Both children were interested in ice skating. For their son ice hockey seemed appropriate, as did figure skating for their daughter. Within a few months the son had expensive knee and shoulder guards, a hockey stick and a colorful uniform. The son was playing on a team and the games were receiving newspaper publicity. The games took place in a stadium with scores flashed in lights and loudspeakers announcing the activities of the boys. The fathers of all the boys took off every Tuesday evening to sit together in the stands, cheer enthusiastically for their sons, and went out with them afterwards to "talk like men" about the game.

Their daughter went to figure-skating practice where no one watched and no one cheered, except occasionally her mother. The daughter was jealous of all the attention her brother received, but didn't see any outlet for the jealousy; she couldn't pin down any specific injustice. Both of them were doing what was appropriate—presumably "what they wanted." When her mother noticed the jealousy and asked if she would like to join a girl's hockey team, she reported that her daughter was incredulous: "Can I play hockey too—me, a girl?" When her mother answered that she would form a team the daughter was jumping with happiness.

Football is not the only sport which is narrowly chauvinistic. Baseball considers its national champions world champions—winners of the World Series. In the Olympics (which are not limited to one sport and for the most part are based on individual achievement) *every individual represents a nation*. When an individual wins a gold medal it is clearly a reflection on tes nation. Germany under Hitler made an extraordinary effort to train Olympic stars to prove the success of Hitler's efforts to breed a master race; hundreds of articles appear during every Olympic year implying the superiority of the political systems of the United States or U.S.S.R. based on a handful of individuals' achievements. In identifying with the athlete representing the nation the fan is stronger than he is in actual life.

SUPER-JOCK

While on the surface it appears as if only the Donahue's daughter was being slighted, in fact both the son and daughter were being hurt in different ways. While the amount of attention the girl receives is minimal, the attention the boy receives really places considerable pressure on him. Every time the announcer broadcasts the achievement of another boy, the pressure for him to perform or score increases. With the lights flashing and his father shouting the boy has much more than his self-evaluation at stake. The rewards after the game are sweet for the achiever but bitter for the non-achiever. There is no overt punishment, just the punishment of being left out. The boy who did not even make the team is relegated to being completely "left out."

"Well," most fathers will reply, "this is all in fun, and besides, any *real* boy learns to take the ups with the downs." In some ways boys do—they soon learn to take it by learning to become well-defended. Sarcasms, witticisms and put-downs become the common mode of communication with their "friends." Underneath, though, boys do not learn to "take it."[12] Few boys escape adolescence without an ego so fragile that only a woman who will spend her life supporting it can be tolerated. Secretly they all yearn to be a super-jock.

The physical striver, as we have seen, is in fact quite insecure. The surface toughness, independence and masculinity of the football player often masks his need to be dominated. Meggyesy discusses the many ways in which the "father-son relationship is football's cornerstone."[13] He describes how players look up to, respect and desperately want approval from the coach. The coach who is respected is tough; he never shows feelings. The players need to be dominated and controlled by such a strong man.

A coach will chastise a player by saying he looks "almost feminine" on the field. Meggyesy points out that "this sort of attack on a player's manhood is a coach's doomsday weapon. And it works, for the players have wrapped up their identity in their masculinity, which is eternally precarious for it not only depends on not exhibiting fear of any kind on the playing field, but is something that can be given and withdrawn by a coach at his pleasure."[14] Not only does the coach exploit a fragile masculinity but he exploits a firm fear of femininity.

With women, though, the athletes are free to do as they like. In high school, players are encouraged to behave in a rough, aggressive manner both on and off the field. Players are even bailed out of jail and gotten out of other trouble by the coaches. The coaches view these activities as "sowing wild oats."[15]

Both coaches and players consider it "healthy and manly" to get drunk, lay a girl and "maybe even rough her up a bit." Meggyesy explains that to the football player "wives are virginal creatures keeping the home and children; other women are meat on the rack."[16] However, a lasting relationship is viewed with suspicion and even considered immoral.[17] There is a lot of bragging about sex among football players, but when a woman is around their self-doubt and nervousness shows:

Football players work up to approaching a woman just the way they work themselves up into playing. They range somewhere between boyish shyness and a heavy-handed caricature . . . players seem to see sex as something close to athletics. That is, they worry a lot about "staying power" and "performance" and dream of being able to inspire a string of orgasms in a woman the same way they dream of singlehandedly making a long series of tackles. I've always been struck by the fact that football is filled with language that is heavily sexual: "hole," "hitting the hole," "sticking it in her," "thrusting ahead," and all the rest. Using his body as a weapon in the game seems to carry over in the player's private imagination.[18]

A man who is interested only in meeting a challenge, running after elusive approval (from the coach), or conquering, tends to find himself unable to have a lasting relationship with women. He is too impatient to sit down and become involved with the entire gamut of emotions. Victory has little patience for feeling. Yet not every boy can conquer on the football field. If he is a lower-class boy he may choose gangs; if he is a middle- or upper-class boy his conquests are business, politics, foreign affairs or domestic secretaries.[19] As the lower-class boy becomes a lower-class man he has a high propensity toward homicide; if he is a middle-class man he has a high propensity toward suicide.[20]

These patterns have changed but little in recent years. In all classes the violence has become more sophisticated. In gang warfare, old reliable sawed-off shotguns have been replaced by more sophisticated weapons, ranging from .22-caliber pistols to machine guns. Walkie-talkie communications systems make the violence more efficient.[21] The members' respect for life is minimal. The fact that at this point the groups are not whites fighting blacks, or blacks fighting Puerto Ricans, or one ideology of any type fighting another,[22] points to the fact that other needs must be motivating the formation of these groups.

Talcott Parsons, the renowned sociologist A. K. Cohen, and W. B. Miller[23] agree that a relationship exists between masculinity and "ganging." Miller writes:

Gang members fight to secure and defend their honor as males; to secure and defend the reputation of their local area and the honor of their women; to show that an affront to their pride and dignity demands retaliation. Combat between males is a major means of attaining these ends.[24]

One gang member described his feeling as follows:

I have my mind made up I'm not going to be in no gang . . . then here come all my friends coming to me . . . then they tell me what they gonna do. Like, "Man, we'll go out here and kill this cat." I say, "yeah." They kept on talkin'. I said, "Man, I just gotta go with you." Myself, I don't want to go, but when they start talkin' about what they gonna do, I say "So, he isn't gonna take over my rep. I an't gonna let him be known more than me." And I go ahead just for selfishness.[25]

A continuing and persistent problem for gangs is a real and imaginary threat of attack by other gangs. The "threat" of attack is often used by violent gang leaders in a way somewhat similar to Fidel Castro's use of the "threat" of a Yankee invasion of Cuba: it mobilizes the group, takes members' minds off internal gang problems and personal problems, and provides the boys with a common enemy toward whom they can express their hostility.[26] ("I didn't want to be like . . . you know, different from the other guys. Like they hit him, I hit him. In other words, I didn't want to show myself as a punk.") [27]

A boy will often employ violence to demonstrate that he is somebody. Gang members use violence for upward mobility to acquire prestige or raise their "rep."[28] When a gang member has "made it," the need for him to engage in illegal violence is diminished. As W. B. Miller's studies of gangs demonstrate, lower-status gang members committed crimes between four and six times as frequently as higher status members.[29] This was the same phenomenon that we noted in relation to participation in suicide squads in football. The insecure rookie was the most likely recruit.

When the expectations for the achievement of masculinity are too high for an individual boy to achieve, he will often resort to forming gangs or rioting as a way of proving he's masculine. From a class perspective, the middle- and lower-class man's masculinity is threatened by a gap between the vague expectations of the man and his actual life conditions. For the ghetto dweller, sociologist Robert Merton suggests, the incitement to riot occurs when the distance between his values, or his goals, and his actual conditions of life is greatest. This distance creates frustration and aggression.[30] Recently, the ghetto dweller has become aware at an earlier age that if his expectations are not filled it may be the system's hypocrisy that is at fault. This minimizes his sense of personal impotence.

Meanwhile, the middle-class man often interprets the gap as one which exists because *he* is at fault, not the system. He feels inadequate and impotent because, unlike the ghetto dweller, he learned that *anyone who tried and is halfway intelligent could make it to the top*. The fact that he tried and did not make it often leads him to some negative conclusions about himself. He and the system were working as allies and *he* let it down. Thus the middle-class man is still feeling impotent while at least some ghetto dwellers are attacking the system rather than themselves alone. Neither, though, questions the *expectations* of the system for a man.

The expectations of masculinity are self-defeating from almost every perspective. Those who live up to these expectations end up being hard and competitive; those who think they are failing to live up to the expectations must prove themselves through delinquent acts when they are young; as they get older, those who "fail" have to feel superior to women or to racial groups or criticize unnecessarily those who have "made it."

In all classes crime is obviously a major political problem, and in all classes men commit most of the crimes.[31] If men's liberation affects men in ways which diminish their need to perform crimes, then this will obviously address some major political problems—only the most obvious of which are the alleged need for law and order, the debate over police recruitment and training, and the balance between security and freedom.

SUPERPOWER

The values of toughness, aggression, physical prowess and "smartness" (duping the other guy) can be seen as middle- and upper-class norms when the middle- and upper-class American male deals in international politics. W. B. Miller has said that gangs fought each other in defense of their masculine honor, pride, dignity and reputation. He adds:

It happens that great nations engage in national wars for almost identical reasons. It also happens, ironically, that during this period of national concern over gang violence our nation is pursuing, in the international arena, very similar ends by very similar means.[32]

The invasions of Cuba, Laos, Cambodia, the Dominican Republic and Guatemala, plus the emphasis on settling conflict physically in Vietnam, are but a few examples of the use of physical prowess rather than rational mediation in solving international problems. Nixon even failed to pay the regular lip service to the norm of peaceful means in his speech given during the invasion of Cambodia: he admonished the American nation not to become "a second-rate power" and "accept the first defeat in its proud 190-year history" by acting like a "pitiful, helpless, giant."[33] The extent to which these norms are upper-class norms when it comes to international decision-making is illustrated clearly by the class backgrounds of the decision-makers, as listed in the Pentagon Papers.[34]

When the man incorporates violence into his personal and family life, it becomes an inevitable part of his reasoning about political goals as well. He may know his country can already obliterate the "other side." However, *adequate* defense is not enough for him. He must be a member of *the* most powerful nation.

Participation in this distorted version of "America First," of course, varies from active belief (followed by action or vocal support) to passive toleration. The right wing tries to get society to approve of as much aggression as possible in the name of law and order. We have already seen how the soldier in Vietnam is ready and even eager to do the Army's bidding. In the political sphere the military trains its soldiers to see the enemy as faceless and totally bad while hymns are sung to America or to whatever the men identify with. Their lives—like the bodies of the football suicide squad—are expendable. It makes little difference whether the participant is a member of the Green Berets or the Green Bay Packers—the system will expend him if he is unquestioning enough and in need of enough approval to allow the system to approve of him by unquestioningly sacrificing his life for its cause.

In some ways the super-soldiers, like the super-jocks, are "guys who don't know any better."[35] For example, one of the first all-volunteer units in the country, the Bravo Company in Fort Dix, New Jersey, has an average educational level of 11.3 years: in other words, its average member is a high school dropout (1972). Army volunteers—with the elimination of the draft call—are often adolescents with a minimum of other alternatives and an awareness of this fact. They are, in essence, men with few alternative ways to prove themselves, and they have come to like this way because it gives them external recognition and rewards. The salient point is that the public is as responsible for the violence as the participants. Without the public there would be no rewards for the violence and participant able to "prove himself a man" by societal approval. Clearly, if war is to be cut back the values by which a society chooses its leaders might be modified to include the choice of men with less masculine and women with some traditionally feminine interests. Leventhal and Shemberg find that people who possess some of the women's hierarchy of values are able to be aggressive when necessary[36] and to avoid justifying violent stances and feelings because they cannot inhibit them. The women's movement has been systematically training women toward this end through "assertiveness training."

ON AGGRESSION

The lay person will occasionally remark, "Men just have an aggressive instinct," or "Boys will be boys," thus de facto assuming the inevitability of male aggressiveness while biologists and psychologists are still debating about its innateness. Assuming aggression to be natural, the "constructive theorists" talk about how natural aggression can be most constructively channeled.

The examples often given possess a subtle fallacy. They do not suggest that the *encouragement* of aggression be minimized, but only that aggression be channeled once it has already been encouraged. For example:

If we block normal outlets of aggression, we may turn it inward. When we pacified the bopping gang of a decade ago, its members turned to narcotics and self-mutilation. And middle-class hippies (also without aggressive outlets) followed in the same path, adding their own variations.[37]

These examples, though, are specious. Pacified gang members and hippies grew up in an environment which encouraged many of the aggressive activities considered natural for a boy. Aggression is stimulated in boys through almost every avenue of socialization.

Most biologists today agree that men do not have natural aggressive instincts, but that aggressiveness is a product of two factors—a tendency and one's environment—and that the two interact to produce aggressiveness or passivity.[38] The implication is that environment is a variable and that by its very nature, aggressiveness is open to environmental influence.

The question should be whether the environment should reinforce that aggressiveness or discourage it. Should we encourage aggressiveness as if it were good of and by itself, or should we channel what aggressiveness there is and do no more to encourage it than is considered humanly functional? Conversely, should a woman's alleged tendency toward passivity be encouraged to the point of dependency, or should her family and school make an effort to encourage at least enough aggressiveness to enable her to assert herself and function independently? *Our logic about aggressiveness compares to the logic of a doctor who says, "Boys naturally have more iron than girls; therefore, boys should take even more iron tablets."*

In fact, we do give more of these kinds of "iron tablets" to boys than we do to girls. This socialization process starts with dollhouses, football and children's literature, and continues through the double standard of the courting and sex life of most people.

According to Sears, Maccoby and Levin (1957), a significantly larger proportion of boys were permitted to express aggression toward their parents; boys were allowed to show more aggression toward other children, and were more frequently encouraged to fight back if another child started a fight. Girls got somewhat more praise for "good" behavior, and were somewhat more often subjected to withdrawal of love for "bad" behavior. Physical or antisocial aggression is less sanctioned for girls than boys in our culture, and physical aggression is expected and rewarded for boys more than it is for girls. Bandura (1965) [39] showed that preschool children's imitation of aggressive models was easily encouraged by positive reward.

Boys were also more subject to hostility and aggression from their parents than were girls. Girls more often than boys reported that both parents were affectionate and less often than boys reported that parents were rejecting, hostile and ignoring. Both sexes said that their mother gave more affection than their father.

Aggressive behavior to a certain degree is certainly positive, but our association of aggression with virility masks its dysfunctional qualities in the everyday life of the average male. We know that the masculine personality type is patriotic and conservative, wanting to do what is best for his society.[40] However, Leventhal and Shemberg find that *men scoring high in masculine interests do not inhibit aggression even when the approval of society is in question* concerning the aggression's suitability.[41] (This finding was contrary to their hypothesis.) However, women expressing feminine interests were able to be both aggressive in societally approved situations and inhibit aggressions in societally disapproved situations. This was also true of men who did not score high in masculine interests.

Since aggression may in some cases be protection against the blows of others some may fear that a breakdown in sex roles would lead to "passive men who cannot even defend themselves." Meanwhile Jerome Kagan, a leading authority in child development, finds that it is the boy with a weak identification with his father and a moderately strong one with his mother who is likely to be passive, feel inadequate in comparisons with his peers, be reluctant to defend himself against attack, and have difficulty suppressing anxiety.[42] When sex roles are broken down, however, the father will have a much greater opportunity to provide a stronger identification for the boy, since he will be free to be with the boy more often once he stops his striving and shares responsibility for child care.

The insecure man is one who often gets trapped into proving himself a man. *It is through this need that society can manipulate him.* He is especially subject to being manipulated into committing violent acts by the approval of the football coach or the Army general, the gang leader, other peers, their parents, the public or fans. The one thing he cannot do is defend what he believes in against the clamor of the crowd. It also may be doubted that he really knows what he believes in.

Passivity is termed a woman's value. Part of what allows us to be so comfortable with aggressiveness is merely the fact that it is *men* who are aggressive and men's value system predominates. Even if there is an innate tendency toward violence and aggression in people, it is our obligation to curb rather than reinforce this tendency. Instead, we have been either unduly reinforcing it or actively creating it.

Six

Masculine Images
in Advertising

The women's liberation movement has frequently protested the degrading image of women portrayed by advertisers in developing product appeal. The counterpart of the media's housebound-mother-wife-maid-mistress is the infallibly successful, accomplished, virile male. Men may be even *more* restricted in their identity as *human* beings. Men can climb to the top of a wide range of occupations to fulfill their image; but they are even more restricted than women in the contempt they receive should they deviate into a feminine role or fail in the masculine one. For example, little girls are allowed to be "tomboys" (ever heard of a "janegirl"?); "Josephine" is permitted to be a plumber (can men be househusbands?). Women can smoke Marlboros, yet no man dares smoke Eve; women wear pantsuits, yet no American male wears a dress.

A study by the author of advertising in numerous magazines, newspapers and TV programs reveals a process of subtle and complete role definition of "male" in our society. Advertisers use both conscious and unconscious messages to pick up on insecurities resulting from role expectations taught by parents, teachers, children's books and toys. They do this by creating a fantasy life connected with the perfect male and female.

Advertisers employ both verbal and nonverbal symbols: Some areas, like masculinity and status-striving, "are rarely discussed in words."[1] Even if specific symbols are not recognized as such, or even if an ad is not read but just seen, it will still have a gradual cumulative effect.[2] The fact that the product is less important than the image people are buying is underscored by the fact that a blindfolded tasting test of cigarettes revealed that a majority of the tasting panel not only could not recognize their favorite brand (and cigarette "brand loyalty" runs relatively high) but could not tell whether their cigarette was lit![3]

Marlboros are a perfect example. Marlboros were originally marketed as a woman's cigarette, until it was decided to completely reverse this appeal.[4] There were specific techniques used to achieve this new image. Marketing analyst Pierre Martineau explained that the first step was to eliminate all women from the advertising. All models were to be virile men, "chosen as successful, forceful personalities to inspire emulation, identification with an admirable figure."[5] The second step was to choose the symbol of virility—originally a sailor, recently a cowboy. Thirdly, the image of virility must be reinforced in subtle ways. Martineau explains:

Each man had a plainly visible tattoo on his hand. These were all standard U.S. Navy tattoos, and very eloquently—far more eloquently than any words could say—this symbol gave a richness to the product image, bringing it all into focus:

—Here is a successful, achieving, virile man.

—In his youth he slipped and had a romance, although he obviously wouldn't do it today.[6]

The tattoo disappeared when the Marlboro sailor was replaced by the cowboy, but the image and its effect, as described by Ernest Dichter in the *Handbook of Consumer Motivations,* remains the same:

The Marlboro cigarette man represents for the viewer the masculinity, strength, ruggedness, and the intensity of pleasure that one associated with sailors. It is hoped, of course, that these attributes will be transferred to the product. Research indicates that under favorable circumstances these symbols do in fact aid in defining the product for the respondent.[7]

Are men really manipulated by this masculine reassurance or do they make decisions on a realistic and practical basis? The history of advertising shows men often do not make decisions on a practical basis if they think their virility is at stake. For example, a major advertising campaign in England showed that Englishmen could not be sold on installing central-heating systems by advertising their advantages in terms of warmth and comfort. This affronted the Englishman who wanted to think of himself as so strong that he didn't need the "effeminate effect of central heating." The sales campaign became effective only after it reassured Englishmen that their virility was not endangered by feeling warm.[8] A false image of masculine superiority actually diminishes the supposedly rational sex's rationality at the same time that it maintains that his irrational "rationality" is superior.

THE MASCULINE AURA

Certain commodities—tobacco, automobiles, alcohol—almost invariably manipulate men by a direct appeal to masculinity. An advertisement for Field and Stream Tobacco, captioned, "A man's place . . . a man's enjoyment,"[9] pictures a rugged-individualist type handsome man standing in a snow-covered rocky terrain and holding a rifle while looking off into the distance—pipe in mouth, of course. It might seem somewhat presumptuous to arbitrarily assert that the snow represents masculine "coolness"; the rocky terrain, "toughness"; the rifle, "power"; and the distant gaze, "aloofness," until one notices the pattern prevalent throughout ads like this. Marlboro cigarette ads invariably show a tough cowboy[10] (leather chaps, leather face) reining in a prancing horse (often considered a Freudian symbol of sexual prowess) in a snow-covered wilderness (male aloofness and adventure). Once again there is the distant stare and the cigarette just touches his lips—occupying his barest concern.

Television often goes to even greater extremes. An ad for Winchester Little Cigars features a rough-looking he-man (rugged mustache plus beard stubble) in Western gear who comes upon a sophisticated couple who are horseback-riding. The protagonist proceeds to beat the tar out of the sissy, who is dressed insipidly in an English riding habit. As the vanquished man flees in terror, the victor leaps up behind the passive female and gallops off toward the horizon. All the action takes place to a rock tune entitled, "You've Got to Change Your Evil Ways."

While men learn the necessity of playing it cool and infallible, they also receive images which instill a fear of appearing at all like a woman. Television can draw this image quite graphically. In an ad for Peter Pan peanut butter the man is asked to make the sandwiches when the ones already made are not so good. Of course, he is represented as a completely asinine, fruity Peter Pan, who crawls in through the window and jumps around like an idiot (one of the kids, awe-struck, says, "He's *weird!*"). It becomes all too clear that any man who knows how to make a better sandwich than Mother *must* be weird.

In one of the few instances in which a man is not a buffoon but works intelligently in the kitchen (not only does he advise his mother to use Ajax Dishwashing Liquid but he actually starts doing the dishes—most unusual for TV), the viewer learns that he washes dishes *for a living*. Suddenly he's elevated to a professional status and he must embarrassedly qualify his domestic advice with, *"professionally* speaking, Mom . . ." It's then all right for him to be in the kitchen without being emasculated.

A more subtle example of the way television broadcasts the masculine image can be seen in an ad for Sears' "Toughskin" Jeans. A young boy is bouncing on a trampoline around which are gathered several boys and girls. The male voice-over describes the product, selling the jeans to both sexes. But he stresses that the jeans come in a "girl's style" *or* with a "double knee [for boys] to make them even tougher." The boys watching are taught that they are expected at least to be tougher than girls, if not tougher than other boys.

Advertising can become an extension of the "locker-room" effect, discussed below, in which unrealistic goals are set for boys who know they can never fully meet those goals, fearing at the same time that most other men have achieved them. By presenting a consistent, unattainable myth of what every man should be, the advertiser hopes that the consumer will identify with the product that is associated with this image, settling for a vicarious realization of this standard. Men are therefore manipulated into purchasing (via desultory products) a myth that leaves them with ulcers if they attain it and defense mechanisms if they do not.

ADVERTISING A WAY OF LIFE . . . OR DEATH

Cars have become the modern measure of a man's worth, an image not lost on advertisers primarily because advertising was instrumental in *creating* this image. An examination of car ads reveals how advertisers exploit this masculine image. American Motors' Jeep, bucking over a mountain road, is called the "Toughest four-letter word on wheels,"[11] implying conquest of geographical and sexual (four-letter word) terrain. Ford's LTD is "Strong. Luxurious. Quiet."[12] The accompanying photograph shows the car in the foreground of a bucolic setting with an attractive couple in the background. They are holding hands. The woman leans casually against a tree; the man stands free, facing her. He is not allowed to lean on the tree or onto the woman for support. This becomes a relevant point when one realizes that these two people are never seen in reversed positions. The woman's dependence feeds the man's independence, her need for his success feeds his need to be successful.

Recent Cadillac ads reinforce these values. One boldly states, "Cadillac. Because you play to win."[13] By examining the ad we can see exactly what expectations a man must fulfill to be a winner. The full-page photograph includes an angular shot of the automobile against a luxurious felt-green background which dissolves into a shot of three men sitting comfortably around a polished dark-wood table. The central figure, silver-haired yet youthful, impeccably dressed, is cradling a golf putter. The other two men look on admiringly, yet they are also well-dressed, confident, and polished to just a cut below the central man. The silver on the table complements the three large silver golfing trophies which adorn the shelf. Every component of success carefully tells the male what is expected, especially the admiration of other males. Another Cadillac ad with a similar format boasts, "If ever there were a thoroughbred of cars . . ."[14] and juxtaposes the car against a mounted male jockey in the winner's circle, surrounded by admiring well-wishers. The point is clear. Cadillac equals the masculine values of achievement, status, superiority, security. Buy a Cadillac and others will admire you, too, as a full American male. (If others admire you, you must be worth something.)

Alcohol, with a highly masculine connotation, also perpetuates this myth. Johnny Walker Scotch ads usually consist of a stark shot of a bottle of their scotch against a rich, dark background with a copy lead like, "As you're fighting your way to the top it helps to have a taste of what's up there."[15] A Seagram's V.O. Canadian Whiskey ad is headed, "For people who really know how to live,"[16] which is accompanied by a picture of a ruggedly handsome man, drink in hand, with a beautiful woman literally hanging around his neck. In double exposure in the upper background is a shot of a lonely beach at sunset with the two of them on horseback riding alongside the ocean. The masculine success symbol is again linked to the degrading image of women. A woman's goal is to wait until a "successful" male comes along, then collar him. The components of ads like these are only part of the overall effect; it is this *total* impact which is crucial, as ad men realize. Ralph Glasser writes that "when an advertising campaign for whiskey portrays an interior with an obviously successful man entertaining friends . . . the advertisement will 'sell' the desirability of the whole way of life that is portrayed."[17] A real man achieves each component of masculinity and ultimately a way of life.

Once the way of life is established the door opens for other advertisers to exploit the need of men to prove themselves. For example, clothing manufacturers claim that "wool . . . is seen as strongly male by men and women alike. To be 'male' in our society means, among other things, to be 'without inner weakness'—and wool almost perfectly conveys this impression. . . . Wool is best for presenting the impression of unquestioned ability to withstand the rigors of the world."[18]

The superficiality (or "inner weakness") of the masculine success ethic is reiterated in ads like those for *Gentlemen's Quarterly:* "No matter how successful a man is, the world won't know unless he looks the part. His entire *appearance* must say, 'I'm a man who's on the way up' [Italics mine]."[19] It continues, "How about your image? Are you telling the world that you're about to reach the top? If not, you need *Gentlemen's Quarterly.* . . . Each issue will bring you a step closer to the image that says prosperity is coming your way." Every step of the masculine value system encourages the need for external approval and appearances of success rather than internal approval or human satisfaction.

Another way in which men must measure their worth is in monetary terms. An ad for The Bank of New York shows a well-appointed businessman standing in front of a distinguished-looking hotel. The copy reads, *"Well, how much are you worth this morning?"*[20] *In a sense, every American male is obligated to answer this question every morning.* He tries to answer it by the way he dresses, the cost of the house he has slept in, the attractiveness of the wife he has slept with, and the prestige of his job.

A man feels that he is expected to be the authority on everything, to have all the right answers. The NOW report on sexism in WABC-TV programing documents the fact that the most significant authority figure in any commercial—the voice-over—is consistently a male voice, even in the case of traditionally feminine commodities, such as cosmetics and baby products. "Regardless of the resulting expertise that might be expected, male voice-over authorities took over 89.3% of the commercials."[21] Men are expected to solve not only problems in which they have a background, but to take care of *any* problem at any time. It is in this way that the improvement of women's self-image helps the man not have to maintain a false image and false ego structure.

Obviously, there is nothing wrong with a desire to succeed per se, but there *is* something wrong with the way it has been perverted into an unquestioned rationale for potentially destructive behavior. The masculine image is clearly destructive. "Real men" smoke stronger cigarettes than women, and their death rate from lung cancer in 1972 was over four times as high.[22] Men drink more heavily than women, and in general die at a younger age. Men are more reckless drivers than women, and are involved in nearly 80 percent of the serious accidents.[23] *Ralph Nader concentrates on making automobiles safer by building in more safety devices, but consider the increased effectiveness of his crusade to cut auto deaths if he could convince men that it isn't necessary for them to drink heavily and drive fast in order to retain their masculinity.*

PRESSURE FOR MEN, CONTEMPT FOR WOMEN

In the Donmoor ad for boys' clothing a poem by a fifth-grader is superimposed on a photograph of three boys frolicking in a meadow. The poem reads:

I'm Glad I'm a Boy

I don't like girls, I do not, I do not,
I know I didn't like them when I was a tot,
Girls hate lizards and rats, and snakes, bugs and mice.
And all the other things that I think are nice.
I sing a gay song and jump up for joy,
For I'm very happy that I'm a boy.[24]

The worst thing this boy can imagine is to be a "sissy." This type of ad, by appealing to mass insecurity, reinforces that insecurity in the masses. It does this by coupling male exclusiveness with a disdain for women, keeping both men and women in their place. The man is manipulated by an ego massage which establishes male solidarity by the degrading of females, in exactly the same manner as a country's patriotism is established by degrading other countries. Each is its own chauvinism. This image hurts men even more because it affects women's expectations of men as well as men's expectations of themselves. The reverse is also obviously true: The degrading image of women in advertising affects men's lives almost as much as it affects women's lives.

The parasitic female is an image of women which creates a burden on any man who does not need the massaging of his false ego structure. An ad for New York Life Insurance prompts men to "Tell your bride you just guaranteed her financial security."[25] The *man* can do this by buying one of their insurance policies. "You can depend on it to protect those who depend on you." Providing equals masculinity. Insurance salespersons (another male club) know it; employers know it. *The male club is in actuality a club of men exploiting other men.* The man overproduces to guarantee his masculinity and her security, leaving an unhappy woman waiting at home while the man lives with the illusion that he is doing "what he must" to make her happy.

Another example of the burden placed on men is the tag line for the Certs series of ads: "If *he* kissed you once, will *he* kiss you again?" Men are expected to initiate any sexual move. A woman cannot.

A series of ads by Allied Van Lines starts by advising "It's a rare wife who can face a strange town, unfamiliar neighbors, and somebody else's empty house without at least a mild attack of the slumps."[26] It is automatically assumed that the man, with masculine success values, will favor the move, while the woman, with her domestic values, must follow. Another Allied ad runs the copy head, "Behind every transferred executive there stands a woman with a moist hankie."[27] Once again husband and wife are set at odds. The advertisement goes on to declare that when a man is appointed manager, "Mrs. Newly Appointed Manager starts in on her special brand of worrying." She "worries"; she is given no credit for what she worries about—usually the bulk of responsibility for packing and organizing the move. In addition to the obvious condescension, this ad defines the woman in terms of her husband, not as an individual. Women are degraded, and men have the burden of having to define two identities.

The Allied ads are also examples of the way the corporation is able to control the man's life through appeal to his ego, and control the woman and family life, in turn, by controlling the man. There is the tacit assumption that a man will risk disrupting his whole family for the sake of a career promotion. It is as if no alternatives existed. Indeed, this type of thinking is so pervasive that for many men no alternatives *do* exist.

As the division of roles leads to a division of labor, a division of interests results. Husband and wife grow further and further apart; the contempt increases; when the children grow up and leave home, couples often find no reason to stay together. The confining images of men *and* women portrayed by the advertising media have merely served to make communication and understanding between the sexes more difficult.

Not unexpectedly, advertising serves to reinforce existing values. The profit motive has been interpreted as demanding this. Copywriters cannot take risks which will alienate any part of a given audience. Therefore, marketers find the lowest common denominators and exploit them. Ads which are not based on a specific profit goal, such as public service ads, tend to express a greater variety of values—as, for instance, ads calling for equal opportunity for minorities, a position few commercial interests would have dared to take if it had not been for strong social and legislative pressure. However, the insecurities of deviating from stereotyped roles are so ingrained that even public service ads consistently appeal to sexual differences.

The profit-oriented advertisers can be induced, though, to effect changes in their appeal. For example, heightened awareness of the manipulation involved in the blatant "sex-sell" method of advertising has forced advertisers to soft-pedal this approach in fear of arousing a backlash against their products. In the same way, heightened awareness can negate the impact of the masculine myth. Perhaps it will take the pressure of a men's liberation movement to accomplish these changes.

The liberation of human beings is not automatically harmful to commercial interests. The present policies of sex-role stereotyping result in many products appealing to only half of the existing market. The market for golf among suburban women is touched so minimally that golf courses are nearly vacant during the week and overpopulated during the weekend. The sale of golf equipment, therefore, also touches only a fraction of the market. The industry did expand the male stereotype with colored shirts, pants, ties, new hair styles and colognes, and although these also have their limitations as values, they did combine the breaking down of an even narrower concept of masculinity with the expansion of profits. By shattering their own myths about men and women, advertisers stand to gain a potential market twice the size of the present one. The market for men's purses is almost totally untouched, as is the market of dolls for boys. Advertisers do not need to lose money by encouraging individuals within our culture to expand their choices in determining their personal role in society.

Seven

The Family:
Redefining Motherhood
and Fatherhood

The current attack on the family as an institution[1] often serves as a huge cop-out; it allows us to avoid examining the problems of the individuals who make up the family. The division of labor between male and female exaggerates any differences in interests the couple might originally possess. It is largely these differences which make them incompatible whether they are in a commune, an extended family (for example, with grandparents), or in the nuclear family (just mother, father and children).

The family does discourage flexible arrangements such as rotating child care among four or more adults, and it does overemphasize privacy, prudishness and possessiveness to the point of exclusivity. But while alternatives to the family, such as the commune and extended family, should be encouraged, they can still confine men as breadwinners and women as housekeepers. None of the "Ten Commandments of Masculinity" are automatically overcome, In fact, in many communal settings this division is still maintained. The women center their labor around the commune and they gradually assume less interest in anything outside it. The men's job-striving lessens their interest in the commune. The men and women learn to take pride in their respective areas of responsibility, even as their interests part.

Pride and habit keep the women cooking and the men building, the women in the commune and the men in the office or studio. Frequently, the division of labor leads to the same division of interests found in the nuclear family. In fact, with the larger number of persons in a commune the need is less for the man and woman to communicate with each other about their interests.

The family per se is not totally bad. For example, a child's attachment to the family does not necessarily mean dependence on it. In fact, Lane finds that the paradox of good family socialization is that a supportive family creates the means for *self*-support.[2] In the same way, I have found from my experiences with consciousness-raising groups that a man or woman can help an attaché to become self-supportive in both family and nonfamilial settings.

A healthy attachment to the family can also serve to deter authoritarian values. In Nazi Germany children who were allowed to speak up were not likely to become Nazis despite the societal pressure at that time to so conform.[3] Good relations with a tolerant father enables a child to criticize society independently of the father and provides a basis for independent political action.[4]

For these reasons it is important to examine the problems of sex roles, and to do it in the setting with which most people presently identify, the family—under the assumption that if the underlying problem is resolved in one of the most difficult settings it will be resolved in extended families, communal arrangements, child-care centers, and in so-called open marriages.⁵

The importance of men's behavior and attitudes rests partly on the fact that *fathers usually care more than mothers that their children learn "proper" male or female behavior.* Fathers are particularly concerned that their sons learn to act like men. Fathers think their sons should learn "masculine expressive movements (such as swagger), aggressiveness, obstinacy, power, suppression of emotion."⁶ Furthermore, the fact that fathers often act this way themselves in relations with their wives, children, and other men establishes a role model for sons to emulate.

Why are these methods of child-raising maintained when so many persons have had so much experience with raising children? They are maintained partially because experience qua experience is considered good, and anyone who has it, whether good or bad experience, feels te can pass it on without evaluating it. We forget that people who have an investment in a method often lose their perspective. We criticize a Communist who discusses Communism as biased, and yet we declare that a parent discussing parenthood is *experienced.* Our receptivity or criticism really depends on whether or not we want to hear the point of view expressed. We accept the fact that a husband or wife who has experience driving may have trouble teaching the other to drive, and yet we entrust the infinitely more complex process of child-raising to word-of-mouth and trial-by-error experience. Little careful study, evaluation or systematic exposure to different points of view is done by either sex and men do not feel an obligation to serve even the most meager apprenticeship as babysitters.

"Love" is also employed to enforce stereotyped roles in child raising. Somehow our parents let us know that to deviate is to show a lack of respect or love for them; we sometimes forget ourselves that it is often a reflection of the love we received to become independent enough to be different. Like primitive tribes, we pass on myths from generation to generation. When we finally recognize them as myths we call them "old wives' tales," another phrase symbolic of our disrespect for women.

Prospective parents believe they cannot make valid observations about child-raising until they have their own children. Then, if they have children and are sorry, we tell them they should have thought about those things before they had them. In two joint consciousness-raising groups I attended, eight out of nine couples with children admitted they never made a conscious choice to have or not have children. As one man expressed it, "We got married, waited three years and had children—it was like being programmed. We're devoted to them, but if we had really thought about it we would have done some other things first." Child-raising is often undertaken with a "devoted resentment" that children resent until they have their own and can resent the devotion they are forced to give.

THE MYTH OF THE MATERNAL INSTINCT

One important key to the women's and men's liberation movement is a *sharing of the responsibility for raising the children.* In practical terms this can be interpreted as both parents having an equal share in the care of the child during its formative years. An apt aphorism for this might be "Balanced parental care means balanced children," which collides head-on with the myth of Mom.

The motherhood myth is an amalgam of the following beliefs: every normal woman has a maternal instinct (but the father has no paternal instinct) ; a woman cannot be fulfilled without children; the mother's constant attention to *her* child is irreplaceable and beneficial; the father's attention to children is important in theory but "impractical" because of the demands of his role as breadwinner; a working mother is asking for juvenile delinquency and marital unhappiness— especially if the family does not need the money; any woman who tries to deny these things is trying to be a man and should feel guilty about her lack of maternal love and the neglect of her children.

The notion of the maternal instinct becomes popular when women's labor in the job market is not needed. During wartime it is rarely mentioned. In the United States, studies of the heroines in women's magazines revealed a high percentage of career women during the war and a strong emphasis *after* the war on the maternal instinct and breast-feeding, the importance of a mother's attention and the glorification of the isolated suburban home managed by the mother.[7]

Is there a maternal *instinct*? In an experiment undertaken by Seay, Alexander and Harlow, monkeys were deprived of their mother immediately after birth so that they had no *environmental* models of motherhood. When they became mothers themselves, they were not able to care for or handle their children. In fact, one monkey "often terminated periods of nursing with violent assaults on her baby. She often dragged her infant across the floor, ignoring its screams, and struck it without provocation. On several occasions, this monkey was observed to hang from the ceiling of her cage and beat the infant with her hands."[8] Seay found that *all* of the monkeys without maternal experience in their environment were totally inadequate mothers themselves, and none of their babies would have survived without intervention from the laboratory staff. "Two mothers were violent and abusive and the other two were primarily indifferent and withdrawn."[9] Men and women may both have instincts for parenting, but the instincts must be learned through teach-

ing. Our culture teaches women, discourages men, and then
claims the instinct for parenting is unique to women.

In defense of the uniquely maternal instinct men usually
respond: "But the woman has breasts which are obviously
needed to feed the baby—and hasn't it been shown that breast
feeding is superior to bottle feeding?" In fact, as Heinstein's
experiments have shown, *the common belief that breast-
feeding is automatically psychologically superior to bottle
feeding is not supported by evidence.*[10] What is important is
the personality of the person doing the feeding and the
environment in which the child is fed. Under some conditions, such as when a mother's personality is cold or less than
stable, or in an unfavorable environment, Heinstein finds that
formula feeding is actually superior to breast-feeding. The
myth of the superiority of breast-feeding is maintained by
misleading statistics. For example, a mother from a broken
home in a poverty area who must work to support the family
probably cannot breast-feed, but the statistic only registers
that the child grows up poorly, and not whether it is because
of the broken home, the poverty surroundings or the lack of
breast-feeding. When everything else is equal, whether the
child is breast-fed or bottle-fed makes little difference.

Why do the same men who claim "you have to have children before you comment on them" make claims about the
maternal instinct without ever claiming to have one themselves? Men have an investment in the maternal instinct.
*It is easy for a man to suggest having children if he knows
his wife's maternal instinct will mean she is the one to take
care of them* and the same instinct means she will love them.
Why do men want children? It took over a year for the five
men with children in our consciousness-raising group to talk
openly and searchingly about some of the reasons. Among
them were "Curiosity—I wanted to see what type of parent
I would be," and, "Underneath, I've always wondered if I

was sterile—when I had children I knew I wasn't. I know that's a pretty stupid reason, but it's honest." In short, the maternal instinct serves as an excuse to assure a man of his sexual potency; it serves to round out his image of himself as a father, as a way of having his wife assume the responsibility the image entails, and as a way of keeping his career goals undisturbed without feeling guilty.

Once the maternal instinct comes into question, so do a number of other assumptions. If there is no maternal instinct, but just a human love for children, then a woman does not need to consider her life any more unfulfilled if she does not bear children than does a bachelor. She and her husband are psychologically freer to adopt children, since if the maternal instinct is seen as no more valid than a paternal instinct, it then becomes invalid to automatically assume the man should earn the money and the woman care for the children.

THE MYTH OF MOM

Some men, in explaining why their attaché stays at home, say: "Instinct or not, my wife knows more about children than I do" (or "Listen, man, that's her bag"). But why should *all* women be good at raising children any more than all men are good at breadwinning? The myth of Mom has forced women who otherwise love children to reach the point of diminishing returns in their love, while it has simultaneously forced men to reach the point of diminishing returns with their jobs. One finds high rates of alcoholism among both lonely housewives who have lived only through their children, and their job-striving husbands[11]; depths of depression among housewives, leading to hospitalization;[12] feelings of powerlessness, leading to 69 percent of attempted suicides by women, and career failures, leading to 70 percent of actual suicides by men (with housewives comprising the "largest single category of both attempted and completed suicides") .[13] For women, drug usage is becoming an increasing problem. Also, *most* children who are abandoned are abandoned by their mothers, and many more women than men are involved in killing their children—using methods ranging from drownings to burnings and strangulations.[14] This is particularly telling in light of the small number of homicides normally committed by women in comparison to men.

The man who explains that his attaché knows more about children than he does is ignoring the possibility that he may be more suitable and more skilled with children *after he has tried it.* He is also ignoring a myriad of studies on the damage to both the father and any child who is brought up by women alone,[15] to say nothing of the damage to the woman. (Doubtless children brought up by men alone, especially if the men had no fulfillment outside of the children, would suffer similarly.)

As families become smaller, each child becomes easier to dominate. As women become more educated, they tend to be more aware of their ability to influence. All of their intelligence is poured into one or two children rather than five or six. These educated mothers face a double jeopardy—they may dominate maternally and dominate their children in a professional and intellectual sense. The child becomes more a case or a specimen than a child. The result is poorly adjusted children.[16] In addition, *girls actually develop a higher level of IQ when they are relatively free from the restrictions of a dominant mother*—free to explore, develop and be creative.[17]

Ironically, among the effects of overprotection of a boy is the prevention of his achieving normal relations with other boys.[18] This is ironic because the parents who divide roles so carefully are usually most concerned with their children's adjustment. The mother-dominated boy is not only excessively passive in many cases, but develops many of the very traits of traditional femininity, such as lack of self-confidence, which we are suggesting is harmful to either sex. A mother *or* father who dominates a child transmits the single most devastating social disease—the deprivation of the child's ability to control tes own life, one of the key requisites for personal liberation. When this is compounded by the domination of just one parent it adds problems of overattachment to one sexual role to the problems of inability to extricate oneself from that attachment.

The second irony is that many studies of homosexuality indicate that the combination of a "super-heterosexual" job-striving father who pays little attention to his son and an overattentive mother creates conditions for homosexuality—especially if the father is also unsympathetic and autocratic. Statistically the association is very high (.001).[19] The father's rigidity makes his child internalize guilt and fear about his homosexuality. The development of homosexuality, of course, can be a product of healthy reasons as well. The point here is that neither heterosexuality nor homosexuality should be the product of an unbalanced parental relationship.

An overattentive mother who emphasizes niceness, neatness and spirituality, while deemphasizing roughness, also creates a likelihood of rebellion for the boy.[20] The boy identifies the mother with both goodness and femininity and reacts with destructiveness and masculinity in its most inhuman sense. Nye finds that children of mothers working part-time are better adjusted than children of mothers who are full-time housewives.[21] In addition, the children's attitudes toward the parents are more positive when their mothers are working. Girls are more likely to cite working mothers as the type of woman they would like to be.

The motherhood myth leads intelligent parents to become

concerned that should their child not receive proper *mother-ing*—especially when te is young—te will grow up delinquent, and it will be their fault. The problem is the implicit neglect of proper fathering. In Chinn's study of 1,000 delinquents, *problems with the father were found to be twice as important in producing delinquents as problems with the mother.*[22] Andry also finds that rejection by the father is more important than rejection by the mother.[23] The same is true with disturbed and maladjusted children. Eisenberg's study of 100 disturbed children revealed that 85 had fathers who placed work before the family, were rigid in their child-rearing ideas, were cold and undemonstrative, and insulated themselves from their children and wives.[24]

The motherhood myth is perpetuated, as discussed above, by the tendency of almost every researcher doing a study of maladjusted or delinquent children to ask "what is wrong with the child's relationship to the *mother?*" Just as frequently there is a deficiency in the father's care, and in the case of boy delinquents, an even greater deficiency. Blaming the mother alone for delinquency also ignores other factors like poverty, subjection to parental marital conflict or racial discrimination, growing up in a bad neighborhood, or other traumatic conditions. When all these conditions are considered, the father's importance looms large.[25] The poorly thought out research has created considerable apprehension on the part of parents who have heard this data but are not aware of its deficiencies. It provides perfect material for the romance magazines, which encourage women to leave the job market in order to breast-feed their babies, but it is not academically sound.

The discovery that the mother and father are equally important to the child's development creates further worries: "We can't both afford to work part-time in order to care for the child, and even if we could afford it, I doubt we could both find satisfying part-time jobs." There is no need, though, for either parent to work less than full-time, *as long as:*

1. Full-time does not mean overtime;
2. Adequate supervision is provided for the child;
3. *Both* parents make a special effort to communicate warmly and givingly with the child when they are home.

A careful investigation of the background of delinquent boys by Ferguson and Cunnison indicated that while delinquency was associated with bad environmental conditions, there was no correlation between the mother's employment status and delinquency. On the contrary, for boys between eight and seventeen, delinquency was, if anything, *lower* among the sons of employed mothers.[26]

Maccoby concludes that adequacy of supervision is the key factor in determining the effect of a parent's employment on the child, and adds that most parents do not bother to arrange for adequate supervision.*[27] For all the talk of the

---

* Adequate supervision is defined by Maccoby in *A Modern Introduction to the Family* on pages 528 through 531. Its essential features are that the surrogate parent exert both nurturance and discipline in about the same ratio to the total time spent with the child as does the actual parent. That is, the actual parent should not have to make up for a lack of discipline and too much nurturance or vice versa. Second, the caretaker should be consistently aware of the child's whereabouts, not leaving the child to roam the streets unchecked. Third, the mode of care of the substitute parent should not be too much at variance with that of the actual parents when the child is young. Fourth, in group care, the adult-child ratio should be small enough so as not to force the child to have to resort to making trouble to gain attention.

Maccoby points out that while one applies these standards to substitute care it should be remembered that the actual parents are often deficient in one or more of these areas—that "adequate supervision" may in some ways be better supervision than that provided by many actual parents. Maccoby also explains that a built-in benefit of adequate supervision (especially in groups) is the experience the child receives of a nonrigid concept of parenting. (Maccoby's research deals with mothering. I have used the word "parenting" based on other research findings on the importance of the father.)

importance of raising a child, parents often try to hire help for slave wages and then complain they cannot get adequate supervision. Without federally sponsored child care, poverty families are often unable to obtain adequate supervision and the children do suffer, but among poor families the woman usually works because she has no choice. For the middle-class family that can provide adequate supervision this should not serve as a deterrent as long as both parents return home promptly and pay attention to the child upon returning.

Finally, it is hypocritical to expect children to develop a sense of equal opportunity or even a sense of democracy if, as Gilman pointed out in 1911, each man has "one whole woman to cook for and wait upon him. The boy with a servile mother, the man with a servile wife, cannot reach the sense of equal rights we need today."[28] A critic may respond, "but the man is also waiting on the woman by earning the money." This belief ignores the fact that the children see moment by moment, day by day, their mother cooking, sewing, and cleaning directly for their father, receiving money and even permission from the father as would occur in an employer-employee relationship. Though he is also serving the mother and children, the father is not doing it in front of them and generally has a mystique attached to his work, whether he be a garbageman, policeman or doctor.

Some men still react to a woman involved outside of the home by objecting that "even if it doesn't hurt the children, it will have a bad effect on me—I like a woman to come home to. This type of situation could lead to divorce." In practice though, this is not usually the result. Danish studies, for example, report significantly fewer divorces in the families of working wives.[29] The key factor in American marriages appears to be the *man's attitude*. If the husband disapproves of his wife working, the result is poorer marital adjustment.[30] This does not imply that a man should force a woman to work even if she does not want to, believing it will bring marital harmony, since this attitude also leads to a poor marital adjustment.[31] But in a well-integrated family, divorce neither increases or decreases when the woman works full-time.[32] The ultimate goal is to free both men and women to have a choice of different types of jobs and at least occasionally to be able to take off from work. The male complaint, then, that if his wife wants to work it will have a bad effect on him is without merit unless he wants to create the bad effect.

THE MASCULINE MYSTIQUE AS
THE MASCULINE MISTAKE

In the same families in which the mother dominates and overprotects, the father is often absent or even when present is still involved in another world. In fact, one of the reasons women lavish attention on their sons is because of the lack of attention they receive from their husbands. Women who have a satisfying sex life, for example, are not as likely to be overprotective of their sons.[33]

Male polygamy—a man married to his job and wife (but barely to the latter)—causes many men who believe their devotion to the job will bring them love to find it has instead alienated them from those they love.[34] This situation embitters many men, since they have invested their lives and status in something they expected would bring appreciation. Instead, they are ridiculed and resented by their children; and they find their marriage unsatisfying now that they have the money to make it work.

The alienation from attaché and children which occurs as men start their devotion to work soon results in the men using their work as an excuse not to come home. Studies of working-class men on night shifts reveal that for a number of men the night shift is a refuge from the home.[35] The same is true of executives who put in long hours. Vance Packard's study of executives showed that the executive uses the office to avoid the home "and on weekends retreats to his golf club where everything is well-ordered and his status confirmed at every turn."[36]

A major problem with executives making their way up the ladder and with four million working-class moonlighters is that these men *are working at this heavy pace when their children are young and need them most.* A survey of moonlighters showed they were married men between twenty-five and forty.[37] Money is doubtless a motive—and certainly the one used to justify this behavior—but the man involved in his job is often avoiding involvement on a more personal level. He cannot be openly passive—that is a sign of weakness—but he can be so "needed" at the job, or need the job so much for money, that these outside needs can serve as a cover for his avoidance of family needs.

We discussed above the damage to the child of the over-attentive mother, but the counterpart absentee father also damages the children he neglects. A deficient relationship between the father and son can result in delinquency; it can result in destructive gang membership;[38] it can result in difficulties relating to peers,[39] to behavior problems in school,[40] and to schizophrenia.[41] Winch's survey of over 1,000 college students revealed the maturity and sexual adjustment of the men to be significantly lower if they were either from father-absent homes or dependent on the mother.[42]

The damage the job-striving father does to the boy may be greater than to the girl, but what little research there is in this area shows it is damaging to both. Johnson finds that girls may also be damaged by an inattentive father because normal development of their sex-role orientation is partially dependent on identification with their father.[43] A recent investigation of the backgrounds of stripteasers revealed that almost all of them had received little affection from their parents, but especially little from their father.[44] The father was generally absent from the home by the time his daughter reached her teens.

When the girl with a job-oriented absentee father does identify with the father, another problem occurs. She may feel she must either imitate him and his tougher, hard-driving qualities or marry someone like him. If she marries a job-striver she may be considered "adjusted" even though she has never been given the chance to identify with a warmer and more loving type of man.

Although girls are believed to mature early, it may be a deceptive maturity since the mother is omnipresent and the maturation may be in substantial part the girl imitating her mother. More importantly, a girl's identity with a mother who is always around is the most narrow and confining type of maturity—a training for housewifery without other options (as opposed to being a housewife after other options are considered).

The boy with an inattentive father often reacts by an exaggerated effort to be masculine,[45] to compensate for his fear of developing the feminine traits of his mother. He may idealize his father even more than the son of an attentive father because he has only a vague knowledge of how to be like him.[46] The only intimate knowledge such boys have is of their unidealized mother.

In some cultures the image of women as unworthy of men can narrow men's desire for women to such an extent that they become either latently or overtly homosexual. In Yemen, for example, women's extremely low status has made men turn toward homosexuality out of a necessity for companionship.[47] While homosexuality per se should not be discouraged, neither homosexuality or heterosexuality should be encouraged because of a lack of alternatives or a contempt for one of the sexes.

In an autobiographical essay, one of the men in Lane's interviews discussed the effects of his father's emotional constipation: "My father is generally undemonstrative of emotion and I have received little affection from him. I can recall even at the tender age of five a feeling of repugnance when asked to 'kiss Daddy.' In fact, my family is particularly loveless. . . . Seemingly as a result of this atmosphere, I find it difficult myself to demonstrate emotion. I have had few sexual experiences and my relations with the opposite sex have always been characterized by varying degrees of inhibition."[48]

In the final analysis, the son becomes like the father he idealizes. His contempt for and protest against his mother distorts his attitudes toward his own wife. He also becomes a father whose job comes before his family, whose absenteeism and lack of ability to express love will produce a son like him and his own father.

The pressures which make the man so inattentive extend beyond his obligations as sole breadwinner. He is also burdened with providing the status and job title through which the family defines itself in the community's eyes. An income which provides a living is not enough; it is the "standard of living" which counts (and is there a standard which can't be improved "just a little?"). The pressure is always on to improve it. Parsons points out that even when women in America work they do so within this framework: "They have 'feminine-expressive' jobs and do not compete with their husbands, if they have them, for chief status earner."[49] When a man is freed from this pressure he becomes free to take a creative job that would incur a loss in status.

The father who pulls far enough away from traditional values to consider child care and job both important reestablishes contact with an area of himself he may not appreciate at first—*the childlike part of his personality.*[50] Interaction with children brings out an enthusiasm many

men repress on their job in exchange for masculine sophistication and an air of knowledgeability.

THE FATHER REDEFINED

A distinction needs to be made between the man who is
active with the family and the man who communicates with
the family. The first is "Dad" as epitomized in the popular
magazines and TV ads. The second is reaching beyond masculinity. Playing ball with the children on weekends, cooking
a barbecue dinner or watching TV "together" on week nights
does not necessarily involve the warmth, reassurance and
opening of self required in communication. Just as sexual
activity does not necessarily encompass sexual communication.

Even communicating can be deceiving. Some men think
they are communicating when in fact they are trying only to
influence. They are simply exhibiting a power motive—the
need to influence either for pleasure or out of a fear of
weakness.[51] The problem with this motive is that the sons of
these men "clearly seek and value what they were deprived of
in the home: power."[52] Fathers who control their children
prevent their children from controlling their own lives;
fathers who have not reached beyond masculinity needs will
produce sons with the same needs. *The type of communicating which offers boys the strongest masculine model (but a
new masculinity) is done by fathers who offer warm positive
affection as well as providing discipline.*[53] These boys can
display confidence as well as warmth.

The father's presence should transmit a *new masculine
identity* based on the type of human values likely to be found
in a man who cares enough to be a parent to his children.
The man with a human identity—the basis of the new masculine identity—is as free to choose to be home with his children

while his wife works as vice versa. He is free to choose a job which is really forty hours a week—not sixty. He is not manipulated by his job striving, leadership striving or physical striving. This freedom is an obvious prerequisite to his being home more frequently. Once he is home, his sons and daughters are seeing a new image of masculinity—*a father who shows respect for the domestic setting by participating in it*—within a society which offers approval for that image.

Even with the options suggested in the alternatives chapter, a commitment to the family and to personal freedom for the man requires at least some sacrifice. If the man is unwilling to make the sacrifice, there is no reason he should expect his attaché to do so. If he does make it, he is certain to think twice about demanding more children. One cop-out, "The nature of my work requires too much commitment for me to cut back," ignores the reasons why the nature of the woman's job does not require that type of commitment; and also avoids another alternative—that if both jobs do require such commitment then perhaps the couple should not have children. In fact, in examining the decline in the birth rate as of 1974, Mary Rowe, MIT economist, discovered, "When men's time must be spent caring for children, the decision is usually made not to have children. This is the backbone of the reduction in the birth rate."

THE FAMILY REDEFINED

The new type of family, where the mother and father constantly have role choices opened to them, where the images for children are options for children, lays the foundation for true equality. The solution does not mean making the woman into a man or the man into a househusband, but rather for the man and the woman to share the responsibility for both breadwinning and family involvement.

Studies of families with creative children find that in these families the father interacts both "strongly and positively with the child, and the mother also interacts strongly but is sometimes ambivalent in her maternal feelings."[54] Actual observers of the children describe their characteristics as both masculine and feminine, but "not characterized by markedly effeminate manner or appearance . . . They showed an openness to their feelings and emotions, a sensitive awareness of self and others, and wide-ranging interests, many of which are regarded feminine in our culture."[55]

Developing a liberated man does not mean substituting new pressures for the old. Showing an openness to feelings does not mean a pressure to always express feelings as a mark of manhood. Once we establish a norm for masculinity, men will strive to prove they are not abnormal.

Will the absence of an enforced model to strive toward make a person insecure? In practice, having no enforced model helps a person feel secure in whatever te chooses rather than feel secure only if the model is achieved. *Insecurity comes from a conflict between the search for a self and society's (or one's family's) expectations of what one should be.*

Condemning society for establishing expectations or values must be qualified. Expectations of a positive human contribution and personal happiness must obviously be encouraged, as should many of the human personal traits discussed in "The Masculine Value System," but these expectations are different from the pressure to make money, hold a position or fulfill an image of the ideal male or female. The family redefined is the family that can be any type of *living unit,* but is not pressured into being any one type. It is the living unit that offers the support for the child to develop its own strength and values—even "conservative" ones. The family redefined is the family that *first* examines alternatives and *then* defines itself.

Eight

Concrete Alternatives:
Toward a Men's
Liberation Movement

As individuals change personal behavior they seek new societal alternatives. The alternatives in this section start with ways to share breadwinning and child care and conclude with a concrete program for a men's liberation movement. However, the individual involved in personal change is often trapped by a low sense of political efficacy—an ability to see oneself as effective in changing society or taking advantage of those alternatives offered by society.

In my experience women frequently express this confinement by saying, "I already tried to do that but it didn't work," usually meaning, "I mentioned that once but someone objected." Men's escape is, "If I just keep my mouth shut for a while, I will be in the position to really do something." They forget that the person in that position probably said the same thing and is now so caught up in responding to daily pressures that te does not have a chance to initiate new ideas. Ironically, the person who does initiate often finds tirself newly respected as an innovative thinker, finds te has new visibility and, more often than not, a higher promotion than the one te worried about forfeiting if te "didn't keep my mouth shut."

The key to implementing alternatives is to become that daily pressure—but in a way that makes allies out of former opponents rather than in a way hampered by ego needs of "I told you so"—the subconscious need to stand alone and play hero. In most cases the alternatives can be implemented through one person's efforts, if the person attempts to organize others who *agree*. For example, a woman friend of mine wanted to work but could not find an interesting job and did not trust leaving her children with just "any old child-care center." She put an ad in a local paper saying that she wanted to form a child-care cooperative, and was startled to receive over forty responses. She soon found herself coordinating a child-care center, which took care of her problem of finding a job and also obtained a suitable place for the children. She organized those who agreed with her.

With the exception of the family, child-care centers have perhaps the most potential for either forming or eliminating sex-role channeling. By the time children reach early elementary school age they are imitating their parents and exhibiting the sex-differentiated behavior seen all around them.[1] By the age of five, the children view the mother's role as housekeeping and caring for children and the father's role as related to earning a living.[2] When they see their parents performing each other's function they interpret it as "helping" the other parent.[3] The child-care center—especially if it admits children at the age of six months, as is the custom in Sweden—can be an important factor in eradicating the thousands of models which channel children into limited perceptions of themselves.

Child-care arrangements range from sophisticated professional care with extensive facilities and meals to simple arrangements which are often overlooked.

DO-IT-YOURSELF CHILD CARE ARRANGEMENTS

The most simple form of child-care arrangement is to get enough parents together to pool resources to take care of children. In almost any given geographical area there are usually dozens of mothers who would like to make some arrangements for child care but who do not because "There are no centers around here." Despite their experience with children, they don't consider starting their own center. The first step in starting a simple child-care arrangement, however, is simply to advertise a few weeks in succession in a number of the local papers, companies, supermarkets, and NOW newsletters. The ad should indicate the desire to get parents together who are interested in child care that doesn't reinforce sex-role sterotypes. The second step is to get a book on family day care (see special child-care bibliography in back of book).

An important third step is getting the men involved. Despite the initial difficulty, ultimately this will mean that enough persons will be involved to enable each individual's commitment to be small enough to maintain a full-time job while also participating in child care. For example, participation by ten couples* means each person must take only one

* "Couples" is used only as a convenience. Persons divorced or absolutely unable to take off any time from work can usually pay extra money into the center to pay someone who would like to work at the center in a paid position.

day per month off from work; involvement of the men also has the obvious advantage of breaking down the sex-role models of only mothers taking care of the children.

A center with approximately fifteen children should have two supervisors. If twenty parents are involved, they can hire either a professional person or one of the parents to supervise overall arrangements and be a full-time supervisor at the center. The second supervisor is drawn from the parents on a rotating basis, so, as already mentioned, each one might contribute one day per month. Taking off one day per month may not seem feasible without giving up vacation days. However, companies without their own centers may be amenable to working out either reimbursement for child care or a "parent leave." A parent leave is a policy in which employees who have children five years or under can take off one day per month without losing pay. It is a method by which the company can contribute to child care without having to invest in its own center. Employers reluctant to do this at the outset may be more amenable to it when they are presented with the possibility of losing good employees completely, retraining the employees and dealing with high absentee rates.

Employers can be helpful in efforts to start family day care by establishing an Information Referral Service. The service coordinator looks into requests common to certain neighborhoods, advertises in the neighborhoods and checks out companies in the area that might wish to pool resources to start a child-care center. It is an inexpensive way industry can help parents start their own center or pool industrial resources to start an industrial child-care center. A homemaker who is looking for a job might create one by selling tirself to an employer as an Information Referral Service coordinator and then proceeding to help the parents in tes community get a family day-care system established and be paid for it. (The research to gain the expertise in order to sell oneself to an employer can also be paid research by writing an article on, say, family day care or information referral services for a magazine.)

If the parents wish to keep the child-care arrangements simple and inexpensive, they can use the home of the parent who is taking the day off from work to be the co-supervisor rather than rent space for a permanent center. Although this arrangement will require the center to operate informally, and technically without legal sanction due to licensing needs, it offers the children different home settings, and enables each child to solidify tes identity as the other children see where te lives. The warmth and involvement of the parents provides a stability which balances the diversified home settings. The parent supervisor can be responsible for planning special activities, even an outing or trip for that one day in the month for which te is responsible. The enthusiasm of a parent involved only one day per month will doubtless be higher than that of a person who returns to the same job and same place every day. For the children each day is a new surprise. Yet the children have the continuity of the one professional full-time supervisor.

The advantages of such an arrangement are its low cost, informality, and lack of red tape in planning. The disadvantages are its dependence on a competent and flexible organizer to organize the parents, and on a cooperative group of committed parents whose philosophies are not radically divergent. In an informal arrangement creative flexibility is essential. For example, sliding scales might be developed to accommodate parents with more than one child or those who cannot take off under any circumstances, for families who cannot make their home available or for those who can supply extra time or facilities.*

* A few publications are listed at the end of the book to provide more information on starting child-care centers.

INDUSTRIAL CHILD CARE

Child-care centers can also be established in the physical location of a business or plant. When properly undertaken, industrial child care can be an important input in cutting back absentee and turnover rates, and therefore retraining expenses, as Control Data's Greater Minneapolis Day Care Association discovered. The investment a computer manufacturer makes in training systems engineers runs into the tens of thousands in dollars per person. The retraining of secretarial and clerical help is also a drain on the time of the employer and other secretarial staff, to say nothing of the time lost by the inefficiency of the new secretary. The Office for Economic Opportunity estimates that the recurrent cost per child for a program with sixty children is $2,050 per year, although the regional variation is wide. This include teachers, administrators, caretakers, and a part-time nurse and cook.[4] Even if a medium-sized company were to "lose" $100,000 per year on child-care facilities, if the facilities attracted two top persons who would otherwise have worked for another company, it might well be saving the company money. There is no way to calculate the financial benefits of the increased leverage industrial child care offers in the recruitment of the best personnel on all levels. *Child care can be one of the few employee benefits that also benefits the employer* (unlike increased salaries, vacations or pensions). An outstanding model industrial child-care center is so needed that its costs may well be paid for in the national television, magazine and newspaper coverage alone, otherwise costing the company hundreds of thousands of public relations dollars.

The father or mother using the center where te works has the advantage of spending the extra commuting time with tes child. Because the child can accompany tes parent to work, the heart-rending cries of "I want to go with you," or, "Don't leave me behind," are eliminated. The child who accompanies the parent can identify with the parent. The mother or father can reinforce this by visiting during lunch hour, and is always available should an emergency arise. In addition, an intelligent company management understands the investment potential of hiring the type of people who can identify and work on emotional problems of the child in their early stages, since these problems eventually affect the parents' job performance.

The potential for massive yet quality industrial child care is exemplified by Kaiser Ship Building Corporation's effort when it needed women employees during World War Two.[5] Thirty-eight thousand children were served in varied locations during twenty months. Each center had an atmosphere rich in toys, recreational equipment and facilities especially scaled to a child's size. Meals were well-balanced and the staff highly trained not just for a custodial type of supervision but for actively teaching the children manipulative and cognitive skills. Extensive education programs were conducted for the parents, and the center undertook research on child-rearing to constantly keep abreast of the newest thinking and techniques.

While these centers were stopped with the return of the motherhood myth after the war, the more recent trend toward two parents working is encouraging many companies to reinvestigate centers, and a number, such as Chesapeake and Potomac Telephone Co., Control Data Corporation, and Avco in Roxbury, Massachusetts, have already started operations. Unions can often be recruited as allies of industry-based child-care centers. The Amalgamated Clothing Workers of America opened seven centers as early as 1966 and have since opened numerous others. A number of organizations, such as the National Council of Jewish Women and the National Organization for Women, have members who have helped start industry-based child-care centers, and would therefore serve as good resources to contact.

In some cases a company may be too small to "get into the child-care business," or find it has such diversified needs among its staff that starting its own center is not practical. The Ford Foundation's solution is to reimburse its lower-salaried employees (under $10,000) $75 a week for every child under six in a child-care center. This offers the employee (and two men are participating) the total range of choices should some want experimental or "progressive" centers and others a more traditional setting. Information referral services, mentioned above, are another inexpensive method of industrial participation.

Child-care centers, though, can reinforce sex roles as thoroughly as the normal family arrangement if precautions are not taken.[7] Many recent child-care manuals still speak in terms which assume the teaching staff are women. This is particularly harmful to the large percentage of children who presently attend child-care centers that come from fatherless homes and from homes receiving welfare under Aid to Families of Dependent Children (AFDC), in which over 80 percent of the children come from fatherless homes.[8] Male teachers are especially helpful for the dependency problems developing among the boys.[9] *The crucial element in the involvement of men, though, is not only the male per se, but the involvement of men who are trained not to reinforce all the stereotyped masculine traits such as aggression and insensitivity.* The crucial factor in the involvement of such men is the supportiveness of *women* colleagues. If the women make the men feel like "sissies," the men usually withdraw (just one more connection between women's and men's liberation). Sweden has found it necessary to undertake extensive teacher reeducation so sex roles are not unconsciously taught by habitual acts such as giving dolls only to girls, or not encouraging girls to be involved in active sports, or pitting boys against girls in certain activities. Experimental programs in Sweden encourage men to enter the child-care and

preschool nursing fields as a career. For a transitional period
men are allowed to enter with less preservice qualifications,
to compensate for past discrimination against them.[10]

A competent staff for child-care centers is crucial if a
backlash against the centers is to be avoided. Trained staff
knows how to complement parental care—knows, for example, that a "good" father or mother who is overly concerned about tes child's success may create anxiety problems
for the child. This is a common problem among young children, since anxiety has its basis in early parent-child relationships in which parents treat their children as ego extensions
of themselves. A competent staff will recognize that anxiety
is best handled by allowing the child to operate in a more
structured setting with more positive reinforcement and realistic standards.

Of course, child-care centers serve little purpose if no jobs
are available for the parents while the children are in the
centers. For this reason the Swedish government has under-
written extensive education and retraining programs for
housewives with minimal education.[11] The housewife is classified as unemployed, which qualifies her for vocational training, and incentive allowances are offered by the National
Labor Market Board. An American adaptation of this program might include incentives for men to retrain part time
or at night while they take off time to be the primary parent.

A NEW WORK SCHEDULE

The Shortened Workweek

One of the easiest methods of freeing time to spend with
children is to work forty hours per week over a four-day
period rather than over five days. Changes such as a four-day,
forty-hour workweek (ten hours per day) seem impossible
for an individual employee in a large company to effect. Yet

in many of the 700 companies now either using a three- or four-day week and in the 1000 transferring to it,[12] the idea started with one or two persons who thought they had little chance of accomplishing it. Company attitudes shift quite quickly from negative to positive when they are presented with the data. According to an American Management Association survey of companies using the four-day week, *efficiency increased 22 times* more often than it decreased and actual *profits increased 13 times* more frequently than they decreased (51 percent to 4 percent).[13] Furthermore, 98 percent of the employers who were operating on a four-day week felt employees had to spend less time and money commuting to and from work, and almost two-thirds felt working mothers had an easier time over all. Gallup Polls also show substantial support among workers.[14]

An example of the options for child care opened by the four-day work week are the father working Monday through Thursday and the mother working Tuesday through Friday. This frees at least one parent for child-raising on Friday, Saturday, Sunday and Monday. It allows a balance between the father's and mother's attention and a third person's or child-care center's attention. It also leaves the weekend free for both parents to spend together with the child, while both parents have a day alone with the children on Monday or Friday.

Example of Distribution of Child Care
Under Four-Day Workweek

	SUNDAY	MONDAY	TUESDAY	WEDNESDAY	THURSDAY	FRIDAY	SATURDAY
Person caring for child	Father and Mother	Father	Substitute	Substitute	Substitute	Mother	Mother and Father

Perhaps the most appealing aspect of a four-day week (as an alternative—not an automatic requirement) is that it provides a balance between the parents' attention to the child

and the child-care center's attention. The child has a stable
base of love and attention at home but te is not smothered by
it. The child takes no one person for granted and yet is not
the victim of random shuffling.

Staggered Hours

Staggered hours are a second alternative allowing women
and men to work at overlapping times and be with children
for longer periods, if desired. For example, if the mother
works from 7 A.M. to 3 P.M., and the father from 11 A.M. to 7
P.M., this means the child is with a surrogate parent only four
to five hours a day (from just before eleven to just after
three). In this example, when the father comes home the
young child will already be in bed so he may spend some
peaceful hours with his attaché. Yet he will also have the
opportunity to spend from three to four hours (depending
on commuting time) each morning with his children.

Companies, such as the Lipton Manufacturing plant, have
made the problem of child care even easier by combining a
three-day week with staggered hours.[15] Even if only one
partner were working on this plan while the other was still
working a normal Monday-through-Friday week there would
be absolutely no need for anything more than a part-time
baby-sitter while the parent is sleeping. Half of Lipton's
shifts, for example, are from 7 P.M. to 7 A.M. during which
time the attaché working a nine-to-five, Monday-through-
Friday week would be at home.

The political and economic possibilities of bringing about
staggered hours is greater than might initially be expected.
Its appeal to corporations which rent facilities at exorbitant
prices in cities is enormous. Using facilities for only one-third
of a day (eight hours) represents a percentage of waste which
would not be tolerated from an employee. A company pays
no more rent for fully utilizing office or factory space twelve,
eighteen or twenty-four hours per day than it does for eight.

This would save many companies millions of dollars per year in rent. The success met by companies which have staggered hours indicates the idea is no pie-in-the-sky concept. In lower Manhattan alone, 255 business concerns staggered the hours of 89,000 employees within two years. Eighty-five percent reacted favorably to their new hours while only ten percent were less satisfied.[16]

The city in which the company is located also benefits by staggered hours. Urban facilities such as mass transit are now extremely overloaded during rush hours. For example, the mass transit running from New York to New Jersey (PATH trains) has as many passengers during the two rush hours as it does during all the remaining twenty-two hours of the day. In most cities rush hour crowding could be eliminated or substantially reduced by staggered hours. Even in Manhattan, which presents the most difficult case, experiments which staggered hours for just one-fifth of the work force in downtown Manhattan reduced congestion at three major subway stations by 26 percent.[17] Staggered hours, then, are a viable alternative for the implementation of sharing child care.

Two-For-One; Three-For-Two; Flexi-Jobs

The value to both employer and employee of part time and flexible jobs hit home for me when a friend of mine and I both advertised for a research assistant in New York City. My ad asked for two part-timers with flexible hours; his advertised for one full timer with prescribed hours. I received seventy-six responses; he received eight. An increasing number of employers are discovering similar results on the recruitment end. On the productivity end, the Massachusetts Department of Welfare found that the fifty caseworkers it hired on a half-time basis, for half-time wages, *each* got 89 percent of full-time workers' productivity. They also had a lower absentee rate and only one-third the turnover rate of full-timers.

Two-for-one jobs (two persons holding a full-time job) enable a couple with children to have one full income while never leaving the child without at least one parent (if that should be desired). The employer always has a back-up person should one be sick and generally has some leeway to ask the employee to work overtime in busy periods. The one caution here is that all employee's fringe benefits be prorated. The Smithsonian is hiring two lawyers this way, and the Progressive Insurance Company in Cleveland and the Nowland Organization in Connecticut have had success with similar arrangements.

Three-for-two jobs (three persons holding two jobs) have perhaps even more potential for parents with children who are willing to have their children taken care of part-time but do not want to be away forty to sixty hours per week. Three-for-two jobs amount to about a twenty-seven hour week per person, which provides about the right combination of income plus child-care time. It allows the employer even more flexibility than two-for-one jobs and virtually never leaves the employer with no one in a job or with no one to train a new employee.

Flexible jobs need not be part-time. Massachusetts Institute of Technology has had such success with full-timers working forty to sixty hours per week, but on schedules which allowed employees to be free, say, two weekday mornings or afternoons, that it is now looking into implementing this on all administrative levels. The advantage to businesses of having offices covered on Saturday at no extra cost is considerable. John Hancock Insurance Company is instituting flexible scheduling and finds it can be handled with the same computer operation as the four-day workweek.

HOMEMAKER PAYMENT

Housework will always be the domain of an oppressed group (in our society women, blacks or Chicanos) until payment for it is similar to any other labor. Cooking is woman's work, unless one is paid for it; then one is a chef, and usually a male. In Norway a person is, under the law, paid for housework. In most cases the woman still does it, but she is legally entitled to an equal share of whatever income the husband makes.[18] Some Norwegian pressure groups are working to implement this by having half of the check made out directly to the woman, in the automatic way that part of an American worker's check goes to social security. This might be called the "homemaker payment." The philosophy behind it is that in a given relationship each attaché's or living friend's labor is worth an equal amount—creating the economic basis for an equal relationship. No one has to depend on the *good will* of the other to obtain money, or threaten divorce to receive the legal allotment.

Payment for housework gives both the woman and the man incentives for making the sacrifices involved in a woman's development of her own career, since if they are both working each receives a full check rather than dividing one check with the other person. In most families, since housework and child care appear "free," parents feel unwilling to pay much to have someone do it. However, once the family values the housework at half the amount normally made by the man, they are likely to be willing to pay more to have it done. This minimizes the tendency to oppress a maid by giving her low wages to do something that is normally done for nothing. It will tend, also, to spur the expansion of professional housecleaning companies which will be able to receive decent wages as the demand warrants it.

For the man homemaker payment is the first of many steps in gaining the psychological freedom to care for his children, since he now has a legitimate income—the same psychology that makes homemaker payment important for a woman. The man gains the freedom to make an income from the housework if he should choose to do something home-based, such as be a student, paint, or free-lance write. Working-class jobs also have home-based potential. An auto mechanic or delivery person can run a small business out of tes home if te goes into partnership with another, with one person taking orders and doing the billing and advertising from home, while the other does the mechanical or delivery work. Thus the pressure to produce in a normal factory or office environment is relieved.

The problems of housework and child care transcend class boundaries. Chase Manhattan's study of the time consumed by an average woman's work revealed that it was 99.6 hours. The more the husband makes, Blood and Wolfe found, the more work the *wife* has to do in the home—in *all* classes.[19] But the more he makes, the less work *he* does, because he's "so absorbed in his career." Although the same division of labor exists in blue-collar marriages,[20] the increase in the woman's responsibilities are even less recognized by the professional man whose concern with his job and simultaneous belief that the housekeeper is taking care of the housework blinds him to the burdens of planning and the responsibility for hundreds of details not assumed by most housekeepers. In brief, the woman's housework escalates to keep up with his escalating image.

PROGRAM FOR A MEN'S LIBERATION MOVEMENT

Each of the above areas of flexible work schedules is an important element in the goals of a men's liberation movement. Some of the programs of the National Organization for Women's Task Force on the Masculine Mystique offer con-

crete alternatives to the present system while presenting a
tentative snapshot of the forthcoming men's liberation movement. The Masculine Mystique Task Force was founded in
September 1971. In June 1974 it held the First National Conference on the Masculine Mystique at New York University.
Hundreds of facilitators were trained to return to their local
communities to form a nationwide network of men's and
joint consciousness-raising groups and to carry out national
demonstrations and "actions"* such as those listed below.[21]
Most of the programs are in areas identical to those on which
NOW and other women's groups are already working, but
are designed to confront the problems directly related to
men, expanding what is now a women's movement into a
women's and men's liberation movement. (Other resources
for a men's movement are listed in the bibliography of resources.)

Industry Affirmative Action Programs. All businesses dealing with the federal government are now required to submit
programs showing an affirmative action program to improve
the status of women.[22] The upper-level management usually
submits such plans only to find them ignored by the middle-
level management responsible for implementation. The
underlying attitudes of the mostly male managers toward
women is an important barrier to implementation. For this
reason modified consciousness-raising sessions or "management awareness programs" have already been established in a
number of companies such as General Electric and IBM to
change the hiring and promoting behavior of managers resulting from their attitudes toward women. The sessions are
similar in format to the consciousness-raising sessions described at the end of the book, but the topics discussed are

---

* Actions include the whole range of nonviolent activities, including demonstrations. Nonphysical actions range from research presented to management as a tool for negotiation, to complaints to human rights commissions
  and writing exposé articles.

oriented toward employer-employee problems. In most cases they are a regular part of management development courses, encompassing management in all divisions of the company.

Topics discussed in "management awareness programs" include such management problems as getting managers to listen to women employees with the same seriousness as men (phrased as "Does our social image of women become our employment image?"). For example, does the sexual focus on women who are attractive and a sexual turn-on influence whom they hire as receptionists, secretaries and stewardesses? Do they justify this with a statement such as "This is what the customer wants?" Does the woman's attractiveness become a qualification for her initial job but a disqualification for promotion ("What guy could keep his mind on what a broad like that is saying?")? Does their image of their own male role create a personal drive that closes their minds to the possibility of committing themselves to caring for children (for example, taking off a day per month from work)? Is their lack of concern for children making them place company child care far down on the list of priorities? To what extent does their need to "make it" as a man lead them into specializing, refusing to take the risks involved in being creative and questioning, afraid to expose themselves to others, work flexible schedules, and so on?

Employment and Labor Unions. Which jobs are men kept out of as "women's jobs"? Thousands of factory piecework jobs are closed to men for fear of unionization and pressure for higher wages. So are jobs for secretaries, receptionists, stewardesses and telephone operators. Token efforts to hire males in these areas do not dispel the fact that discrimination against men in these areas is even more complete than it is against women in management. *The belief that only women work in inferior and low-salaried positions is part of the same belief that says only men work in superior and high-salaried positions.* When men share these jobs equally they will, practically speaking, become unionized and more highly paid, neither of which is presently the case. Jobs on all levels must be integrated before "job determined by sex" can be eliminated.

College men can undertake effective actions in the employment area if they time them carefully (an important step in all actions). In the early summer months college men are hard hit with discrimination in factory jobs. They can probably best be organized at least a month before and immediately after final exams. Exacting concessions from one or two factories and using the gains as leverage for others is an effective method of maximizing resources.

Child Care. Paternity leaves are fundamental to the sharing of responsibility for child care. Ultimately the terms "paternity" and "maternity" leaves should be replaced with "parent leaves." Court cases for parent leaves, such as the suit against the New York City Board of Education, must be encouraged. Industry must be pressured into making a "one day per month plan" available for parents who wish to take off one day per month for two or three years at a neighborhood-formed child-care center, as discussed above. Legislation must also establish guidelines or even graduated quotas for the hiring of men in child-care centers.

Education. Until recently the only pressures brought on the publishing industry about sex roles were to bring about changes in the image of women in children's books by showing women "making it" in industry, politics or the professions. While the production of books with titles like "Women Who Work" must be continued, a men's movement must pressure publishers to produce children's books with titles like "Men Who Care," with pictures of men in the home, men cooking, expressing emotion, wanting sympathy, crying, admitting they are wrong, and especially asking for help and being dependent (even on a woman). Most importantly, men must be pictured loving children and staying home with them

occasionally out of choice, rather than in the blue strait
jackets of a policeman or businessman (and the accompanying authority symbols of attaché case or gun) . The Masculine
Mystique Task Force of NOW organized just such a demonstration on August 26, 1973, in New York City. It was the
first major "action" of a men's liberation movement focusing
on the injustices to men resulting from traditional sex roles.

Demonstrations before toy departments might encourage a
broader range of dolls for boys—not just G.I. Joes—to prepare
men for fatherhood; and an end to separate male and female
areas in toy departments with Mighty Mike Astro trains, guns
and tanks for boys, while dolls and Susie Homemaker sets are
the fare of the girls' department.

A national effort must be made to involve men as elementary school teachers, nurses and guidance counselors.
This implies pressure on colleges to undertake speial cam-
paigns to attract men to prepare in these fields. In colleges
the R.O.T.C. and war research as well as money used for
football or wrestling teams should be questioned from a
masculine mystique perspective. Courses in sex roles and
men's liberation might be financed instead as a way of expanding the feminist studies curriculum.

American educators often complain, "We open our home
economics courses to men and no one shows up. What can we
do?" Sweden has found that schools must do more than open
up courses; they must actively counteract the biases of the
mass media and environment by undertaking *critical* analysis
and discussion.[23] This critical analysis is incorporated into
every subject, from geography to home economics, civics, and
biology. Commenting on some of the concrete curriculum
changes actually made in his school, a school principal noted:
"It turned out that differences of achievement between
pupils didn't have anything at all to do with sex. The boys
often sewed their own athletic uniforms. Many knit jersey
gloves and mufflers. The girls learned to use tools that were

brand-new to them. They sawed and planed, hammered nails and glued things together."[24]

Reproduction and Its Control. Actions encouraging research to make male birth control realistic by making it reversible might focus on hospitals, universities and governmental agencies such as the National Institute of Mental Health. Because of the lack of research into male birth control, vasectomies are not reliably reversible, and semen storage methods are still not perfect. The research must be accompanied by a massive education program both to help men overcome psychological effects of vasectomies and semen storage and merely make them aware of its existence as an alternative.

Image and Aggression. The image of war, crime and violence as exciting, and the corollary excitement attributed to men who enter war, solve and even commit crimes, are perpetuated daily by television, radio, and papers.

The six volumes of the U.S. Surgeon General's report of Television and Social Behavior made it repeatedly apparent that publicizing violence leads to imitation of violence. Specifically, crimes in newspapers should be listed similarly to obituaries—mostly in small print in the back pages of the paper with an occasional one listed on the front page, not because of the amount of blood spilled but because of its implications for society.

Reporters should be freed from chasing crimes and enabled to do research on conditions which are likely to lead to crimes. Masculine values, as we have seen, are conflict, power and external action rather than human cooperation, careful background work (except to investigate or create conflict), and internal values. The media reinforces and encourages these values. The pressure to change the media, though, will have to include the most careful strategizing, since demonstrations play right into their hands as a form of conflict and violence, and nonviolence allows them to dismiss efforts to force change. Among the methods which are both effective and have a minimal chance of backfiring are lawsuits, research followed by sit-ins with demands, and alternate radio and television stations (e.g., the WBAI and Pacifica radio stations and cable TV stations) .

PART II

Women's Liberation
as Men's Liberation:
Toward a Change in Behavior

Nine

Factual and
Self-Fulfilling Myths*

FACTUAL MYTHS

Two of the barriers that prevent men from changing are factual and self-fulfilling myths. Factual myths are merely beliefs that can be disproven by presenting the relevant facts. They usually contain some truth, but fail to hold up when the whole picture is presented. Factual myths are of particular importance because people can use the new information in discussions and soon find themselves supporting the changes that flow from the new information.

---

* This section includes myths which have been countered in much of the women's liberation literature, but are included here as a result of findings that most men who have been exposed only to the media's interpretation of women's liberation still do not have the information to counter these myths.

Many men express the belief during interviews that *women have at least "come a long way, baby" in the last ten or twenty years.** In fact, this is not true. In 1955 women's full-time year-round median wages were 64 percent of men's while sixteen years later, in 1971, they were only 59.5 percent.[1] The percentage of women attending universities is lower than in the 1920's. In 1870 women were one-third of the college faculty in the United States. In 1970 they comprised one-fourth; in 1972–73, 22.5 percent. As the rank goes up, the percentage of women goes down—only 6.6 percent of all university full professors were women in 1973. The proportion of women graduate students was *less* in 1972–73 than it was in 1930.[2] The percentage receiving M.D. degrees also declined from 10 percent in 1950 to 9.1 percent in 1973.[3] Women have made gains in some areas, mostly in the last year or two, but they have been countered by the little-publicized losses facing all groups whose childhood psychology discourages the self-confidence required for success. Even affirmative action programs, for all the defensive reactions created in men, have resulted in no appreciable gains for women as of 1974; the central method of hiring is still "the buddy *boy* system."

In politics, despite the dramatic gains of certain individuals, the number of women in state legislatures declined from 392 in 1963 to 344 in 1970, and has only risen recently, to 441 in 1972 (still only about 10 percent of the total) . The percentage of women in Congress for the past twenty years has fluctuated just above and below 2 percent, dropping from a peak of nineteen in the Eighty-third Congress to sixteen in the Ninety-third.[4] The number in the Senate has decreased from two to zero between 1953 and 1974. The women who do get elected are usually widows. Only four women have served more than a year in the Senate, and they have *all* been

* Factual myths are italicized.

widows.[5] Twenty-three of the fifty-seven women who have served in the House have also been widows of congressmen.

Myths about women's sexual desires have actually represented two opposite views at different points in history. The early Christians, Hebrews, Romans and Arabs considered womens' sexual desires insatiable.[6] Accordingly, Arab women were closely guarded and suffered severe punishment for sexual deviations; adultery warranted their being stoned.[7] In contrast, the Victorians completely denied that "decent" women had sexual desires.[8] Both views of sex, though, reinforce the same conclusion: *There's something wrong with women sexually,* and men are not to blame if women are sexually unsatisfied. "The male is left, sexually speaking, off the hook."[9]

As is the case with most myths about women, men are also the victims. By assuming responsibility for sex, men have been forced to initiate sexual encounters and to develop the fantasy lives which always surround the master plans of the initiator. The resulting erections are confined to the lonely solitude of their pants. By exaggerating his own sexual capacity and suppressing women's he forces women into a longer "warm-up period" to enjoy sex. By that time he is fluctuating between bursting and turning soft. When she is ready for her second and third orgasm the only thing he has left which is hard is his finger or his vibrator.

It is said that *women in women's liberation groups want equal rights but not equal responsibilities.* Many men interviewed have mocked, "I'm willing to give women equal rights, but then don't expect me to give them a seat on the bus." In addition to assuming it is men who give women equal rights, the very statement reveals incredible shallowness about what equal rights entails (to say nothing of the number of men I have ever seen forfeit a seat). Moreover, the statement itself is clearly untrue. Almost every women's liberation group strongly supports the Equal Rights Amendment which may subject them to the draft, and will abolish protection against working overtime or lifting heavy loads. They explicitly refused to support a U.S. Senate rider to the amendment permitting laws protecting women and giving them special privileges.

Employers who are trained in cost-benefit analysis in numerous areas, have not thought of applying it to their women resources until recently. Even now, the myths about women employees are so ingrained that they often block even the start of such investigation. Many employers still feel that *"Women are less dependable employees; they're absent more from the job."* Yet the Department of Labor reports that "the work time lost by persons 17 years of age and over because of illness or injury averaged 5.3 days for women and 5.4 days for men over the same period." The myths about women's menstrual cramps creating excessive absence is just that—a myth. The same male employers never discuss equally valid forces which affect men's productivity—tendencies toward fantasizing about women, luncheon drinking, ulcers and ultimately premature death due to heart attacks, all predominately male statistics. These employers hurt their company by ignoring women's capabilities and hurt themselves by driving themselves past the point of diminishing returns, to their level of incompetence.

A related myth maintained by employers is that they *should not hire women for career and professional positions since women quit much sooner than men to bring up children or move with their husbands.* Women, of course, do quit for these reasons, which is why women are fighting for reforms such as child-care centers or the sharing of responsibility for child care; and fighting the assumption that they must automatically be the ones to move with their husbands rather than vice versa. (Ironically, it is just the employers who use these reasons not to employ women who are most against these reforms.) Yet despite the pressures on women to quit, the turnover rate of workers is only very slightly more for women than men 26 per 1,000 women and 22 per 1,000 men. The Department of Labor reports that "labor turnover rates are influenced more by the skill level of the job, the age of the worker, the worker's level of job stability, and the worker's length of service with the employers than by the sex of the worker."[10] Both men and women in boring low-skilled positions often look for stimulation in a new job. In like manner, women, as well as men, who have landed jobs on higher rungs of the career ladder and who are involved and committed to their jobs are not likely to quit.[11] Many employers are not aware that some companies report a 36 percent dropout rate of male college graduates during their first three years of employment—a figure exclusive of the draft.[12] The Prentice-Hall report concluded that "female employees may be a 'safer' investment than men."[13]

Another "fact" held against women is that *women get their degrees, get married and quit.* Yet 90 percent of the women holding doctorates are working and are very stable in their employment patterns.[14] Still, many employers explain, "We must take it slow on this affirmative action stuff. *Women must have a chance to develop qualifications they do not yet possess.*" Women, though, have the qualifications in almost all fields to a greater extent than they are being hired. In the academic field of psychology, for example, women earn 23 percent of the doctorates nationally. Yet at the University of California at Berkeley not *one* of 42 faculty members is female. At Columbia, the Department of Psychology grants 36 percent of its doctorates to women and hires *none* to teach there.[15] Why is this? Advertising is just one reason. The Department of Psychology at City University of New York advertised in 1970 "prefer male, but will consider either" (imagine, "prefer white, but will consider either"?). Discrimination forces women to teach at junior colleges or community colleges, where they comprise about 40 percent of the faculty.[16] There they are exposed to considerably fewer research and grant opportunities, less pay and much less status. This unequal treatment for equal qualifications ultimately also means they are considered unqualified to compete for posts at major universities with men who received initial teaching posts with more status and research opportunities. In this case the factual myths turn into a self-fulfilling prophecy.

A series of factual myths militates against women in the professions. For example, it is still occasionally thought (although seldom said) that *women do not have the brains and talents necessary for legal and medical work.* However, women medical students and law students graduate consistently at the very top of their classes.[17] It is more frequently claimed that *women are more apt to drop out either for personal reasons or when the academic going gets rough.* This is also false. For example, the percentage of men and women completing medical school is about the same, 84 percent.[18] In Finland, in fact, where fewer barriers to women exist, the majority of physicians and dentists are women.[19]

Another common myth is that women are more emotional than men. It is true that women are not emotionally constipated; they can get their emotions out of their system. However, we have distorted women's ability to express emotions to add to the "proof" that *women are emotionally less stable, more likely to break down under conditions of stress, and are "not the type whose hand you'd want on the nuclear but-*

ton." Men, though, are the ones who break down under conditions of stress more easily than women. During World War Two, almost 70 percent more men than women broke down and became psychiatric casualties as a result of the bombing of London and Kent.[20] In this country, more men than women have been in mental institutions consistently since the 1920's,[21] although women are also driven to mental institutions for problems growing out of their role. The number of men drivers designated as assigned risks is also greater than the number of women by four to one, even though male drivers only outnumber women three to two.[22] According to a pamphlet from the Auto Safety Council of the American Medical Association, women are better drivers because they are *less* emotional (meaning emotionally unstable) than men. If rape, murder and other crimes are considered indicators of emotional instability, then the male capacity to express his emotions in a form not harmful to society is clearly placed in question. Compare the rates of emotional crimes performed by men and women: homicide, more than 5 to 1; assault (excluding rape), more than 7 to 1; disorderly conduct, more than 6 to 1; all crimes (including rape and prostitution), almost 6 to 1.[23]

To document an area in which women are *presently* "better than" or "less likely to commit something" than men is not to conclude that women are *naturally* superior to men in that area. It is only to say that the socialization process to this point has given women this advantage, and that therefore each of these advantages to women is an area of potential *liberation* for men as men's socialization is altered. Once the alteration occurs, if men or women are still found to have deficiencies in relation to the other, society may wish to encourage compensation for these differences rather than reinforcement of them.

When myths about sex roles are answered on a personal

level some men will then tranfer to societal reasons for maintaining sex roles. One rationale often offered is that *"each sex having its role" helps maintain a stable society.* This is not true. Countries such as Sweden, Finland and Norway are among the more stable and peaceable countries of the world, while in the Latin American countries, where machismo and "woman's place" permeates society, instability is widespread. Among the Arab countries, Syria, Jordan and Iraq are both highly unstable and highly differentiated in their sex roles. In Lebanon, usually considered the most stable of the Arab countries, sex roles are the most fluid.[24] Even among tribes, the few peaceable ones found by Geoffrey Gorer were the few in which sex roles were not polarized.[25] Since the threat of instability has often served as an excuse to dehumanize society, understanding that freedom from sex-role stereotyping is compatible with stability lays an important basis for human liberation.

SELF-FULFILLING MYTHS

A more difficult type of myth to detect because of the subtlety of its origin and its surface accuracy, the self-fulfilling myth is a statement assumed to be true—such as "John is more independent than Sue"—that is followed by doing everything to make the assumption true—such as giving John every opportunity to be independent. The assumption is a myth (as well as a prophecy) because at the time it is first stated it has no basis in fact; it is based on a mythology of expectations. The major agent for creating the self-fulfilling myth is the interacting process of socialization by parents, peers, the media, and institutions such as schools and churches.

The self-fulfilling myth colors our interpretations of actions by men and women that are essentially alike. Once we have stereotyped women as concerned with the home and family, as scatterbrained, catty and "out to get married," we read this into all their actions.[26] When a man has a picture of his family on his desk it is a reflection of a solid family man. A similar picture on a woman's desk reflects a woman more concerned with her home than her job—a "doting mother at heart." When a man's desk is cluttered it belongs to a busy, overburdened executive; a woman's desk to a disorganized, scatterbrained female. When a man talks about his colleagues, it is constructive criticism or office politics; when a woman does the same she is "catty." When a woman expresses happiness with her marriage it is assumed that she is expressing total fulfillment; for a man it is "extra credit," a nice thing to have *in addition to* his competence at work.

One self-fulfilling myth is that women, by nature, are physically the weaker sex. To create this myth we define physical weakness only in terms of muscles, a definition appropriate to the male value system. This allows us to ignore evidence which might point to women's greater physical strength in terms of resilience and constitutional longevity. For example, women are better able to endure devitalizing conditions such as starvation, fatigue, shock and illness. They have greater stamina and live longer.[27] They also develop many aspects of physical control better and more quickly. They are quicker to develop control over hand and body muscles,[28] and have fewer speaking, hearing, vision and stuttering problems.[29] Four times as many boys as girls stutter[30]; they stutter more severely and are less likely to outgrow it.[31] Young boys also outnumber young girls 4 to 1 in having vision, hearing and speech disorders.[32]

If physical strength were defined from a genetic perspective, the woman would still have an advantage. The Y chromosome, the distinguishing chromosome which creates a male, makes him vulnerable to over 50 diseases;[33] there is no comparable disadvantage in the X chromosome of the female. The larger size of the X chromosome plus the presence of two

X chromosomes in females results in women's cells being about 4 percent greater in chromosomal value than men's. This makes for "a substantially richer, genetic capacity than the male," according to Drs. J. H. Tjio and T. T. Puck, the researchers who discovered the differences in sex chromosome size (1958).[34]

After avoiding alternative definitions of physical weakness and ignoring contrary evidence, we make our myth self-fulfilling by encouraging women to spend their lives *reinforcing their muscular weakness* rather than trying to minimize it. We do this by teaching women never to be aggressive or competitive in physical activities such as baseball, football, track, tree-climbing, weight-lifting, wrestling and boxing. Finally we are able to declare the "obvious" difference between the twelve-year-old boy in our family and the twelve-year-old girl, even if she is taller than he at that age. Girls do their part in enlarging this difference by accepting the social restriction that certain activities, like certain toys, are for boys. They learn their "place," shy away from activities that would develop their strength, and then declare their lack of strength to be "natural." (What is most devastating is not the definition of physical strength as muscular strength, but the willingness of both sexes to reinforce whatever weakness they consider natural rather than minimize these weaknesses. It is like telling persons with a sugar deficiency that it is natural for them to stop eating sweets!)

We forget that whenever in our own history we have needed women, we have dropped these myths and women have assumed what was otherwise "men's work." During the Civil War, Andrew Sinclair points out, Midwestern men came east to fight and then "women were in the field everywhere, driving the reapers, binding and shucking, and loading grain, until then an unusual sight."[35] When women have been needed by the economy, as during almost every war, they have suddenly done men's work in the factories and in the fields. When they are needed more desperately, as in Israel, they are even used as soldiers.* To create a myth of weak women when that myth suits economic purposes and destroy it when it does not is a highly manipulative use of human potential and aspiration.

Women and men want things the way they are—a perfect example of the self-fulfilling myth. We tell both sexes what they should be and imply they have made a choice when they tell us they want to be exactly what we said they should be. We bombard both sexes with television commercials of women with whiter wash for the satisfaction of role number one (woman as a fulfilled washing machine); for role number two (woman as a fulfilled sex object), the woman is transformed into a seductive tigress to be "had" along with an over-horsepowered convertible sports car and a bill for $5,000. The system of education "for equal opportunity" uses schoolbooks rife with men as astronauts, doctors, lawyers and manual laborers, and women as secretaries, mothers, elementary school teachers and nurses. In newspapers, it is the woman pictured when marriages are announced, since she is supposed to "want" marriage most. In fact, though, Kinsey found that single women were happier than single men, that married women were the least happy of all groups and married men the most happy—and this by their own admission.[36] At the end of this process we declare that these roles are what women want, and ask, "Shouldn't women have the freedom to do whatever they want? Nobody is preventing them from becoming a doctor or anything else."

If we looked beyond our borders to see how cultures influence wants, we could see the fallacy of another self-

* When women are needed by the entire economy, as in the Socialist and Communist countries of Cuba, the Soviet Union and much of Eastern Europe, a philosophy of women's equality accompanies the need. (Which underlies the other and the extent to which the philosophy will outlast the need is yet to be finally demonstrated.)

fulfilling myth, that *the roles of men and women are exten-sions of the biological differences.* We do not even look to Sweden, where 75 percent of the crane operators are women;[37] to Rumania, where over 40,000 women hold political office; or to Czechoslovakia, where 70 percent of the judges at the district level are women.[38] What women and men "want" is clearly at least as much a function of environment as innate tendencies.

Vivian Gornick, writing for New York's *Village Voice,* describes how this self-fulfilling prophecy permeated her life. She was brought up to think independently, and yet she learned in "100 different ways, in a continuous day-to-day exposure to an *attitude*"[39] that she, as a woman, had a primary role as a wife if she were to be considered successful. The sexualized definition of success eventually leads even the most brilliant woman to consider her intelligence at best a nice vocation and at worst something she should suppress. Gornick calls it a destruction of inner necessity at an early age: "Always the battle was internal, and it was with a kind of paralyzing anxiety at the center of me that drained off my energy and retarded my capacity for intellectual concentration . . . It took me a long time to understand, with an understanding that is irrevocable, that we are the victims of culture, not biology."[40] One of the most destructive self-fulfilling myths that both sexes help to perpetuate concerns women's intelligence. Some biologists have contradicted Gornick, suggesting that there *are* some biological differences in women's intelligence as evidenced by the fact that their brains are very slightly smaller than men's.[41] This is true, but what is left out is the fact that there is no correlation between brain size and intellectual capability.[42] "However," some men persist, "don't men outscore women on intelligence tests, like on abstract reasoning and in areas like that?" Since this is the type of assumption that not only makes the self-fulfilling myth a myth, but is a contributing factor to men's underlying contempt for women, it deserves a well-documented answer.

On the most respected and well-known intelligence test, the Wechsler-Bellevue Scale, women score higher in almost every area and at almost every age. Wechsler concludes "these differences in themselves do not prove anything, but taken together with other evidence, have led this writer to the belief that it may be possible to demonstrate a measurable superiority of women over men so far as general intelligence is concerned."[43] Girls tend to do better in logic as opposed to rote memory, particularly when the content is favorable to neither sex.[44] They read better and earlier and surpass boys in verbal and language skills.[45] Boys, though, comprise three out of four of the retarded readers[46] and are subject to learning disorders three to ten times more frequently.[47] In the area of spatial and mechanical aptitude tests, preschool girls do just as well as boys. It is only after the experiences that boys have with toys and instruments—basically a cultural advantage—that boys of school age begin to move ahead.[48]

There are too many unanswered questions about the influence of environment to conclude that women are more intelligent by nature. There is evidence that even the timing of puberty is influenced by environmental variables such as handling, and exposure to coldness and warmth;[49] that basic physical growth may be impeded by poor psychological conditions, even when nutrition is adequate.[50]

The more sophisticated men I interviewed did not deny women's intelligence, but frequently explained that "I, personally, would feel uncomfortable married to a woman who is more intelligent than I am." On an even more subtle level, both men and women fall prey to undermining women's intelligence. For example, a series of *identical* professional articles were circulated to college women with instructions to evaluate each article. There was no difference in the articles, just the authors, which were labeled by close-to-identical male or female names, such as John McKay or Joan McKay. After reading the identical articles, *the women ranked the articles with the man's name as superior, whether in traditionally masculine fields or traditionally feminine fields.* The experimenter concluded, "Women seem to think that men are better at everything—including elementary school teaching and dietetics!"[51]

We know environment is a significant influence; it is the one variable that human beings, as opposed to animals, can control. We must therefore ask ourselves whether we want to control it so as to maximize human potential, or instead to create adverse psychological conditions that amount to reinforcing a person's deficiencies with the excuse that they are natural. On the surface one might object to the environmental approach by suggesting that we are imposing values. Exactly the opposite is true. Stereotyping is imposing values. Human liberation means opening options at an early enough age so that the environment is not used to impose certain values on girls and others on boys—except the value of openness. It means changing adult behavior so that children's role models will be different, and adults changing that behavior for their own satisfaction aside from the children.

Men cannot be expected to participate in these changes, though, unless women's liberation is redefined as a two-sex movement which provides enough benefits to men to make change worthwhile to more than the most altruistic, condescending or masochistic men. Since the benefits to men are less obvious because they are not all materialistic and tangible in a society oriented that way, it may help to outline some specific examples.

Ten

Women's Liberation as Men's Liberation: Twenty-one Examples

Two women who were at opposite poles on the subject of women's liberation were shocked to find themselves suddenly agreeing on one point: *Women's liberation is a threat to men.* Men fear losing their masculinity, losing top jobs to women, losing status and power.

It is inevitable that *many* men will *feel* threatened. But I challenge the assumption that men *must necessarily be* threatened by defining twenty-one specific areas in which men can benefit from what is now called women's liberation. (All of these benefits must be seen in the context of the accompanying responsibilities, particularly the sharing by men of the responsibility for child care and housework.)

1. *If a woman has her own life and destiny to control, she will not be as likely to feel the need to control her husband.*

Men who complain, "My wife has too much power already—
she controls the whole house," often forget that an independent woman does not have so much at stake in what he does
because she has her own stakes. She can approach him as an
equal—someone with power, rather than as a vassal needing
to manipulate the power which he alone possesses. Men call
this vicarious controlling coy and cute when they do not
object to it, devious, cunning, and underhanded when they
do. They incorrectly worry about the aggressive female dominating them. As Marya Mannes points out, "The real ag-
gressors are the female killer sharks in the guise of submissive
females. These women use guerilla tactics to ambush and
conquer the male."[1]

2. *The basis for any marriage or living arrangement can be
more genuine.* The man does not have to pretend to love his
attaché to cover his guilt feelings of "leaving her with nothing" when she has "given her best years to him." When a
woman has diverse interests or a career her "best years" are
redefined as all those years in which she makes the most of
herself mentally and as a total person. She is thus not a
physical mannequin subject to a deterioration process from
the twenties onward, nor is she hanging on to the man
because she has no other means of financial security, or
because she knows so little of the outside world she is afraid
to enter it without her husband's protection. If the man and
woman do not get along and the children are perceived as a
responsibility of *both* of them, they can make a decision
together as to whether a divorce is appropriate.

At the outset, this may make the divorce rate rise. Men and
women who merely tolerate each other will not be living
together for artificial, materially based reasons. However,
women's liberation goes a long way toward preventing this
division of labor and subsequent division of interests. Consider what happens to the independent, educated woman a
man marries. The man is thrust into the world and the

woman into the home; one expands and the other contracts. The woman is forced to worry about a world of shopping, cooking, cleaning, diaper-changing and child-raising. If she is a college graduate she is probably married to one, and when he comes home he is confronted with his wife's conversation about "Johnnie's soft doodie" or the price of meat.

Society makes a woman's world the house while men laugh at her overconcern with the home. Women may discuss problems of child-raising with their husbands for the first twenty-five years of marriage, but then the husband often cannot understand why his wife is suddenly so boring after the children are raised. The separate "places" of women and men and the mental separations that occur because of them go a long way toward explaining why the divorce rate soars after couples are married twenty-five years and their children have grown, despite the investment of memories, the material complications and the social embarrassment of divorce.

The irony is that the same men whose disrespect for women is revealed in their jokes about their overdomesticity are also the men who want women to remain in these roles. They are the men who say, "When I come home from a hard day's work, I just want someone there to provide a balance to the dog-eat-dog world," and who mock the Bella Abzugs and Betty Friedans who deviate from their image of a woman.

3. *Sexual interest heightens in an unstereotyped relationship.* Many men wonder privately why sex has become so boring with the same woman with whom it was an undying preoccupation before marriage.[2] One man in his late twenties amplified this: "It isn't that I lost my sexual interest in her as soon as I made her (we made love for over a year before we got married), but my interest seemed to decrease pretty soon after the honeymoon."

The excitement of sex diminishes quickly with the domestication of a woman who is always the same and "always there." Sexual attractiveness deserts a woman who gives up her sense of freedom and her ability to explore. Major studies by both Kinsey and Vance Packard have revealed that the sexual responsiveness of women who have their own interests and profession is also much greater than those who do not.[3] The more educated the woman, the more likely she is to enjoy full and frequent sexual orgasms and the less likely she is to be frigid. The implications of this information for men can be found in Abraham Maslow's extensive study of human personalities, in which he finds that *men* receive much greater sexual fulfillment with a woman who realizes herself and is developing her full potential. When an active man and woman make love, Maslow observes:

What we see is a fusion of great ability to love and at the same time great respect for the other and great respect for oneself . . . Throughout the most intense and ecstatic love affairs, these people remain themselves and remain ultimately masters of themselves as well, living by their own standards, even though enjoying each other intensely. It is a very common report from these individuals that sex is better than it used to be and seems to be improving all the time.[4]

Their sex itself was varied and unstereotyped:

That is, they did not assume that the female was passive and the male active, whether in sex or love or anything else . . . They did not mind taking on some of the cultural aspects of the opposite sex role . . . They could be both active and passive lovers . . . Kissing and being kissed, being above or below in the sex act, taking the initiative, being quiet and receiving love, teasing and being teased—these were all found in both sexes.[5]

A conventional marriage often becomes sexually one-sided. Her sexual interest in him increases because his availability is uncertain, just as hers was uncertain before marriage, when his sexual interest was high. His sexual interest in her decreases because she is always there waiting for him. His mind, if not his body, begins to wander. Meanwhile, she is expected to sleep faithfully at his side.

A man who wants a woman to be sexually exploring and creative with him while castrating her feelings for other men is asking for a sexual schizoid. He somehow does not recognize how the very definition of exploring implies *not limiting oneself*.

One aspect of women's liberation is the demand not to be considered a sexual possession. In a real way this demand is likely to re-create the sexual interest many husbands have lost in their wives. Germaine Greer elaborates on this: "Lovers who are free to go when they are restless always come back; lovers who are free to change remain interesting. The bitter animosity and obscenity of divorce is unknown where individuals have not become Siamese twins. A lover who comes to your bed of his own accord is more likely to sleep with his arms around you all night than a lover who has nowhere else to sleep."[6]

4. *The man becomes psychologically free from the woman's view of him as a security object—a view which governs his choice of goals.* The role-playing, "submissive" female often brags as much about the quality of a guy's school or job ("I went out with this guy last night. He is an engineer from MIT . . .") as he brags about the quality of her body. The man becomes a security object because when the woman lives vicariously the only goal of his from which she benefits is security—and this goal becomes his goal. He becomes so enslaved to the money he's making that he loses his emotional ties to the person for whom he thinks he is slaving. By contrast, a man who lives with a liberated woman can think through his own goals. In my own life I found my reconsidered goals were a lot more human than my original plans. I also find that my attaché now admits that she disliked in me that very self-centered ambition which I believed would

bring me her undying love. It must be disappointing for men to work so hard for those they love only to find that those they love are lost to them.

On one level men recognize how they are hurt by their attachés' overconcern with security. A man in the random sample explained "I wanted to start my own gas station last year, but my wife objected to my taking a bank loan, saying, 'Suppose the gas station fails?' She always wants security. I think women are naturally cautious." Many lawyers and businessmen expressed parallel fears of not being able to move without "a veto from the boss." Few, though, seemed to recognize that a woman with her own life to control does not have to worry about controlling the life of her husband. He pays a price for establishing a masculine mystique out of finance and business: a loss of freedom to take risks and choose goals that excite him.

5. *Sharing of the breadwinning role by a woman frees a man from a great deal of the pressure that the corporation can presently exert on a man afraid to lose his position because he is the sole support of the family.* Many a radical man suddenly turns moderate when he realizes that "I now have a wife and children to take care of." He knows that if he objects to his company's investments in South Africa or even to his boss's petty political preferences, he may lose his job. *The sole-breadwinner status gives the corporation a subtle leverage over its employees.* It stymies creativity and basic questioning. It makes his job a "job" and not an employment opportunity. It defines his manhood as his breadwinning status and makes him sacrifice leaves of absence or more interesting jobs for the raising of his status. It is only when that responsibility for breadwinning is shared that he can afford to take risks on his job which may result in his being fired—since he then knows he is not leaving the family in the poorhouse if he is fired.

6. *A man can devote more time to his children, in a more positive atmosphere.* Tensions which develop between the mother and children during the day are placed in the lap of the father at night. The father who is relieved of the role of "arbiter of accumulated tensions" ("Wait until Daddy gets home") finds less strain in the relations between him and his wife and himself and the children. He is free to develop a closer relationship with the children due to his increased responsibility for them which he can handle because of the decreased pressure from other roles. For example, pressure for the working-class man to work overtime to get time and a half decreases when his attaché is working; when the pressure for the middle- and upper-middle-class man to think he "has to make it" by working a sixty-hour week is alleviated, he becomes freer to spend the other twenty hours with the children.

The children come to view their parents in a different way. If the family has dinner in a restaurant because neither wishes to cook after working, the mother has a chance to talk with her children; the children see her as more than just a servant. ("Mom, you forgot the napkins," or, "Mom, get me more milk.") The servant role keeps the mother "half out" of a sensible conversation and diminishes the children's respect for their parents as partners.

Men will benefit from a number of the indirect changes resulting from arrangements enabling fathers to spend more time with children. For example, a Gallup poll revealed that 45 percent of men would prefer a four-day, forty-hour week to the present five-day week. Only 49 percent prefer the forty-hour week spread over five days,[7] meaning the availability of both as options would meet the preferences of 94 percent of all men. Unions are already beginning to make this part of their demands, at least as an option, and among labor-union families the preference for this arrangement is even stronger. Changes in work schedules are one result of pressure from men and women's liberation for men to share responsibility for child care.

The jealousy which many men feel when a new child is born also diminishes when the man comes home earlier to invest more of his own time in the children and the woman is not spending all her energies in devotion to them.[8]

7. *When his living friend has economic self-sufficiency the man has greater leeway to choose an interesting low-paying position rather than an unfulfilling higher-paying position.* For example, a man who loves teaching is often pressured into administration because of money and status. If his living friend is less educated or skilled he assumes he must make the sacrifice of taking the less fulfilling job rather than making the sacrifices which will enable his living friend to develop her own economic independence. His freedom to take the lesser paying position will be particularly valued once men do not consider themselves a failure if their attachés make more money than they do. The concept that one person should feel better if another person does not do as well is more than absurd—it is destructive.

8. *In poverty homes, if both parents work, the additional money gives the man and his family the basic freedom to keep food on the table and the option of holding the family together.* In other families it offers the resources to travel, take advantage of the high cost of culture or afford better-quality education for the children. It allows middle-income parents to fly to a long weekend vacation spot and to afford a baby-sitter when they want complete privacy.

9. *The advent of women into the market of "men's jobs" can be seen not as competition, but as the lessening of the need to compete.* For example, the man whose living friend has economic independence can take off a year or two to obtain the education and training necessary for a better position—or just to pursue a dream. Many men may still reject this analysis by saying "in the long run men will not benefit

because business will not be able to absorb all these women, there won't be enough jobs to go around and we will all be working harder to share the same pie." Intellectual and liberal/radical men add that women working is just another asset to middle-class families which will help neither the working class or men.

First, if the reason for bringing up the myth of women's place in the home during peacetime and forgetting the myth during wartime is to prevent women from competing, nothing could be a more cynical channeling of human potential on so artificial a basis.* Secondly, middle-class women working hurts neither men or working-class women, but creates a broad demand for services and therefore jobs which these women are now doing for free. Some examples follow:

- The restaurant industry, catering services, the equivalents of Chicken Delight and frozen gourmet dinner industries will all have increased demand from women who are liberated from cooking responsibilities due to working responsibilities. Most persons who wait on tables are of working- and lower-middle-class backgrounds, as are short-order and small-restaurant cooks. This demand opens jobs for working-class persons of both sexes.

- New industries, such as large chains of professional house-cleaning services, are created by a working attaché's demand for relief from housework due to responsibilities at work. Many of these industries have already been started

---

* The extent to which the lack of fulfilling work can drive a woman to madness is discussed in Phyllis Chesler's *Women and Madness* (N.Y.: Doubleday, 1972). The need for redesigning jobs to make work fulfilling is best outlined in the Department of Health, Education, and Welfare's study *Work in America* (1972). One caveat, though: the competitive grind into which men have been trapped should serve as a warning that women's liberation does not mean allowing oneself to be forced into the same ego-oriented rut of upward mobility as men, rather than allowing the freedom to switch jobs, switch careers or just change one's mind. This is the freedom for both sexes that comes from *sharing* work responsibility.

and hire both men and women from the lower- and lower-middle classes, finally desexing housework. As these jobs become more universally unionized these workers can also expect to earn a decent living, which is not always the case at present. Some window washers already claim, though, to be making as much as $17,000 per year.[9]

- The services of cleaners will expand and establishment of more washing and ironing centers will result from the need for clean and pressed clothing for work.

- The clothing and women's apparel industry will need to hire more persons in response to the demand for a variety of clothes to wear to the office, and the increased money women will have at hand with which to buy clothes. This has a large impact on the garment industry, in which a large percentage of lower- and lower-middle-class workers are employed.

- Industries connected with almost all labor-saving areas will expand, such as delivery services for mail-order shopping, or manufacturing of large freezers to cut down on shopping.

- The need of most middle-class working women for cars, mass transportation or the use of highways means an additional demand for jobs employing the working class, such as workers in automobile factories, transit workers and highway construction workers, respectively.

- All industries catering to the consumer, from department stores to supermarkets, will need to stay open later when one sex is not home all day to consume. Stores will need to stagger their hours and hire additional personnel, the demand for which will come from two sexes being able to shop rather than one and the expanded hours of the stores allowing both men and women to have the time to shop each day.

- Child-care centers, many on a sixteen- or twenty-four-hour-per-day basis, are likely to need teachers and professional personnel, offer construction workers jobs in the building of the centers, and make demands on industries manufacturing toys, books, games, play equipment and teaching tools to use in the centers. (Many employers are also likely to establish their own centers as an attraction for workers.) [10]

- The travel and tourist industries benefit both from the decreased pressure on the father to work overtime and on weekends, and therefore the increase in time when the entire family is together and free to travel. The travel industry hires a fairly wide range of personnel.
- The sporting industries benefit from sales to a much wider market of women who no longer see it as their role to stay home while daddy fishes or golfs. These women are likely to participate increasingly in sports such as skiing, baseball, golf, tennis, camping and fishing.
- Numerous service industries, such as the computer industry, increase sales only as other industries expand. Banks also benefit from demands for industrial investment loans. The expansion of these industries provides new jobs in clerical, professional and working-class job areas.

In conclusion, then, the expanded demand on goods and services benefits men, women, industry and all classes of the population.[11]

10. *The man in the poverty bracket whose family presently receives welfare only if he leaves the family can benefit from "homemaker payment."* "Homemaker payment" is paying the man or woman who is doing the housework or caring for children half of the other person's check, which is sent directly to tir by the employer. This legitimate income will tend to make housework and child care more respectable. Then the man whose living friend is able to earn a better living outside the home will feel free to take care of children

inside the home. The benefit to the children of having a father around the home who is legitimately earning an income is invaluable.

11. *The responsibilities of the man within the home, while in some situations becoming greater, will in other situations be lessened.* Women are socialized not to perceive of themselves as assuming many of the responsibilities they might otherwise assume. For example, in a Parker Pen advertisement, the voice-over says, "You might as well give her a gorgeous pen to keep her checkbook *un*balanced with. A sleek and shining pen will make her feel prettier. Which is more important to any girl than solving mathematical mysteries."[12] It is inconceivable this would be said about a man, and if it were said of a black person the company would have a suit on its hands. The point here, though, is the increased responsibilities this image implicity shifts to a man within the home.

Other chores within the home now become the man's by the same narrowness of role definition. These are: painting rooms, painting the house itself, repairing cabinets, mowing the lawn and weeding the garden, shoveling snow, putting up fences, refinishing playrooms and sometimes building entire rooms or occasionally even the house. Some of these chores, such as building, are more creative, while mowing the lawn or shoveling the snow, like dusting, are part of a never-ending routine. The release of men from automatically having to do these chores will appeal to some men. Others will be attracted to the idea of *doing* many of these chores together. Living friends washing dishes together, preparing a meal together, putting up shelves in the study or painting a room together can share an experience which will draw them closer together rather than farther apart. The fact that a man and woman should be able to do things together does not mean they should always do things together. The ability, though, gives them the choice.

12. *Role definitions limit men in responsibilities they might otherwise enjoy pursuing around the home.* During one of my interviews one man named Bill said his wife did not care much for sewing but said that he had wanted to sew some holders on which to hang his tools. He asked his wife for some thread. Her reaction was defensive and threatened. Although she did not like to sew and would have agreed in theory that he could do it "any time he wanted," when faced with the situation she was threatened with a loss of identity and purpose (despite the fact that she has all her credits toward a Ph.D.). Bill explained that he eventually did sew the holders and showed them to one of his neighbors who was with him in his tool shed. A few days later a second neighbor mocked, "Billy, my wife would like you to join the girls at the sewing circle next week." The pressures and kidding which result from any attempt to deviate make one recognize how emotionally attached most of us are to even the simplest of role definitions.

13. *Women's liberation frees a man from being the sole source of his attaché's happiness.* In the interviews one policeman mentioned he didn't discuss his real fears on the beat with his wife because she would "be worried sick" about them all day. If the man feels he must be the only reinforcement his wife has, he not only burdens himself but degrades his wife, since she must then be in the position of jumping around like a puppy dog always looking for a crumb of affection. This degradation in turn becomes one of the thousands of elements contributing to some men's subliminal hostility toward women. The present cycle, then, does her an injustice, and confines him in his masculine tendency to suppress fear and not to ask for help.

14. *The liberated woman can allow a man more autonomy in his personal life.* Since she has not been waiting for him all day she is much less likely to mind if he wishes to have a drink before coming home, stop off at the gym, go bowling or

go out with the boys. The very fact the man needs to go out with the boys after working all day says something about his relationship with his attaché. This point is cyclical. If his attaché is interesting when he does come home, his preference for "the boys" will decrease accordingly. As society encourages a pattern of independently fulfilled women, the need to get away from what the man perceives as a nagging wife will lessen. What men often want to escape now is the woman who is uninterested in his world and who often has nothing in common with him but the same home and children. When two or more persons have responsibility for painting the house, when both can go fishing and bowling or stop for a beer, then the type of beer becomes a topic of mutual interest, and so does the type of paint or the execution of a pass by the quarterback in a football game. When we cease defining some areas of life as men's alone, men will not have to escape their wives to discuss some activities or to do them. When men participate in shopping on a routine basis the price of meat is likely to become as important to them as the price of stocks, and in their mutual concern for the former, a man will not perceive his attaché as petty.

Men and women often meet at resorts on vacation and are attracted to persons they would not have noticed under different circumstances. At a resort they are playing tennis, hiking and enjoying life together. An oppressive power relationship of "do as I say" is not entrenched; both persons are not locked into a barren relationship with each other. Under these circumstances of greater autonomy they most enjoy doing things together.

15. *The reduction of anxiety about one's sex role.* Many men say, "If I don't teach my boy to be a boy, he'll lose his identity. I'll make him insecure." In fact, the opposite is often true. Stereotyped sex roles create lifelong *anxieties* over whether the child is deviating from or living up to the sex-role standards.[13]

Masculinity implies standards of sexual prowess which create anxiety on the part of the man at the same time it dehumanizes the woman. The standards suggest that a real man makes love with more women, does it with a hard penis, does it in many different ways, or makes her have more orgasms. These artificial standards—as opposed to standards of warmth and overall sensuality—turn men into anxiety-ridden performance objects. These same artificial standards turn women into sex objects.

16. *Anxiety about homosexuality decreases as artificial standards of masculinity decrease.* Perhaps Kagan, an important psychologist, best summarizes this point in saying, "The occurrence of homosexual behavior or fear of being a homosexual is often related to anxiety over not attaining the masculine ideal." An adolescent male who is ignored by girls, is slight of build, and has nonmasculine interests often begins to believe he might be homosexual. The anxiety resulting leads him to avoid women to save himself from rejection. He interprets his apathy and avoidance as an indication that he is a homosexual. Kagan explains that this leads to panic and still less initiation of contact with women.[14] The benefit implied here is obviously not the reduction of homosexuality per se, but its reduction as a course taken out of negative reasons such as fear (just as heterosexuality is often developed out of negative reasons such as a compulsive need to adjust to the stereotype of masculinity). When men fear their own homosexuality less they will repress it less and not stigmatize others who are so inclined for more positive reasons. The reduction in anxiety benefits both homosexuals and heterosexuals.

17. *The man can develop a balanced ego as a result of sexual relationships with women which do not always force him to risk refusal.* A man's ego is the second most fragile instrument he possesses. Why? Even in a "liberated" relationship men are still expected to risk the first sexual contact—

before the relationship is secure enough to be certain "the pass" will be accepted. (Seldom does a woman touch a man's genitals for the first time—before he has ever touched hers.) The man is the one who must risk refusal. No wonder his ego becomes sensitive. His physical response to rejection may be to "try harder," but the physical response belies the underlying emotional hurt. He objectifies women rather than risk the increased damage entailed by rejection after emotional involvement. Conversely, a relationship with women balanced by being asked rather than always having to do the asking creates a balanced sense of ego and an ability to be emotionally involved.

18. *Men who learn to listen to women rather than making presentations acquire a new set of values that accompanies true listening.* When I listened at women's liberation meetings rather than "solving a problem," I was at first surprised to find that I learned considerably more than when I was preparing my question/speech and blocking out what others were saying. The fact that the women generally arrived at better solutions to a problem became a contributing factor to my increasing respect for women over the past few years. I believe a number of men will find that developing the ability to really listen will completely alter their perspective on a number of presently assumed values.

19. *Intellectual achievement is a benefit to the boy not caught up in striving to reach artificial masculine standards.* The more intelligent the boy the less likely he is to need to be traditionally masculine, while the boy who has overcome the fear of being called "sissy" for achieving becomes free to use his intelligence in nonstereotyped ways. This intellectual achievement also occurs among girls who are brought up to be more active or "male" than is traditionally considered appropriate.

20. *Men become free of many of the legal burdens which discriminate against them.* Legal changes in the automatic

responsibility of men for alimony,[15] jury duty,[16] and even their later retirement age under Social Security[17] serve to benefit men. In some universities such as Temple, men are not admitted to daytime continuing-education courses. Their freedom to take off during the day to pursue their education is limited. The legal barriers to obtaining paternity leave also limit their ability to participate equally in child care.

Most of these freedoms are closely linked to women's present dependency on men. The women's liberation groups' agreement with the phase-out of the husband's almost automatic alimony payment is predicated on the assumption that the woman's role will change to one of financial independence.

21. *Upon retirement, men's lives will not be as empty as those of men whose loss of position means loss of self-identity.* At present the man who retires often senses a vacuum in his life. Often the vacuum contributes to his death;[18] occasionally he seizes the cooking and household responsibilities as a way to fill it. Ironically, this can effectively kill the woman not only by creating a vacuum in her life, but also by making her brutally aware that those specialties to which she devoted her entire life and on which her husband was presumably dependent, he is now perfecting with reckless abandon. If a couple shares responsibility and halves the burden during their entire life together, however, they would continue to do so easily when retired, and in addition would have an equal amount of leisure time to pursue outside activities.

Eleven

Highlights of Experiments on Changing Men's Attitudes

Can men change, or are their habits too ingrained? What rationalizations do men use to justify remaining the same? Which men are most likely to be able to change? (The educated? The liberals?) What arguments or situations are most effective in bringing change about? Do radical women really turn men off, or do their ideas take root, or both?

To help answer these questions I designed two extensive experiments which focus on whether or not attitude and behavior changes occur, with whom and in what way. The first experiment was designed to see if men could change their attitudes; the second focused on behavior, and is described in the final chapter on consciousness-raising.

192

METHOD OF STUDYING MEN'S ATTITUDES

For the experiment on men's attitude change, I randomly chose two groups of men from matched subsamples. I gave a more comprehensive version of the questionnaire appearing at the front of the book to the first group of 120 men. This was designated the Questionnaire Only group. The second group of 120 men received the same questionnaire *after* they had read seventeen articles from women's liberation literature. The comparison of this group to the group that hadn't read the literature helped to determine whether a systematic exposure to the arguments of the women's liberation movement would produce a positive change, have no significant effect or produce a backlash. The seventeen articles or excerpts amount to about two hours of reading. To be certain that the men actually read the material they were asked to return a comment sheet with their written reactions.

Only after they had returned the comment sheets did these men receive the questionnaire. In order to be certain that it was the literature which produced the effect and not original biases, I tested both groups for the amount of prior exposure to women's liberation and the similarity of socioeconomic backgrounds, and designed a scale to measure whether their original biases were similar. Among the hundreds of background variables there were almost no statistically significant differences between the two groups.

While hundreds of types of men could be found among the total sample of 240, members of only four groups of men were consciously selected—a random population sample and samples of employers, state legislators and college students. These groups were selected as representing men whose attitudes were most relevant to the goals of women's liberation. (Men's liberation was not part of the questionnaire, except indirectly.) The employers' attitudes were important in relation to the economic and business goals of women; the state legislators' in relation to the ratification of the Equal Rights Amendment, and laws on abortion, marriage and divorce. The college students were selected to determine what type of changes we could expect from the next generation; the random sample determined whether there was a substantial attitude difference between the population at large and these key groups.

The key, of course, was getting the men to read the literature. It usually took one or two follow-up calls and a follow-up letter to obtain the response, since all of the men were chosen blindly. This effort to get the men to read the literature will be an important job of a men's liberation movement. Until now, this job has been done by committed women. In fact, *the single most important factor in bringing about men's attitude and behavior change has been a woman committed to that end.* Hopefully, a men's liberation movement will change this—making men want to change for our own reasons, from our own initiative.

WHICH MEN CHANGE?

The most astonishing finding is that almost without exception, every type of man who read the literature changed in a positive direction toward women's liberation.* *Not one man in the entire sample who had a high degree of knowledge about women's liberation opposed it.*[1]

Some backlash was expected from men who were originally opposed to women's liberation, since some of the articles were quite radical, but the men *most opposed* to women's liberation *ended up changing the most.* Even the political

---

* The literature is not reproduced in the appendix since most of the ideas from the literature are integrated in one form or another in *The Liberated Man.*

conservatives who read the literature became much more favorable. Among Nixon voters, for example, 45 percent opposed women's liberation if they did not receive literature, but among those reading it, only 12 percent were opposed. This is an enormous difference!

It had been expected that the men who would spend the time to read the literature would be biased in favor of women's liberation, but instead they were slightly more conservative on the scale testing *original* disposition toward the subject, making their eventual changes even more significant. Yet they almost never admitted to changing or to learning anything from the literature. *Men do not like to give credit to an outside force for reorienting their thinking. Especially if that force is women.*

The effect of reading the literature was obviously quite different for different groups of men. Among religious groups Catholics were the least positive toward women's liberation (only 10 percent agreed who did not read the literature). They changed the most, to 18 percent agreement, but this was still short of the agreement of Protestants and Jews who did not read the literature (23 percent for both groups). The Protestants and Jews also made favorable changes but only to 26 percent and 27 percent agreement, respectively.

The level of a man's education makes a significant difference. Men with little education are strongly opposed to women's liberation. However, reading women's liberation literature has a very strong impact on these men. *A full half of these men who did not read the literature were opposed to women's liberation, but not one man in the group reading the literature was opposed.* This huge shift has broad implications for the potential of women's liberation among working-class families. Most have only been exposed to the mass media's version of women's literature.

Married men are more hostile toward women's liberation

than single men. But when married men read the literature,
they change more than single men, perhaps due to their
ability to directly relate the literature to their personal experience. A married man, for example, can see the immediate
relevance of articles pointing out the basis involved in giving
girl children nursing kits and boy children a baseball bat.
Agreement with women's liberation among married men
increased from 11 percent to 23 percent. Most of the remainder were in the mixed or moderate category.

It made no significant difference whether that knowledge
came from reading the literature I distributed to them or
from other sources. Once they knew a lot about women's
liberation they could no longer remain opposed. Conversely,
if they had little knowledge of women's liberation and did
not read the literature, 46 percent of the men opposed it, 47
percent felt moderate about it, and only 7 percent were in
favor. Once the men with little background read the literature their opposition dropped from 46 percent to 8 percent.
While mere knowledge of women's liberation makes men
more favorable, knowledge combined with an extra dose of
literature that is positively oriented is extremely effective in
moving men in a positive direction.

THE "PLATEAU EFFECT"

Somewhere between theoretical agreement with women's liberation and its practical application—when the man is asked
to undergo fundamental attitude and personal behavioral
changes—there is a leveling-off point called the "plateau
effect." For example, students, the group which most questions sex stereotypes, stall just short of a definite verbal
commitment of time to joining a consciousness-raising group
themselves, agreeing only to *"probably* give it a try." They
wavered between moderate approval and strong approval of

their wife or woman friend joining, although they usually reached the "strong approval" category. Among all the groups of men, they were most likely to agree in theory with articles such as "The Great Toy Shuck," which deplores the way children's toys brainwash children into accepting stereotypes early; *yet only 2 men out of 240 could bring themselves to consider a doll or dollhouse as a "most appropriate" birthday present for their son.* In the same vein, only 7.5 percent of the men considered either of the traditionally feminine toys (doll and nursing kit) as even fairly appropriate for their sons. The literature could not change even the most liberal man's basic fear that his son would become effeminate if he gave him a dollhouse or a nursing kit. It took the men's and joint (men with women) consciousness-raising groups to bring about these more fundamental attitude and behavioral changes.

Men are willing to agree that giving boys one type of toys and girls another involves an unhealthy channeling of youngsters into sexual statuses, yet they are simultaneouly unwilling to stop this channeling in their own behavior. Men become more and more positive in their attitudes toward women's liberation as they read specific examples of the way stereotyping is harmful, but they reach a sudden plateau when asked to apply it in their own lives. This does not mean that their attitudes regressed, since it generally takes such a change in attitude before the behavior change can be carried out. The danger of the plateau is that if the man remains there too long, he becomes afraid to make the jump and inevitably starts a process of retreating from his progress in changing his own attitudes.

ESCAPE MECHANISMS

Escape mechanisms are all the "outs" that help a man do this retreating (or never get there to begin with). The "rugged individualist" position is a favorite escape mechanism, used by employers who think of themselves as rugged individualists to escape facing the way they discriminate. Harold, an executive for a large petroleum company, explained, "I always treat people as individuals, with individual traits." He believes no group has inherent advantages or disadvantages, that everyone can do anything te wants in this society. Yet the rugged individualist inevitably treats boy and girl children differently, expects women to take care of children, but is glad to hire any person according to tes qualifications. There is no recognition of how different socialization creates different sets of qualifications for men and women, or of how the requirement that females care for children perpetuates these differences. In this way, Harold avoided admitting that any barriers applied more to one group than the other.

Harold added that "everybody discriminates against everybody," explaining that he and anyone else might "discriminate" against someone if he didn't like the way te combed tes hair or the glasses te wore. But all Harold was doing, in effect, was to dismiss the discrimination against an individual because of color or sex as meaningless, since we all discriminate in one way or another anyway.

The rugged individualist is among the most difficult types of men to reach or change. Although Harold had a negative reaction to every article on his comment sheet, it was almost impossible to engage him in a direct confrontation. He would consistently employ a second escape mechanism, the out-of-context theory. For example, in an article about sexism in children's books, he automatically assumed that the facts and figures mentioned in the articles were "not representative" and "taken out of context." He would support this by giving *an example* to the contrary. When asked about discrimination against women in employment he cited one women who was a successful executive to prove that there is no discrimination and that "it's all up to the individual." In essence, he used the out-of-context theory to "prove" the articles were erroneous, and then used an example out of context to prove he was right.

Another escape mechanism making a man not only difficult to change, but difficult to reach in the first place, is "Oh, I'm already in favor of women's liberation" (meaning: "Please don't talk to me about it"). An intelligent man in the student sample, Chris, typified this view with his statement that reading the literature was for him "like preaching to the already converted." During the course of the interview, however, in front of his fiancée who later joined us, one example of inequality after another found him declaring openly, "Our marriage will not be a union of equals . . . On a gut level, I really feel men are superior. Yet I realize that's intellectually untenable." He made no further attempt to reconcile the contradictions in his stance beyond pointing out that all societies in the past have been stratified in one way or another, as though this would make the stratification he could not intellectually defend a bit more palatable.

This technique of separating intellectual thought processes from behavioral change and visceral reactions is often disparaged by radicals as being *worse* than a hard-core conservative stance. It is, though, further along on a continuum toward total commitment to a change in life style. This division might even be a necessary step in accommodating major changes in life style. But the key is to make sure that the process doesn't stop with this convenient separation. Discrepancies must be pointed out; escape mechanisms recognized for what they are; and alternatives constantly offered until it is more comfortable for the behavior to conform to the intellect than to deviate from it.

THE IMPACT OF THE RADICAL*

Does exposure to radical feminists through the popular media help increase or retard male receptivity toward their message?

The male reaction is complex, and not nearly as unilaterally negative as generally supposed. The effect seems to occur in four basic stages. During the first stage the men are turned off—even vehemently. Responses like "This gal is full of it," along with strong aspersions on her heterosexuality and complete alienation ("If this is what it's all about, forget it") were common reactions to the four (out of seventeen) articles classified as radical. In the interviews the reactions to "those lib gals on TV" were almost universally negative, with many references made to the bra-burning incident that reportedly took place four years ago but which really never happened.

During the second stage after exposure to radical supporters, feelings are more contradictory. If the radicals were seen on television, the long-term reaction includes a residual aversion to the participants, but also some absorption of the ideas advocated. The reason given for not openly advocating the ideas is the inability to identify with "the dykes and the uglies" who make the statements.

When the men read the literature, they often called it ridiculous, but a week or two later, their responses on the questionnaire were much more positive than were those of the men who had not read the literature. Sometimes during the interviews the men would actually repeat phrases they had read in the literature but would credit them to ambiguous sources—"You know, *they* say that . . . " or "If you

---

* Radical refers here to that portion of the women's liberation advocates of the early 1970's who generally believe that working separately on women's consciousness is the best way of changing the values and institutions of capitalism and men—considered the two major enemies of women's liberation. The real meaning of a radical is someone working on the *root* causes of a problem.

really think about it . . . "—not remembering the article
that made them think about it.

The job of the radical, then, is thankless in the first stage
because it appears to be without effect, and almost thankless
in the second because when the effect does take place, the
man takes credit for the thought himself or assumes it came
from an ambiguous nonradical source.

Although the men exposed to radical thinking did experience increased personal awareness and support for the movement's ideas (as opposed to its representatives), during the
third stage they were generally unwilling to discuss this
publicly. One of the student interviewees was a typical example. He said he could personally understand that when he
and his friends looked out of the dorm windows and discussed
the girls like pieces of meat on a rack, they were being sexist.
He added, "It really gets to be too much after a while." But
when asked if he would point this out to his friends, he said
he would not because they would not understand. When
pressed as to whether he would protest if his friends made
racist comments about blacks, he responded that he would
because he felt more assured of his position and he would not
anticipate an argument because no one is overtly racist any
more. But, he explained, "If you start talking about women's
lib, there are a lot of guys who'll think you're queer, a
homosexual."

The radical women do seem to scare most men from direct
identity with the movement, but they have the effect of
making the old "extreme position" seem moderate. One of
the major effects of the radical literature and television
programs was to enable the conservative men to move to the
left and feel they were still reasonable and moderate. *The
great majority of men were willing to accept almost any
standard as long as they were convinced the standard was
acceptable to others.*

If a man reaches the fourth stage it is generally because the people closest to him are supporters of women's liberation, allowing him to perceive a new reality. *The radical woman who lives with a man becomes that man's reality.* If he feels she is "out of it," this will probably lead to a dissolution of the relationship. If her attitudes become the attitudes of her friends, and if he ultimately joins a men's group or a joint group, this creates a new group of friends to reinforce those beliefs, and these new groups become his new reality. They create a subculture which enables the man to change with security. This new subculture may conflict with old ones, such as the people at his job and his old friends. However, if he has gone this far, the importance of an attaché or living friend who does not appear to be ready to give in is usually greater than the opinion of his associates at work, with whom he can remain silent on the topic if he chooses. The man and woman then begin to drift away from their most chauvinistic old friends, further solidifying their new reality. The danger in this is that in the process of the subculture becoming its own isolated society, it often establishes new doctrines rather than new alternatives. For example, the possibility of living in a family may be eliminated as an option.

This four-stage process is the most common result of close contact with radicals which I have witnessed among men in this country. Most men are never affected beyond the second stage, since their contact with the radical is at a distance (e.g., TV). The need to choose among realities never occurs. In a few countries, such as Sweden, the transformation to a new approach to sex roles occurs without the radical as catalyst. The catalyst is the government. Its support in breaking down sex roles creates a major base of security for any man or woman who has any inclination to make the change. The government legitimizes the change in life style. It becomes an acceptable standard, a new reality. It minimizes the burden on the woman isolated in a suburban home who has to fight the battle alone and face a high probability of divorce, and it cuts down on the need for radical groups to have to constantly chip away new edges on the left to make feminism seem more in the center. It also minimizes the risk of a man being mocked by his friends and feeling castrated and dominated by his wife if he does change. In the United States, the government encourages radicalizing of new movements since it only responds to excessive pressure instead of assuming the initiative for change.

THE SEARCH FOR SECURITY

Much of the hesitation of men to identify with any position they believe is radical originates in their security needs. One example after another on the questionnaire and in the interviews led me to believe that most men are a lot less self-confident than they would have other men believe. One surprising revelation came in response to the following true-false question on the questionnaire: "I think I develop sexual relations with women faster than most men." A reputable social psychologist advised me to exclude this question from the questionnaire since he predicted that 90 percent of the men would want to classify themselves as sexually more aggressive and "more of a man" than the average man on the street. *However, only 17.6 percent of the entire sample felt they developed sexual relations with women faster than most men.*

Men put on a public external appearance of being masculine, but internally fear they are not up to other men. The more insecure a man feels, the more he will resort to bragging about how he fills the masculine image. Ironically, it is this insecure man who is being most damaged internally by the masculine image. He wishes to keep things the way they are because he is vulnerable to accusations that he is effeminate. He is insecure about taking any position which deviates from the norm. When this man becomes convinced, though, that the norm has changed, he is most likely to act in accordance with his new perception of it. Legislators, for example, have a big investment in knowing the norm. They started out as the most conservative of the four samples, with 42 percent opposed to women's liberation.[2] At the same time, they are aware that they must be responsive to any change in norms. When the male legislator read the literature, he made the biggest change, so that his response pattern immediately shifted to the norm where it was almost identical to the random sample of men. After reading the literature, only 9 percent of the legislators opposed it, similar to the 10 percent of the random sample. The literature persuaded the legislators that the norm was changing, and that they would be more secure in changing with the norm than in deviating from it.

What is the fear that sparks this insecurity? It might be capsulized in the defensiveness of the one interviewee who did admit to playing with a doll: "A doll was among my most prized possessions . . . of course, I'm very masculine, so it didn't hurt me at all." The chances are slight that a woman would have been as defensive about playing masculine games as a child. In both personal and job situations, men's insecurity stems strongly from the fear of being associated with femininity.

Twelve

Changing Behavior:
The Subtleties and Barriers

Behavior change is the extremely difficult process which largely follows attitude change yet interacts in such an integral way with attitudes that sometimes the two are indistinguishable (a condescending attitude toward a woman is also a type of behavior). Examples of behavioral barriers are found throughout the book. This brief chapter serves only to alert the reader to some of the subtle ways in which every attempt at change involves overcoming both attitudes and behavioral barriers.

A man's willingness to change behavior is tied to his psychological security. If he feels his attaché and children like it the way they are, he is unlikely to risk that security by rearranging the entire balance of power in the family, with the instability, insecurity, misunderstandings and even resentment likely to emerge. For this reason, few men change without a woman who is similarly committed—and few women change without at least a partially cooperative man. Once the change process has started the firmness enables a man to at least have some sense of security from his environment. The male-female relationship is like a dance—it takes two to tango.

A second type of security necessary for behavior change is internal security. An illustration from an Ohio consciousness-raising group can be helpful here. One man revealed that before he married he wanted his wife to be Mrs. John Seymour. When he had developed a secure relationship with her, one where he felt not only unthreatened in her presence but also wanted his wife to fully develop herself, he did not object to her referring to herself as Alice Seymour. The fact that she was still referring to herself as Seymour should not obscure the point that as the husband's security increased, his need to "possess" his wife in his name decreased.

Can a man ever be secure if we set the expectations of every man far above what he is likely to achieve? What happens to a talented man when he reaches his forties and recognizes he will never be president of his company? If he has been taught that the most important value is inner fulfillment as a human being he will be able to accept the idea—and will probably be glad that not having to achieve that external goal will free him to keep developing himself as a total person. However, if he has been socialized to recognize the achievement of external goals as the only ones for which he must strive, goals which only a handful of men can achieve, he may never be secure. He is likely to display this insecurity by finding mistresses, by trying to have his children succeed where he could not and by showing his wife "who the boss is." In essence, *it takes a secure man to want a liberated woman, and developing secure men means break-*

ing down the emphasis on external goals, the achievement of which is linked to masculinity.

A second illustration from another consciousness-raising group involves Karen and Ralph. In the men's group Ralph had said he wanted his wife to develop her intelligence and be able to speak up. He is intelligent and speaks well himself. Karen, though, hesitated to speak up in conversations although theoretically acknowledging its importance. When they communicated this in a joint group they resolved to make a more serious attempt to involve Karen in future conversations.

The following week another couple visited Ralph and Karen. The four sat down together, and after a few minutes a serious discussion evolved. Ralph started to respond to a pertinent comment, but kept quiet to "allow Karen a chance." A gap of silence followed. Neither of the women said a thing. Ralph felt embarrassed and slowly responded, leaving pauses should Karen want to interject. Ralph noticed that his company seemed less impressed with him than usual. He also observed he was leaving the impression of being bored. Five or six times that evening Ralph did this; sometimes the conversation was picked up, sometimes a dead silence ensued. As the evening ended it seemed like no one had much in common. When the company left Ralph got mad: "I gave you every chance I could, and you hardly said a thing." Karen responded, "I don't always feel like saying things. I don't always have something to say like you, big mouth."

This appeared like a superficial argument until the consciousness-raising group questioned the dynamics of what happened that evening and made an attempt to understand the socialization process prior to that evening. Part of what became Karen's personality both while she was dating and while she was learning her entire role as a female was that it was not polite to dominate—especially men. She also learned that it was polite to be a good hostess or to help the hostess. When she went to the kitchen, this usually left the men talking. To the men the conversation had continuity. When new points were to be made the men had the benefit of the entire conversation. When she returned from the kitchen she had to listen to pick up where things were at. She was literally "half out of it." She was also diverted by having to pay attention to the next course, to more crackers and cheese, or to the placement of ashtrays. Also, Ralph considered the essence of his life as concerned with the outside world, while Karen had come to consider the home the essence of her life. Karen, over the years, had become less able to respond quickly in conversations, less able to mentally prepare arguments, less knowledgeable about events outside of the home and, most importantly, less concerned about being knowledgeable since it did not appear essential to her role.

It took the consciousness-raising group longer to pinpoint the problems in Ralph's socialization process. Finally, though, they questioned why Ralph was so concerned with impressing his company. Ralph discovered that most of his friends were job-related or "in my general area of interest," and he therefore never knew when they might be important to his career. Slowly he saw what he was doing—objectifying his friends and choosing friends for career reasons rather than human reasons. The need to impress left him much more tense at any awkwardness in the transition process with Karen.

What the group never did question was everyone's assumption that Ralph was "allowing Karen a chance" to speak. No one considered the benefit to Ralph of "allowing Ralph a chance" to listen. It took a year more for Ralph to admit that he had to stop taking Gelusil for his acid stomach and had lost the "knots" in his stomach—his adolescent ulcer pains.

Understanding this process would also have made Ralph and Karen see a most important second fallacy: the "isolationist fallacy" of "we can work this out by ourselves." As the consciousness-raising group questioned Ralph and Karen it discovered that their company had directed all their questions at Ralph, making it all the more awkward for Karen to reply. If the company had been conscious of Karen's desire to overcome this passivity and if they had also been conscious of what was doubtless a similar situation on their own part, the entire evening might have proceeded differently. The gaps in conversation would have been understood, creating less tension and less nervousness; fewer questions would be directed exclusively by the men to the men. The trips to the kitchen would have been arranged on an alternating or all-together basis, or while the conversation was at its lightest points rather than at its heaviest. Karen explained, "When a conversation gets heavy it seems like an invitation for 'the girls' to retreat."

Behavioral change in the area of housework is compounded by the tendency on the part of men to oversimplify the chunk of unable-to-be organized time consumed by housework. Men often miss the distinction between helping and *sharing responsibility* for housework. An incident from another consciousness-raising group illustrates this. A complaint one of the men had about his attaché was that she always bothered him just when he was busy or tired: "She bothers me about the smallest things—like 'Do you think we should serve broccoli or squash with dinner tomorrow night?' It seems she always picks a bad moment to ask."

This "nagging" was particularly annoying to him since he now helped with the dinner and felt the least his wife could do was not bother him about all the little details beforehand. However, he was not assuming the responsibility for *planning* the dinner. It was only when he began to do the planning that the situation began to change. "We were sitting in bed the other night and my wife was reading a book. I wanted to plan the shopping list for the company. Suddenly I

blurted out, 'Do you think we should use cream of mush-
room sauce on the rice?' She responded, but a minute later I
asked 'Did you like the *brown* rice the Samuelsons served last
week?' After the fourth time Joan finally looked up at me
and asked, 'Now who's nagging?' "

The fascinating aspect of examining everyday interactions
is that it becomes easy to see how all the lip service for equality is usually undermined by both men and women the
moment they open their mouths. It also happens in the way
men touch women. It is so unconscious that consciousness-
raising is almost essential to bring it to a person's attention.
Some overall distinctions between the way men and women
talk were found both in my own studies of consciousness-
raising groups and in a study by Ceil Coberly of male-female
conversation patterns. Men, for example, tend to speak intellectually (not personally). Women tend to speak socially.
Men hold the floor for longer stretches while directing their
talk principally to one person. The women vary their attention more frequently among talker and listener, more likely
to include the entire group.[1] Coberly found that in an
equally balanced mixed group of eight the pattern deterio-
rates. "The women talked less in amount and less frequently
than the men . . . Men tend to 'dominate' women, who
accept a 'submissive' role."[2]

The division of interests resulting from the division of
labor between men and women is acutely apparent when
guests arrive. The women's labor in the kitchen encourages a
physical separation as it did with Ralph and Karen. In a
larger group, unless sexual attraction is keeping the sexes
integrated, one can find the men grouped together involved
in the male crutches of depersonalization—sports, business,
politics—and the women grouped with other women talking
about the house, decorating and children. The barriers are so
great that if a woman walks over toward a group of men
talking, one can notice the entire tone of the men's conversa-

tion change from a deep-voiced, prove-my-point pitch to a high-pitched voice: "Oh, hi-yah, sweetie—you made a great dinner." The superficial pleasantry, the brevity, the change of tone are all a clear indication to the woman that she is an intruder, that the rules of the game must change if she intervenes; that the men do not mind a moment's relief but that she shouldn't interfere in the substance. If a man comes to the woman's circle it is usually to get something ("Do you have the car keys, honey? I think I left my pipe in the car"). It is rarely with the thought of joining as an interested and equal participant. If he lingers more than a few seconds, a woman usually asks him a question ("What do you think of that, Bob?" or "Hasn't that been a problem we've been having with Jimmy? I've just been telling the girls about it"). His sense of authority is inevitably played to by "the girls," who ask him questions to which they doubtless know the answers as much as he. He may stay in the group as long as the attention is on him, but try counting to twenty after the attention has left him.

The women's reaction to the male interloper is frequently one of immediate willingness to forfeit the conversation with the women in order to receive the man's advice or authority. The very least some woman will do is take a half-step back to provide room for the man to join and explain, "We've just been talking about such and such." Generally the man smiles, starts putting up his hand to politely refuse, but instead lightly pats the woman's shoulder and responds, "Oh, that's nice." There is not even an obligation to acknowledge the invitation with a thank-you. If the man does join even for a moment (which will occasionally happen if his opinions are sought), the women's conversation flows less freely, lowers in tone, contains less expressive body movements directed at other women, and will occasionally even move to the man's area of topic security. Because, due to individual differences, these patterns do not always occur, and because we are usually participating in them, few observers notice them until they do a timing or counting. The conversations, though, are only microcosms of the problems caused in the larger society by the division of labor and, therefore, the division of interests between the sexes.

An understanding of the ingrained nature of masculinity and femininity can make persons like Ralph and Karen recognize from the outset that their task is going to require infinitely more effort than just "an equal chance"; that it is going to involve more than hostility, but a consistent and unrelenting effort by both parties; that it will usually also require the support of others making similar efforts.

THE PRIMARY PRODUCER PRINCIPLE

A third case, of a couple we shall call Jim and Betty, reveals even more fundamental barriers to changing behavior. When we first discussed this in the consciousness-raising group we thought it would be fairly simple to at least overcome the barriers to, as Jim put it, "helping around the house." First, we questioned the concept of "helping"; "Why should Jim just help Betty? The housework should be both their responsibility." While Jim and Betty accepted this in theory, they ran into a fundamental barrier, which the following case illustrates.

Jim had only been in his new position for about a year. It looked like he had a chance for promotion. He was making $14,000 and the promotion would bring him to $16,500. However, obtaining the promotion would be assisted by his staying late at work a few evenings per week and doing some extra work at home. The dilemma: If he participated fully around the house he would be likely to lose the promotion and the $2,500. This did not seem like a temporary dilemma. Prior to this Betty was working while Jim was going to school and the reason for Jim not sharing the housework was to accomplish their primary goal of completing his schooling. In the future the stake would again be more promotion possibilities. If Betty had been allowed to put more emphasis on her position she might eventually have moved from a good secretary at $7,000 to an office manager of the secretaries at $7,600. The $600 did not compare to the potential $2,500 at stake in Jim's position.

The underlying problem that created Jim and Betty's dilemma was this: Both their primary goal and society's primary emphasis is on the husband's work, the husband's schooling and the husband's career. Once this is accepted, simple cost-benefit analysis speaks in favor of providing the conditions under which the primary producer (Jim) can best produce.

In conclusion, what often appears as a simple attitude change toward housework or a simple "helping each other grow" requires in practice a much more fundamental change in attitudes toward both women and masculinity—attitudes which develop from the earliest interactions between parent and child. It must be a change which recognizes the very essence of a woman's productive role outside of the home as one on which the family *depends*—not just enjoys as an extra. From this it follows that the children and functions *inside* the home must be dependent on some equitable distribution between the man and woman. It is only when men or the family *depend* upon women to produce that the woman's productive role will be taken seriously. When this is combined with a willingness on the part of men to admit they are wrong, to listen and to raise their consciousness on a systematic basis about the myriad of barriers to change, it is possible that attitude changes will become behavioral changes.

PART III

*Men's and Joint
Consciousness-Raising:
Toward Human Liberation*

Thirteen

Men's Consciousness-Raising: Tools for Beyond Masculinity

The questions this book poses for any individual cannot be covered in any one book; no one book can reverse a life style developed over twenty to sixty years, with daily reinforcement by family and peers. But there is one tool that has facilitated this change for hundreds of thousands of women and perhaps a few thousand men: an ongoing consciousness-raising group—a group of persons meeting regularly to develop each other's awareness of alternative ways of overcoming the limitations on our lives that have evolved from our view of ourselves as masculine or feminine. The consciousness-raising group creates a subculture which encourages questioning and experimenting in ways that are applicable to one's personal life.

Men's groups have started in every region in the United

States. As I began to participate in, organize and observe consciousness-raising groups for men, however, I could not help noting that most were highly inefficient, escapist, afraid to discuss themselves in a personal way and afraid to discuss women's liberation in *any* way. The most personal groups often became one-sided—all therapy, all marriage counseling, all women's liberation, all homosexual. There was always a gap between the speeches made about men's liberation and its application to one complex individual. *The bigger the group, the bigger the idea, but in our minds we harbored little doubts and little fears.*

I harbored many of these doubts and fears as I entered the room of my first men's group on a winter evening in early 1970. I had been attending women's liberation meetings (any I could get into) for three or four months—since November 1969. I could barely pronounce what the group was calling itself—a men's antimale-chauvinism consciousness-raising group.

At the beginning, like most men, I didn't really think I needed to go. Since I had read a lot of the literature published by that point, I thought I had a pretty good grasp of the issues. My initial attitude was a mixture of curiosity about *women's liberation* and a semiconscious feeling that it would be nice to show the other men what a liberated man was like.

I didn't know what was coming. None of the information I came with ("The salary gap between men and women increased between 1964 and 1970," and so forth) was being used. When I referred to it the group continued as if I had not spoken. Then I began to notice the difference between their interests and mine. They were talking about themselves—their own experiences; I was talking about facts, statistics, trends, generalities—not about me. The power of the consciousness-raising group lies in its ability to get its members to build liberated relationships in their own lives. Its purpose is not to teach the Bible of women's and men's liberation at its weekly meetings or to give psychic rewards to the members who know it best and who couldn't care less about who applies it. This recognition came to me slowly because statistics appeared to be much less refutable than just one person's experience. Statistics were a combination of the experiences of thousands of real people, I had reasoned. However, statistics were the aggregate experience of *others,* and knowing them demanded nothing of *me.*

Because we had no leader, each of us was encouraged to assume the responsibility for speaking up when we felt a man was being sexist, egocentric or biased. But without a leader we found it easy to withdraw from personalizing. Collective responsibility was our theoretical strength and our practical weakness. Fear of getting too personal lest our comments make us vulnerable sidetracked us into issues such as "liberation and the socialist revolution." The diversion to the seminar approach was, in my opinion, the group's downfall. This was ironic since this group was so effective in helping me see the value of personalizing.

This first group—connected with a "free" university called Alternate U.—had another deficiency. Although its consciousness of the nature of oppression was high, its philosophy of the coming Socialist Revolution was its excuse for the avoidance of incremental, "revisionist" approaches to social change. It served to keep the men's ideas confined to a small group, since dealing with the media was "playing footsie with the Establishment." It therefore avoided stepping on the Establishment's feet. That deficiency made the incremental action orientation of NOW appealing.

NOW pressures the system from the outside in order to improve women's opportunities on the inside. While it has radicalized and broadened its base since 1970, its concern at that time for consciousness-raising was minimal. It was the only women's liberation organization admitting men, but for this it paid a price. At plans for the first August 26th Strike for Equality one man lectured, "You girls ought to be more careful about your image. If you want us men to like you and agree with you, you should at least have your girls put on dresses when you march. And it's not just convincing the men I'm talking about. Other women, too." At each meeting a few men could not resist "solving" women's problems and defining them through their eyes. They could not allow women to define themselves even at a meeting held for that purpose. It was this same assumption of dependence on men which made the phrase "if you want men to like you" so grating.

This male attitude made the need for a men's consciousness-raising group apparent. A second impetus for me was the hope of changing men's attitudes. The persistent requests of NOW leaders such as Jacqui Ceballos and Ivy Bottini for me to draw on my experience with the Alternate U. group and "Please, do *something!*" did much to stimulate my attempt to gather some men together for the first consciousness-raising group meetings. The men were drawn from three sources: attachés of women attending NOW meetings; men who attended NOW meetings by their own motivation for reasons ranging from a civil rights type of benevolence to "picking up a liberated chick"; men who read or heard about the sessions after our first few meetings.

The initial participants ranged in age between twenty-three and fifty-four. Most had living friends or attachés, about half with children, a couple were divorced, and a few were unattached. Most were from New York City and a few from the suburbs. Politically, all but two men were to the left of center.

For which men was the group effective? Most unattached men who came because a casual "girl friend" wanted them to did not stay, but if their attachés or living friends persuaded them to get involved *and* were themselves involved in women's liberation, the chances of their remaining were much higher. Frequently, these men also made the most substantial changes. But the motivation to join a group does not necessarily have to come from women. In fact, if books like this one's goals are achieved, the motivation will come at least as frequently from men.

The following pages deal with some of the recurrent questions encountered in the Alternate U. and NOW group as well as in the hundred or so groups I have had an opportunity to organize around the country in 1971 through 1974.

DISTINGUISHING CONSCIOUSNESS-RAISING FROM THERAPY, SEMINARS, AND MARRIAGE COUNSELING

A most frequent series of questions from men is the following: What does a consciousness-raising group do? What is it actually like to sit around with men for three hours without talking about business, politics or sports? How do we prevent the group from turning into another all-male bull session? How do its methods resemble or differ from various kinds of psychotherapy or counseling? How does it actually help people to change their thinking or behavior?

Therapy and consciousness-raising are not mutually exclusive. Many men enter consciousness-raising only after learning to communicate in therapy groups. Men's groups often fail to make a distinction between consciousness-raising groups and therapy groups, issue-oriented seminars on women's or men's liberation, and—especially in the case of joint groups—marriage counseling. The distinctions are important. A therapy group is led; it can delve into *psychological* explanations as to *why* behavior occurs; it generally teaches one how to *adjust* to the societal norm; the leader is trained to encounter participants on a broad base of problems, and it is assumed that a leader can best help the participants deal with the complications acompanying change. A consciousness-raising group is more specifically focused, dealing predominately with problems resulting from the attempted adjustment to sex roles. Its members encourage each other to question sex roles, rather than to depend on a leader to help them adjust.

Perhaps the distinctive characteristic of men's consciousness-raising groups is that each man learns to ask a *peer* for help rather than an authority for help. As each man does this, he learns that all men have similar problems—that he does not need to be insecure about the expectations he never met; as he sees that many men have not met these expectations, he comes to regard these unmet expectations not as unique failures in need of psychological help, but as false measures of manhood. He comes to understand that his main weakness is having the expectation of not being weak. The process of each man slowly opening up before a peer rather than an authority is the first step in learning how to be open in front of neighbors, friends and colleagues. It is a crucial step in the liberation process.

This process of lay persons supporting each other in change and questioning every behavioral and psychological restriction of sex roles has become a major contribution of feminism to therapy—to the point where feminist therapy has become a rapidly growing field.

An important additional distinction between consciousness-raising groups and therapy is the more supportive nature of consciousness-raising rather than the encountering nature of many, although not all, therapy groups and therapists. Women's groups are almost entirely supportive. Men's consciousness-raising groups combine supportiveness (through understanding common problems in socialization) with challenging each other to change. They support other men not only by highlighting the expectations on men, but by understanding how these expectations become pressures, how pressures become anxieties, how anxieties give us feelings of powerlessness and *how anxieties about powerlessness, combined with expectations for power, make us fight to be in control.* Men support each other in understanding how our hang-ups about masculinity affect our relationships with other women and men. They can both support and challenge each other to change by the use of "follow-through hours" at the beginning of new meetings as a way of showing the concern for the changes each man has experienced during the week.

In the effort of many traditonal therapy groups to get their members to *adjust* to sex roles, they often work with a man to become a better breadwinner or a woman to become more confident and sexually attractive or a good mother. For example, an executive-development program (therapy style) develops the male executive, but it still leaves the woman in the home. It may perpetuate the Dale Carnegie-type ability to speak on "any subject" rather than encourage the man to express weaknesses or spend more time with his children. Men's consciousness-raising concentrates on the latter—on overcoming the problems of masculinity.

While both consciousness-raising and therapy groups can lead individuals into depression without replacing the depression with guidelines for solutions, consciousness-raising tends to avoid this by the more voluntary nature of most men's attendance. Most men will quit rather than put themselves through change that is too uncomfortable. Since they are not usually paying if there is no leader, the commitment to stick out an unpleasant process is minimal.

Ellis and Harper, two psychotherapists, point out how techniques such as consciousness-raising can be beneficial to changing behavior.[1] In fact, Ellis has sponsored consciousness-raising weekends at his well-known Institute for Rational Living in New York City. He explains: "All that seems to be necessary is that the individual *somehow* come up against significant life experiences *or* learn about others' experiences *or* sit down and think for himself *or* enter a relationship with a therapist who will help him reconstruct his basic attitudes toward himself and others."[2] "With or without psychological sophistication, an individual can read or hear about a new idea, can forcefully set about applying it to his own thought and action, and can carve amazingly constructive changes in his own psyche."[3] If a gap exists between one's emotions and intellect, Ellis and Harper feel, there is usually something unresolved intellectually, and that can be tapped by examining a person's present thinking and behavior. Adler, Fromm, Horney, Rank and Sullivan also emphasize this analysis of present problems.[4]

Despite areas of overlap between consciousness-raising and therapy, the risks involved in therapy for untrained lay persons can occasionally lead to too great a potential for destructive outcomes. Also, therapy tends to become so all-consuming that the participants forget to examine their lives from a men's and women's liberation perspective. I have been especially struck by *how difficult it is for men to discuss women's liberation seriously and personally in a men's consciousness-raising group*. This is obviously not all that men should be discussing, but men do seem afraid to even read women's liberation literature: "I've read plenty about it in the media—I know their arguments" is a standard reply. *It is as if they are unwilling to admit they can learn from a woman.* Some men will read an interview with Germaine Greer in *Playboy* and never recognize the chauvinism involved in continuing their subscription to that while not subscribing to even one feminist publication. When they do claim to have read a given book, they oversimplify its thesis into one or two points which usually start out like, "Well, the book was good, *but . . .*" ending always with a criticism or an "I didn't really learn anything I didn't know already." There is never the deep respect and careful discussion that there is of Marx or Marcuse. There is never a discussion marked by curiosity, openness or the discovery that "maybe this applies to me." If a feminist publication discusses male dominance the men find a woman who dominates and assume, therefore, that it isn't a male problem. (Few men dismiss Marx because of one working-class man who isn't for revolution.)

Consciousness-raising is also distinct from issue-oriented seminars on men's and women's liberation. I have seen some groups, especially among academics, undertake an issue a week for fourteen weeks and then disband, feeling they were more liberated. In fact, they are more *educated*, but there is no guarantee they are more liberated. Whether or not anything has changed in their own lives as a result of their education is an unexplored question.

The strong relationships between women's and men's liberation often makes persons ask *whether there is any real difference between consciousness-raising and marriage counseling*. As with therapy groups, the two overlap and can contribute to each other. There are some differences, though. In marriage counseling couples often feel they have a *unique* problem which only an experienced counselor and large outlays of money can solve. In consciousness-raising groups, problems are seen as almost inevitable given the way both sexes have been socialized. Only a few marriage counselors are fully in tune with overcoming sex roles. For many couples consciousness-raising is more supportive because of the challenge it gives *the couple* to overcome the culture, rather than fight each other. Consciousness-raising also has the advantage of establishing a new subculture of friends who offer support for each other's changes. While a marriage counselor cannot offer collective support, if te has overcome advocacy of sex-role stereotypes te can offer a trained perspective which will often be missed by even the collective assistance of the group.

ASKING RELEVANT QUESTIONS ABOUT MASCULINITY

The importance of treating women's liberation seriously and personally in men's consciousness-raising groups should not overshadow the need by men to focus on the confines of masculinity (particularly how we are still manifesting these signs today). This means asking ourselves questions for which we are *presently* accountable, not just explaining to the group how we *used* to have a problem, which we have since overcome, and then offering our ready-made solution. For example:

- When was the last time I spoke of my feelings for children?
- Was there a situation I faced in the last few days where I would have expected a woman to cry? Why didn't I cry?
- Do I quietly develop my knowledge of wines and subtly let the knowledge fall on appreciative ears? Do I want to stop doing this, and if I do, do I resent the pressure of those ears being appreciative? (If those ears are those of an un-liberated woman still trying to construct a man's ego, can I begin to resent the way an unliberated woman adds to my pressure to maintain a pseudo-masculinity?)
- Do I talk around women of the differential in cars, as if I were born with the knowledge?
- Do I enjoy talking about the wattage of my stereo system more than talking intimately with another man (or woman)?
- Do I feel particularly concerned about not having some-one contradict me in front of another woman?
- Am I overly concerned about the way "my wife" looks and how she speaks when I am at a party (that is, do I like the status of her being intelligent, but not so it casts a shadow on my intelligence)?

- Do I resent some women's pressure to keep a steel penis at all times, or to make love in fifty-seven varieties?
- Do I feel comfortable talking about my sexual inadequacies, real or imagined?

If a man has a feeling of sexual inadequacy, such as a small penis, and cannot talk about it with other men, he creates a shield of protectiveness and unfeeling coldness which makes him, as so many women complain about men, "hard to love." To the extent a men's group helps us counter our emotional constipation and be vulnerable without being defensive it establishes the framework in which women can express feelings and emotions without feeling uniquely "just like a woman." When men are also expressing feelings, such expression by definition becomes a human characteristic.

PROBLEMS

Leadership

Some problems are both recurrent and important enough to the men's consciousness-raising group that the participant should be aware of them from the outset. One of these is the dilemma of leadership. Perhaps the experience of Steven best summarizes the dilemma. After almost a year in our group, Steven, the most politically radical member, organized some groups in New Jersey, determined "not to impose leadership on it." He related his experiences to me as follows:

The first group I formed completely fell apart. When the men got together, they looked to me for leadership, but I refused to lead or provide them with direction 'cause I thought that was condescending, and I couldn't stand the idea of another structure with another leader. Well, they spent hour after hour supporting each other in their misery, downing the women in their lives and complaining of the plague that had overcome their marriage since this "women's liberation stuff." Warren, the Movement out here in New Jersey has changed these people's lives something fierce. But the men won't discuss women's liberation from the women's point of view for even a moment. They are ruining themselves with their bitterness. The group didn't get anywhere. The guys didn't develop any understanding of anything, *including themselves,* and it just fell apart. They didn't know what to talk about or even where to start. I realize after that experience that these guys have to have something to go on or they'll just be reinforcing the status quo—and I guess that's not very radical.

Steven's second experience with starting a men's group was quite successful. It involved a gradually decreasing leadership role in the group, after which he had the men rotate a "facilitator" role to ease himself out of the leadership role (after about two months). As facilitator, he mostly introduced techniques and stopped the group for comments. The men kept moving toward collective responsibility for working with each other.

Self-Listening and Self-Revealing

The problem of self-listening is a recurrent one in men's groups. (Self-listening, described in more detail on page 11, is basically the process of catching the gist of what a person is saying and then starting to think to oneself of a similar incident which the supposed listener can bring up the moment the talker pauses, in a way that transfers the focus of the group to tirself.) While men dominate conversations about "issues" to the point where we self-listen, when it comes to *self-revealing* we are silent. For example, a woman friend of mine noted that when she and her attaché returned from work, she would respond to his question "How was your day?" by describing some of her successes *and failures,* intermittently asking, "Do you think I handled that okay?" with a plea in her eyes for reassurance. But it would often take days for him to reveal his failures, and when he did, they were usually couched in terms of "me and the bad guys." Many of his failures were suppressed, only coming up months and sometimes a year later in another context; in the meantime they had taken their toll on him internally.

In the joint groups (men with women), women are guilty of not listening in a different way: they *pseudo-listen*. The woman's face may be strained with "fascination" at the man who is speaking, but her "fascination" is only a way to get the man's attention to focus on her. Pseudo-listening is also a defense for the woman who feels unable to state an opinion worthy of a man's attention; *it is conversational cheerleading*—a method of attracting the attention of the main performer without sharing the responsibility for the performance. Like all cheerleading it puts even more pressure on the performer to maintain his isolated performance, to maintain his image of being "fascinating." The man feels unable to ask a question lest he shatter the image (imagine a football player asking a cheerleader's advice on the next play). He continues to self-listen rather than ask questions for which he does not already know the answer. Unfortunately, it took much more effort to eliminate the self-listening problem from men than to stop women from pseudo-listening.

Being Specific

In both the men's and women's consciousness groups vague charges such as "chauvinist" were often used to avoid a more specific and intimate complaint, like "You never volunteer to do the dishes." Choosing vague words avoids the intimacy and vulnerability that comes with zeroing in on the exact nature of a problem.

Cautiousness-Raising

There is always a group skeptic, or cautiousness-raiser, who "foresees" all the negative possibilities to anything the group might try, thereby discouraging the group from experimenting. Usually a male, the cautiousness-raiser loves his aura of "father protector"—one who cannot bear to see the group hurt itself. By making the person suggesting the experiment appear naïve and pollyannaish in contrast to himself, the cautiousness-raiser helps the group forget that the real reason they do not want to try something new is because of their own insecurities which he is now compounding. *The cautiousness-raiser thereby deprives the group of the most important part of consciousness-raising—obtaining the security to try new things.*

Touching—Fears of Homosexuality

The inability of men to touch each other makes touching a more important topic for a men's consciousness-raising group than a woman's. Group exercises such as sitting in a circle and holding hands, first concentrating only on the physical contact and then on attempting to speak normally while holding hands, can eventually help men overcome the self-consciousness involved in touching other men. Holding hands also tends to make men more hesitant to compete and interrupt. The contradiction between warmth and verbal aggression becomes painfully apparent while everyone is holding hands.

Relating to Relationships Outside the Group

In all-men's groups, it often takes a long time to reverse roles in a way that helps men understand the power plays involved in their relations with women outside the group. For example, in campus groups discussions about a man and woman living together usually deal with the *woman* living in the *man's* apartment. This offers untold advantages to the man which extend beyond familiarity with the apartment and the area. For example, the woman has to notify all her friends of her changed telephone and address. This increases her emotional commitment more than his. If she changes too often she seems flighty or even like a prostitute, while he appears stable. Finally, in describing why a man seldom moves into a woman's apartment, Gail Sheehy may have expressed it best: "It happens rarely because think what it means when the Breakup hits at four in the morning. They stand in the middle of the bone-chilling bedroom, with the damn window open on his sensitives . . . facing each other in pocky-mouthed indignity . . . *and he is the one who has to leave.* Ignominy! He, the man, alleged lord and master of the house, must scramble up his socks and toothbrush like some creep Private Hargrove and crawl out *her* door."[5]

Joint Consciousness-Raising vs. Separate Groups

When I overcame the dogma that men's and women's groups *must* meet separately, this opened up all the possibilities involving joint groups. However, it is important that men's and women's groups meet separately first for two to three months. If they meet jointly before meeting separately the meetings often turn into the normal male-female game playing—the men self-listen; the women pseudo-listen; and neither sex learns how to be truly supportive of the same sex, since they are competing for the attention of the other sex.

The joint groups are most successful when the men and women can return to their separate groups the week after the joint meeting to analyze among themselves the ways in which they lapsed into stereotypical roles when they were with the other sex. In a sense, *the joint groups serve as a laboratory to put into practice the theories everyone agrees to in the isolated comfort of separate groups.* I find that if the groups remain separate for too long, the men and women both start building up distorted stories of "I would love to have a more liberated relationship if only my wife (or husband) would cooperate." The joint groups communicate directly with the attaché to determine whether the "lack of cooperation" is a reality or projection.

In both separate and joint groups the question often arises as to whether older people should be in the same group with young; rich with poor; married with single. The only mixture of persons which seemed to spend time in group discussion from which the others did not benefit was a mixture of people with attachés and single persons. Living friends and attachés quickly became bored with "dating problems," and singles get bored fairly quickly with extensive discussions of parent-child relationships. While theoretically both can learn from each other, in practice the intellectual learning is an escape from confronting problems that are present-day and personal.

For these reasons, when I have organized groups I usually advertise enough in the local papers and NOW newsletter to attract about fifty persons, who can be divided into four groups of about twelve to thirteen each (allowing for attrition to the ideal of six to nine) as follows:

Men's Couples: Men who have attachés or living friends. (The attaché should be in the women's couples group unless gay. Gay attachés may be in the same group unless they desire to start a separate support group.)
Women's Couples: Women who have attachés or living friends. (The attaché should be in the men's couples group unless gay.)

The men's and women's couples groups meet separately for two to three months and then alternate meeting together and separately. If the combined group on a given evening reaches sixteen people, it is helpful to meet in two separate rooms for that evening so everyone has a chance to participate. These same principles apply to groups three and four:

Women's Singles: Women without attachés or living friends.
Men's Singles: Men without attachés or living friends.

Joint consciousness-raising groups have met with more success than I expected when I started writing this book. I did not expect them to be as successful in getting conflicts into the open quickly (although some persons interpret the conflict as proof that joint meetings are a disaster). Once the conflict is in the open, I did not expect joint groups to be as successful in offering constructive alternatives. We found that the importance of mixed consciousness-raising groups for women is that it minimizes the loss of humanity that comes with fighting the entire battle of changing attitudes by oneself. Vivian Gornick makes this observation with vivid insight in her comparison of the painful change process of women and blacks:

But of course that is the whole sickening trickery in life—the idea that one cannot fight for one's humanity without, ironically, losing it—and it is a piece of trickery that the blacks sometimes seem helpless against and the women now sometimes seem helpless against, and, in the final analysis, that trickery is the real enemy, and the very essence of the thing we must continually be on our guard against. For what shall it profit a woman if she gain an end to slavery in marriage and in the process lose her soul?

However, a liberal who was outraged ten years ago at the sheer "unreasonableness" of the blacks and is outraged now at the sheer "unfairness" of the women is a fool, and possessed of the kind of impatience that calls all of this early allegiance into question. For how is it possible that a man in one breath should proclaim his genuine understanding of woman's deeply subordinate position in our society, and in the very next exclaim savagely against the forceful and sometimes "unreasonable" expression of rage now rising in women, an expression which inevitably accompanies the uprising of those who suddenly realize they have been cheated of their birthright and which dies down only slowly and with the healing passage of time that brings real change and increased understanding?[6]

The joint consciousness-raising group communicates the woman's rage, but through the advent of men's liberation, often creates an alliance in the man who finds himself trapped by the same lack of liberation. Perhaps in that alliance rests some of the success of the joint consciousness-raising groups.

THE MEN'S GROUP:
THE INITIAL MEETINGS AND INITIAL ERRORS

At our first meeting we only had about six men. My philosophy was to exert minimal or no leadership, but since I had convened the group and was the only man with experience in consciousness-raising this position took constant effort. I have since retreated somewhat on my no-leadership ideology to one of minimal and decreasing leadership, depending on the experience of the group.

Within twenty minutes the group had agreed the problem lay with the type of people *outside* of the group. Statements such as "If everyone were only like us, there would be no need for a women's liberation movement" were not infrequent; more importantly, they were characteristic of our self-satisfaction and willingness to keep the focus away from ourselves. We didn't discuss how or whether each of us had developed a more liberated relationship; we just assumed we did.

Lewis, a hip-talking men's clothing designer with jet-black hair and unabashed enthusiasm, explained: "I really like liberated chicks. They are into a lot of things; they're fun to talk to, man. I just got back from Europe and those chicks were really cool. They weren't so hung up and frigid, like here."

"Yeah," added Hank, a tall, lanky, blond drug counselor, "you can treat liberated women as sex objects because they're liberated enough to treat us as sex objects, too. Both know where the relationship is at, and no one is using anyone else." There was little objection to this "equal" use of each other.

I was becoming somewhat uneasy at what appeared to be a clouding of the distinction between sexually liberated women and women's liberation, so I interjected, probably sooner than I should have, not allowing other unquestioned assumptions to surface. "I wonder if the woman is still thinking in terms of 'giving' her sex, but more easily, to attract a man for her ultimate marital security, or even just to obtain his approval? The fact that we 'each want something' does not mean we have freed ourselves from looking at women as sex objects or that women have freed themselves from looking at us as—as 'security objects.'" For most of us, this was not a new theory, but we had never seen *ourselves* as providing a basic good (money) and a basic service (security) in exchange for women's basic good (her body) and her basic service (sexual gratification).

Rod (a blond, blue-eyed man of German extraction, schooled in Wilhelm Reich, an avid reader and insightful thinker but also an intellectualizer) explained that women's services extended beyond sexual gratification. "They're also the housekeeper, maid, nurse, typist for our papers, cook and laundryperson. Actually they're a cheap labor supply, a source of slave labor—and just like with all slaves, their body is their primary possession. We're all born with certain markings, like in the Indian caste system, but here it's a penis or a vagina—and the marking makes each of us treat the other with certain expectations, certain limits. Everyone justifies it by saying it offers security and identity, but I'd rather be free to develop my own identity. I don't dig having one imposed on me by birth."

None of us picked up on Rod's intellectualizing—his avoidance of discussing something with which he was having problems. In fact, we were all soon showing the defense mechanisms of which new groups are usually so capable. As the meeting progressed I noticed that Lewis, the men's clothing designer (with thick black hair on both his head and chest, the latter discreetly exposed with two open shirt buttons), was perched on the edge of his seat, sunglasses in hand. His eyes reflected an anxious intensity, and he was shaking his head in agreement as each member finished the first sentence of a new thought. One could almost watch him thinking, "I know what you are going to say." He was nodding his head furiously; with a second's pause by the speaker, he would jump in and say it his way, with his own story and elaborations. When another person was speaking, he seemed to be forming his own parallel incidents related to his own experiences. This was the process we eventually called self-listening.

Lewis used Rod's reference to the Indian caste system as a springboard to his foreign ventures, explaining how "in the United States, I always find I'm in the position of bringing chicks up to my intellectual level—they know so little about clothing, fashions, marketability," and so forth. As I listened further, I could begin to see a number of us were not only self-listening, but were assuming women needed to come up to our intellectual level. I began to see the connection between the two. In the same way Lewis found it difficult to listen to other men, he was doubtless also unwilling to listen to a woman's contribution except insofar as he could relate it to himself. He was almost always unable to understand fully those values which the woman had come to recognize as primary in *her* life. He subtly considered them inferior to "his" values. Self-listening enabled Lewis to avoid all values outside of his own masculine value system. He never marveled at his woman friend's ability to emphathize with characters in a novel, her desire to work with younger children, or her way of expressing emotions. By self-listening he never really had to seriously consider those values and so he could bring her up to his values of marketability and fashions. When one of us alluded to this, Lewis responded, "Oh, I can understand how women have to have their interests, too," but his tone of voice betrayed his *tolerance* of women's interests rather than a sincere attempt to listen for the subtleties which might enable him to respect them.

Self-listening can become such an integral part of a man's personality that even when a woman is operating in the masculine value system the man may not recognize her contribution. This might be called the "power of nonrecognition." A blatant example of this occurred during our third or fourth meeting when Mark, about fifty years old, attended the group for his first and only time. When introducing himself to the group, Mark stressed his experience in the area of employment. Coincidentally a group of NOW members were discussing employment in the room next to ours from which Mark had just come.

As Mark finished his introduction I asked, "Aren't you interested in the program on employment?"

With an air of confidence, he replied, "Not really; what they are doing is really irrelevant."

"Oh. Have you discussed this with them?"

"I've already told the girls how they should do it. You see, their present method is really ineffective."

"You've listened to one of their presentations before, then?"

"No, but if these girls want to do this right they shouldn't be putting pressure on the employment agencies, they should put the pressure on the Labor Department."

The discussion continued for fifteen minutes with all of us asking him questions. Our questions, though, dealt with the substance of the issues and not one with his *attitude* of condescension toward the women or his nonrecognition of the possibilities in their approach. Not one of us asked if he really had such a clear grasp of what the women were doing that he could not have benefited from listening to their presentation.

As the discussion continued around Marc's substantive expertise, one of the men suggested we were not being personal. The spotlight was taken off Marc and *within two minutes he left the room*. None of us commented on this; I did not make the connection until writing up the session.

These first few meetings were a constant temptation to talk about the intellectual and the sexual. We discussed Lionel Tiger's *Men in Groups,* the kibbutz as an alternate life style, homosexuality and bisexuality and problems of women in business. One of the first steps away from this direction was taken by Tim, a branch manager of a large insurance company. About forty, with neatly cropped gray-lined black hair and horn-rimmed glasses, Tim was always impeccably dressed in dark-blue wide-lapeled suits and was a fanatic about wild ties, gourmet foods and wines. He was to be with the group for the entire two and a half years. Tim's dilemma concerned a conflict involving friends, his company and the use of women as sex objects.

Tim leaned forward, took his glasses off, rubbed his eyes pensively and explained: "I'm having a party for my boss. I know he'd like some of his old buddies from Dartmouth, so I called one of his closest friends. He wanted to 'do it up real nice—with some real sexy broads, a floor show and some really good stuff.' The problem is like this: I can recognize how this is what you guys call 'sexist,' but don't I also have an obligation to do what my boss likes? It's his party—do I have a right to impose my values on his party? I'm always looked at as the maverick in the office now. I think I'm inclined to save my objections for when they really count. What do you think?"

Twenty minutes of discussion followed while we deviated on to stag parties and topless nightclubs and took a mental tour of the naked-above-the-waist underground of New York City—never answering Tim's real concerns. Finally one of the men asked, "What about the other guys from Dartmouth? Have you notified them?" Tim answered he had not. "You mean you're *assuming* all the guys are going to have the suggestion this guy has? It could be a lot of them would be just as happy to have an opportunity to talk with your boss as to watch the topless broads—or women, I should say!"

I learned from our experience with Tim the importance of getting beyond the original framework in which a problem is presented, of pressing for more information and questioning the basic assumptions. I can also recall being personally hesitant to suggest alternatives for fear they would not be accepted; as I thought about it, I believe I felt I had to be "right" in everything I said.

Tim's decision also raised the question of the depth of rage any of us could feel about women's liberation. For Tim the decision involved the "balancing of priorities." An important factor in his case was who might be offended. For a woman with her consciousness raised the priorities would have been a lot clearer. As long as we were isolating women's liberation from our own liberation we could only match understanding and sympathy against the self-interest of doing "what we think the boss wants." It was not until we discussed how having "broads" dance at our parties was really a manipulation of *us* into paying money for promises of sex to be dangled in front of our faces that the first traces of anger began to filter through our conversation. As we discussed how the men who were selling these women had an investment in maintaining our fantasies, in giving us just so much of their bodies and no more, we began to feel used and insulted ourselves. Consistently, *the technique of asking "How is this also hurting us?" enabled us to discover how our own self-interest was being threatened by the same phenomena that threatened women.*

During the first meetings of both the Alternate U. group and this consciousness-raising group the words "chick," "girl" and "lady" were used frequently in instances where the word "man" would probably have been used if the discussion were about a male. At the very beginning the word "broad" was not unheard but it became immediately clear in both groups that this word was too direct a focus on a woman as a sex object. Lewis used the word "chick" quite frequently during the first session. None of the men challenged him on this. I toyed with objecting but knew each time I did I risked reinforcing the image of myself as a leader. The more the conversation continued, though, the more I began to sense that the alternative to leading was to continue having nothing more than a bull session. Since men in groups had not stopped to ask these questions for centuries there was little reason to expect that we would do so now.

I finally asked Lewis what image of woman "chick" implied. He looked sharply back at me, his eyes revealing that he knew my point, but then looked back out toward the group and in a hip, cool and confident manner took off on an elaborate intellectualization tracing the word to its etymological derivations of "chicken." "Chick," he explained, "is a perfectly acceptable word." It did not appear that my questioning made much of an impression on Lewis until a few sessions later when a new member, John, joined the group.

John was a law student who had a ready response to all questions, an extroverted young man who had recently come out of the Army, and spoke in highly complex, involuted sentences in eight-to-ten-minute clips. During his third or fourth turn speaking—some of the members might have suggested it was his third or fourth speech—he used the word "chick," and then proceeded to explain how he had done so purposely. Lewis apparently sensed John's attempt to preserve the "liberated" image John thought he was creating, and jokingly assured him that we all made that type of mistake, so why didn't John admit it? "Well," John said, laughingly, with his face turning red, "you got me there."

Lewis then took the initiative of explaining to John, "Whenever *I* think of women in these terms, I end up with a woman I can't appreciate intellectually." As Lewis became more secure he had moved from an intellectual justification of the etymology of "chick" to a personal experience. At only one point during his remaining year and a half with the group did Lewis fall back into using the word "chick." It was immediately after he was verbally berated by the women at the East Village church. He then used the word "chick" a number of times, openly justifying it by saying, "I'm going to say just what I feel—and if that's the way I think about them then that is what I'll call them." Lewis obviously found it necessary to degrade women when he felt most degraded and insecure himself.*

JOINT CONSCIOUSNESS-RAISING: THE FIRST ATTEMPTS

After meeting about five times as a semi-stable group of men (feeling at least as much like a group of semi-stable men), we were asked by a group of NOW women, who had met only once previously, if we wanted to meet with them.

---

* Lewis' reaction to women at a time of insecurity is not unlike the reaction I have occasionally seen by women as they are working through the insecurities of the consciousness-raising process. Consciousness-raising takes women out of the security of subservience before it offers the security of self. It creates a vacuum of insecurity. It is during this period of insecurity that I have felt that some women do try to downgrade men even beyond the point where it appears justified, as if by so doing they are building themselves up. Although Lewis' reaction—of putting another down to compensate for his own insecurity—is similar, the first stage of the process is different. The man starts out from the security of perceived superiority (rather than subservience) ; the second stage, when a semblance of equality is achieved, is an insecure stage for both sexes; the third stage, of recognizing that an equal relationship is one that is far more beneficial than threatening, provides a new security.

Although a few of us thought we still had a lot to learn about where we were before we met with a group of women, the majority felt we had progressed to the point of applying our discussions of self-listening and dominating to our daily interactions with women. We agreed.

As we were about to start, I left the room for a phone call. When I returned a few minutes later no discussion had started. The women's group, which had its own discussion leader, assumed that *I* would lead. The irony was too great. I struggled to avoid even giving a signal to the woman leader indicating my desire (permission) for her to start the group.

What appeared like an hour, and was probably thirty seconds, passed. Nothing was said. A new woman arrived, apologized for being late and asked what the silence was about. A few of us indicated we had not really started. "Oh . . . well, then, can I tell about a problem I had getting hired by this firm?" Almost in relief one of the *men* replied she could. For the next ten minutes the woman explained the full story of how she had applied for a position with a consulting firm and encountered a series of discriminatory responses.

She looked toward the group for help. There were eight men and eight women. The next twenty minutes were spent by all eight men giving her advice. *Not one woman offered advice and not one asked even a single question.* When the first few minutes of this passed and I became aware of the emerging pattern, I glanced at my watch and incredulously watched the next fifteen minutes tick away without one woman speaking. Slowly my stomach was knotting. I could only see each new piece of "advice" as an addition to the underlying problem.

As the discussion proceeded, I began to believe that this pattern of dominance might not be discovered and therefore not resolved. Finally, I burst out in an emotional tone of impatience, "Look what's happening here—we're doing exactly what we were supposed to be here to overcome!"

The reaction to this observation was perhaps the most painful event of the evening. The women explained, "The men know more about employment problems than we do, so isn't it logical the men should help her?" For a moment that did seem logical. Then one of the women did what we had seen was so valuable in Tim's case: She questioned the premise of the statement. "I don't know about that. Let's try an experiment and go around to each woman to see what she might have contributed." With one exception each woman was able to make a contribution to the employment problem. As one woman later put it, "When I saw someone was seriously going to look at me for an answer, my mind suddenly started clicking. Before that I was content to just sort of passively listen. I didn't even know I could come up with a suggestion."

"This is why the feminists distribute two or three chips to everyone and allow a person to speak for only as many times as she has chips. When the dominant woman runs out, the less dominant have to speak."

"We should probably try that," one of the men said. "This is also the first time I can see why women limit their organization to all women."

"Yes, we'll never see other women as helpers if you are solving our problems. But our group should probably have met separately first, too—we're missing a lot of ways we could be helping each other. I'm damned angry that a man had to discover that the men were dominating us."

What was happening, though, was also a strong argument for *ultimately* combining the groups—gaining a laboratory experience of the validity of the points intellectually agreed to in the separate groups. The value of the men's group meeting previously to discuss the consequences of this dominance was that we recognized it immediately and were angry ourselves. By the end of the meeting we were involved in a much more tense but equal dialogue. We were still dominating, but more like 60 to 40 than 100 to 0, and after we did speak we were somewhat more careful to listen to the women's contribution.

At our next men's meeting we discussed the joint meeting from both a women's and men's liberation perspective. John mused, "Boy, does equal pay for equal work seem meaningless once you see how someone can be restrained so easily from making an equal contribution. My image of women really changed in that meeting."

Tim added, "What surprised me was how fast we *all* changed once we were willing to challenge each other."

Rod used the example to draw a parallel with our preconceived attitudes toward homosexuality. "I would suggest that just as we have preconceived attitudes about our mental capacities, we have them about our capacities for bisexuality. If people learn to love and feel warmly toward each other, can't sexual feelings evolve from this regardless of the sex?"

Larry, a muscular six-foot-five physical-education teacher, who attended his first session at the meeting with the women, told a story which further provoked our interest in this area. "Last week I was in the cafeteria. I saw this guy at the other end of the room sort of nudging up to this girl. They were both sitting so they were facing me, so I could see their legs under the table. Both of them stared straight ahead at their food, pretending not to notice each other. All of a sudden I saw this guy starting to move his leg back and forth to rub her leg. I could see him getting more and more excited. Every once in a while he would move up a little off the chair and sort of readjust himself. It was really funny—and the girl wasn't doing a thing, playing like she didn't even notice. A couple of minutes later she just finished her lunch and got up and walked away. This guy, though, was *still* rubbing his leg back and forth the same way. I couldn't believe it so I looked real closely while pretending I was still absorbed in my eating. What this guy was doing was rubbing the leg of the table! He was still getting more and more excited. I thought, 'My God, no wonder she never seemed to notice,' but I could really see from that how much sex is in the imagination."*

"Sure, sex is in the imagination—that's what fantasizing is all about."

"That's what Portnoy's liver was all about, too. If you can get yourself off making love to liver or a table leg, you can do it with another man, too."

"It's more than getting yourself off," Rod objected. "In ancient Greece men *loved* other men. Here people are, well . . . they are *compulsive heterosexuals*. The persons who are really limited are those who are just homosexuals or hetero-sexuals. Both of these groups are limiting their concept of expression and love—but the bisexual has gotten beyond that."

I mentioned to the group a remarkable change which occurred with one of the men in the group at Alternate U. He had been very open about his homosexuality, open enough to make some of us who were limited to our hetero-sexual tendencies seem uncomfortable about it. (At one point, when he had expressed an interest in a few members of the group who were heterosexual, we experienced the uneasi-ness of being treated as a sex object.) Some of our discussions

---

* The film *The Summer of '42* is a humorous but telling commentary on the powers of the imagination and adolescent conversation to build up sexual fantasy and masculinity to its most vulnerable heights. The movie weaves in an incident of a young boy petting a girl's arm in a movie while thinking it is her breast. The sexual excitement he experiences is almost beyond what he can handle, and the letdown he feels when he is informed by his boyfriend sitting next to him in the theater that "the breast you were holding for fourteen minutes was her arm" is a parallel experience to Jim's observation of the man in the cafeteria getting sexually excited by rubbing his leg against the table.

of women at first appeared vaguely irrelevant to him due to his own sexual limitations. After the group had been meeting for about three months, however, he was making more and more frequent comments that some of the respect we in the group had for women was influencing him to have an increased respect for them too.

Soon we were noticing his respect for women developing into a casual interest in women sexually. As we talked more about our own relationships with women, his interest appeared to grow. At one meeting he said, "I have got to tell you something. I met this airline stewardess last week, and she was really a doll and . . . " Well, none of us expected to be in the position of questioning the single most open homosexual on his use of women as sex objects, but by the next meeting this was a topic of discussion. More importantly, though, *the experience of this turnabout made me recognize the possibilities for a person's perception of women to undergo the most basic type of change.* None of us were left unmarked by the extent to which we had seen the immediate environment have such an influence on a person's basic sexual preference—something we had previously considered largely innate.

"Damn it all," Lewis objected, "when I hear you guys talk about bisexuality I feel like my heterosexuality is abnormal."

"Right on!" Rod exclaimed, "Now you know how I feel when you guys are setting the norm. For the last hour or so I could feel my respect for myself go up as you guys were at least considering intellectually the norm of bisexuality. We did the same thing with the women. When the norm was such that we expected the women to contribute, they did, and not until then. This is why I feel a tie to women's liberation. As soon as you break the norm this society yells 'queer,' 'bent,' 'frustrated,' 'maladjusted'—it's always something wrong with *us.* That's what society calls the women in women's liberation—'queer,' 'bent,' 'frustrated,' 'needs a good lay' (heterosexual, of course) .''

At our next meeting a man who had been with the group a few weeks, Jonathan, asked if we had discussed "the meaning of women's liberation to men." Jonathan was a thoughtful and quiet young man, an attentive listener whose silence was only occasionally interrupted by his contributing a perspective everyone else had missed. With an almost inaudible voice and self-effacement he was able to command the complete attention of the group each time he spoke. At this meeting we decided to rotate, letting each member speak without interruption except to ask a question, so the rest of us would listen and the dominating would be minimized. Since Jonathan suggested the topic, we looked to him to start.

"I was married a few years ago," Jonathan began. "My wife and I were both working, but every day she used to call me from work. She could not continue through the day without the reinforcement of knowing I was there with her and supporting her. She had not learned to provide her own stimulus. If she had, I would have been able to share some of my burdens with her. Every day when I came home it was sort of like taking a pump and having to blow her up again. She seemed so deflated. Day after day this got too much for me. I just didn't want to live my life as someone's crutch, especially when I occasionally needed a crutch myself. The whole relationship really limited my freedom to be me."

Hank asked, "Didn't you feel good that she needed you and was coming to you for support?"

"Not really. I guess part of it was that I was just someone who was serving a series of functions—a sort of role. She had been trained to want and need certain things—a man on whom she could depend, one with a college education, one who did certain chores while she did others. She had a pattern a man had to fit and she was more concerned with my fitting it than she was with the real me."

At this juncture the conversation switched to a relevant example by a new member, Dan, but we had not yet trained ourselves to return to the original person speaking; nor had we observed whether Jonathan might be doing things in the group that were contributing to the problems in his relationship outside the group. For example, so far in the group Jonathan had been very personal but each time he spoke he had a ready-made solution (although he never admitted they were solutions). None of us asked whether Jonathan thought his silent problem-solving technique might have encouraged his attaché to use him as a crutch; or if he thought his attaché had been using the helpless technique as a way of getting him to communicate. We did not ask if one of the reasons he married her was because she fed his need to be a problem-solver. It is not as important that our observations be correct as it is that we take the time to pose the questions rather than allowing a new example to distract our focus from the original problem.

Dan's example illustrated how playing a certain type of role could lead to dependence. He was also new to the group but remained for over one and a half years. He has a full, dark beard, is about average height, and describes incidents with the detail and accuracy of a landscape painter and the humorous social commentary of a Jules Feiffer cartoon. Dan is a successful artist whose life revolves around his studio. "I was playing a typical woman's role when I was painting at home (before I had my studio) and Beth was working. I thought I'd love the peace, but during the day the four walls would sort of close in on me. I used to wonder at five-fifteen— 'Why is she late? Is she out with the boss? Am I in some way unfulfilling to her?' These were all the things women were supposed to worry about, but I could see myself doing the same thing as soon as I was in her role. I think it's just that being physically in one place, doing the waiting. The control is all in the other person's hand. She knew when she was coming home but I didn't.

"Even though I had already displayed in prestige galleries I used to wonder if I would establish an identity for myself outside my marriage. When I was in that house for two or three weeks in a row the moment-by-moment sameness made me forget my accomplishments—I had no adult reinforcement. I just got depressed. I can dig the depression your wife must have been going through, Jonathan, even though her reason may have been different."

During the conversation Ralph, another new member who was to be with us for a year, was looking somewhat pensive. To appreciate this, one has to picture Ralph—about three hundred pounds, neatly cropped hair, and a former professional football player for a major team. He explained some of the rest of his background.

"I'm thirty-two now and I got out of the Marines not too long ago. All the guys were always bragging about how they used to meet these broads and belt them around and fuck them. That's all they ever seemed to talk about. So I used to talk about it too. It seemed so sadistic. I don't know how much of it they really did and how much was fake. I never really did it—I just said I did. I was really a loser with women. I guess that's what I didn't like about that type of stuff; it always made me feel more and more like a loser."

We each contributed stories of the way each of us, especially in all-male locker-room environments, exaggerated our sexual conquests. We almost all felt uncomfortable about the uncertainty of whether the other men were exaggerating—in a sense we were all losers. Finally we realized that even in this group, as we told each other how we once exaggerated, we were exaggerating and explaining "incidentally" how we came into the locker room in the first place: "After a good football game (in which I happened to be the quarterback) . . ." We were still involved in setting standards of masculinity for each other which we, but no one else, could meet.

Hank continued on the topic of what women's liberation meant as far as he was concerned. "I see it as an opportunity to spend more time with children, to have a responsibility for them, to love and be with them."

Larry agreed, "I don't see any reason why men can't think about being fathers. I don't want to be thought of as a weirdo for spending a lot of time with my children—and suppose I want to stay home and just take care of them while my wife goes out to work. What's wrong with that? Besides, I think it's really important for a father to be able to show warmth and feeling toward a child—and to be able to show warmth and feeling, period."

Dan retaliated in a tone of amazement, "It's obvious you guys don't have any children [Dan has two]. You don't seem to understand, but the whole housewife role is pretty damn rotten. The child infringes on the life of everyone. There are nice moments, but by and large you are not going to like it very much. Most of the job is shitwork—I can really see what women are complaining about. Everywhere you move and everything you do, this kid is hanging around you—needing diapers changed, wanting to be picked up, wanting to be fed, not sure what the hell it wants. Every minute your eye is half on the baby. One minute it doesn't want to go to bed and the next minute it's crying from being overtired. Then there's all the extra laundry—and try waiting in a supermarket line with a bag of groceries in one hand, a baby in the other, while you're holding onto the other kid with your pinkie and the first one's pants are leaking and this wetness is dripping down your arm. 'Kind and tender'—you must be crazy."

Although Dan's experience with children helped some of us without children to exert some caution before making plans just to "have children," and think it would be a breeze caring for them, Larry's and Hank's attitude is important on a different level. Their intellectual desire to care and be responsible for the children is a type of socialization which mentally prepares one for assuming the responsibility—the only type of socialization experienced by most women prior to childbirth. However, the group could have asked Larry and Hank to be more concrete. For example, were they doing any baby-sitting? Had they looked into the problems of arranging for child-care assistance or obtaining a paternity leave or parent leave?

A parent leave, for example, presents more than mechanical barriers; it presents severe psychological ones as well. A man might object that parent leaves are "impossible in the present corporate structure" but his real objection may be "How can I face myself if I do this in a society where all my friends and family will wonder about me?" or "Imagine my boss looking at my résumé: 'You spent 1973–74 taking care of children?' " To ignore the toll of society's psychological pressures is the essence of the isolationist fallacy. An important function of the group is to create the support to overcome the pressures.

Jerry, a student who attended only once, illustrated this perfectly. "I had to tell my roommates I was going out to do a research project tonight. Last week when I attended a NOW meeting they looked at me as if I were some type of queer. Suppose I told them I was going to a men's *consciousness-raising* meeting!"

Larry mused. "Wow, I wonder how many men have those same fears that we never even find out about. Can you imagine a blue-collar working-class man hiring a baby-sitter to attend a women's or men's liberation meeting?"

The embarrassment of deviating from the norm for one evening gave us a perspective on the embarrassment of deviating in the basic day-to-day arrangement of child care, an arrangement which, for a man, has implications for his career plans and therefore his identity.

Frank, a graphics designer who only attended a few meetings, illustrated how the isolationist fallacy was affecting some of his attempts at behavior change. "My parents are pretty traditional. For example, they know Karen and I are living together but they are always dropping hints like, 'Frank, don't you think you may be leading Karen on?' Well, this weekend after dinner I volunteered to do the dishes. The reaction was incredible—my mother was amazed, my father was more than embarrassed and the company was shocked. It made me realize how little of the housework I ever did. Worst of all, my father, who is usually calm and rational, couldn't seem to quite handle the situation.* He came into the kitchen and said jokingly (at least he made believe he was joking), 'I'm really pissed off at you, Frank.' My sister said, 'What's happened with you, Frank?' and one of the other women guests leaned over to Karen and told her, 'You really have him well-trained, don't you?'

"I was really taken aback by this whole episode, because . . . well . . . I guess I should be honest—I originally wanted to do something which would illustrate my 'liberation' in a more dramatic fashion. I thought doing something like the dishes might just go unnoticed."

It was obvious Frank would think twice before undertaking housework again. His upsetting the equilibrium of the home had upset his father's equilibrium and his routine for handling a normal situation. The isolationist fallacy is the fallacy of the rugged individualist who ignores the importance of the pressures to preserve that equilibrium. Those pressures are an important part of the barriers to changing behavior. Another barrier is Frank's desire to do something more dramatic, a stage common among men going through the first levels of behavioral change.

The allegedly simple "doing of the dishes" created still

---

* Kate Millett and other feminists have frequently said to men, "I cannot discuss this topic with you. You just get too emotional to handle it."

more insecurities. Frank postulated, "My father might have been embarrassed because doing the dishes is not a masculine role and for me to do them might reflect adversely on his masculinity. The problem is that now, with my masculinity in question, I'll find it still harder to even discuss sex roles. Suppose I start defending homosexual tendencies among some of the persons in men's and women's liberation movements?" All of us were beginning to see how much internal security even the smallest deviation required.

At our next meeting one of us remarked how he was just beginning to see how masculinity affected him as he started to deviate from its standards. "I wonder if a good topic for this evening might be how we started developing some of our ideas about masculinity."

Dan picked up the invitation with recollections of early camp experiences such as the "circle jerk" and penis measuring. He continued by explaining, "This, mind you, was just part of a whole repertoire of things we did to prove our masculinity. For example, did you guys ever have a Boners Club? It was just about the time a lot of us were getting our puberty hairs. In the evenings, around bedtime, we would all sit around and try to get a boner. We'd sit and think and think as hard as we could about some girl we couldn't quite get all the way with, and hope we could get it hard. The Boners Club was in the next room, behind a sheet; as each guy got a boner he could enter the area behind the sheet. Everyone already in the club would look at the new guy's penis to see if he really had a boner—and if he did, he made it into the Boners Club.

"Not everyone made it, of course. Some of the guys who were at the stage where they couldn't get a boner would shout 'I have the feeling, I have the feeling, but I just can't get a boner.' If you had the feeling, well, that was at least better than nothing."

Frank contributed one of his early memories of masculinity. "I can remember after a new kid moved into the neighborhood, finding out he was really good at weight lifting and doing push-ups. I guess when he first moved in he could do about forty the right way—which he said was with your chin and chest just touching the ground for a second. Well, me, for weeks on end I worked every day, going from six push-ups to ten, then to twenty, all along telling him push-ups didn't really mean anything, hoping this would make him stop practicing. About a month later—maybe longer—I got to forty. I was so humiliated when he did forty-two. I kept trying and he kept improving until one day I beat him at fifty-two. I can still remember—fifty-two. But then he accused me of touching my chest—of doing 'cheat push-ups' by just moving my head and touching my chin to the ground. We had a big argument about how push-ups were supposed to be done. It really got intellectual after a while; we were going to books and encyclopedias, and all. At the time I actually thought the argument was about push-ups."

"And now you're a phys. ed. teacher," said Tim.

"A lot of the early myths I believed about women's sexuality and how to be a man came from guys who were always trying to show how great they were with women," I recounted. "For example, when I worked in Paris—I guess I was fourteen or fifteen—this American millionaire hired me as a bartender for a ten-day party from July 4 to July 14. It was on the boats of the Seine River. Dozens of GI's and other men came along with about thirty or forty women. Almost all of the GI's thought it was great I didn't know how to make drinks—this way they could tell me, 'Mix about three-fourths gin and some orange juice and that's fine, kid.' Finally I asked, 'Why always gin?' One of them told me: 'Gin makes the chicks fuck. It stimulates them and they don't feel like controlling themselves any more. It's the greatest stuff going, man. That's it, put a little more in there—I can get her the first time 'round.' "

"Yeah," Dan exclaimed, "and what's really powerful is how easy it is to become a part of that. I know last week I was undressing Sue for her bath, and she asked me, 'Peter has a thing here, Daddy'—pointing to her vagina—'why don't I have that?' I told her, 'You have a *fun* spot there.'

"I answered that way purposely because in the past when things like that came up I had said, 'You have a cave,' or 'You have a vagina,' and I've heard some parents tell their children 'You don't have one because you're a girl,' without mentioning what they *do* have. At least when I said, 'You have a fun spot,' she could view her own anatomy as a *positive* thing—something she could do something with and enjoy just like a man can with his penis."

Dan paused. "God, when I told Sue about her 'fun spot' I just remember I had a serious look on my face—I was sort of sheepish and surprised at her question. I think it showed. I think kids pick these things up. I know when I used to diaper Peter I would powder him carefully and look for a rash. If there was one I'd be concerned about it, whereas I wasn't so concerned about a rash on Sue."

"That's interesting," Frank observed, "because on any other part of the body you would have been more concerned with a rash if it appeared on the girl, because she's supposedly more delicate and so on. But when it comes to the penis we treat that more delicately and at the same time expect it to perform so powerfully. Maybe *men* are the sex that really needs protection, since our genitals are exposed and unprotected! At least women can play baseball without getting hit in the balls with a line drive! Ugh! No wonder men are moody!"

MY COMMENTS

The circle jerk, penis measuring, and boners club all create an atmosphere of pressure about the penis and masculinity. One pressure is the concept of "bigger and better." Part of masculinity is having bigger and better penises, being bigger physically and having better jobs; the circle jerk exerts a pressure for bigger and better ejaculations. The male ego is like a penis subject to premature ejaculations: It is preoccupied with being bigger and better, but demands delicate treatment lest it explode into nothingness.

The strength and hardness we were discovering in ourselves matched the strength and hardness required for membership in the Boners Club. The man surrounded by pressure to keep hard until it becomes a part of his image and expectation of himself is not comfortable admitting weakness or displaying softness. In relation to our attachés, we were still trying to overcome the needs to be bigger, stronger: the earner and the protector.

The display of weakness and softness is as difficult for men in business as it is in bed. In bed he must "keep it up"; in business he must be "a person to pay attention to—he's on his way up." He cannot admit weakness to those below him without breaking down that image of strength. He cannot admit it to those above him because they are also looking for "a hard, pragmatic businessman."

Despite men's contempt for weakness, many men seek it in a woman because it lends evidence to their own strength. When a woman displays strength he appears to react negatively to *her* but underneath reacts negatively to himself. When a woman acts strong, his own weakness is most likely to become apparent. He calls her an aggressive bitch as a cover to his own being "exposed" or being "caught with his pants down"—analogies that are not without meaning. He is, in brief, threatened. He is threatened at having to look at

himself as a manifestation of the boy who couldn't get a
boner, whose penis was too small, whose ejaculation was
inadequate.

If a man's ego is so weak, is there then a need to keep
protecting it? *Protection only reinforces weakness.* We need
instead to cease setting false standards which force men to
lose touch with reality by reaching for goals they cannot
attain. This implies ceasing to group "the boys" together—
which creates the environment for comparing their prowess
with girls. It implies rethinking whether boys' and girls'
camps and boys' and girls' gym classes reinforce the feeling of
the "specialness" of each sex and create special activities in
which each sex develops competence as part of its definition
of itself as masculine or feminine. This simultaneously en-
larges the gulf between the sexes.

At our next few meetings the group interacted like a
handful of weakly magnetized marbles, attracted for a moment to one conversation, then to a second, a momentary
attraction for a third and a superficial interaction with a
fourth. It was becoming obvious that our inability to create
deep relationships was a reflection of our inability to listen
with true concern and empathy to other people. We were not
using techniques such as a "follow-through hour" to return to
persons to whom we had offered alternatives, or who had
broached problems which we had skipped over. A number of
men also expressed frustration at my unwillingness to exert
leadership, and I suspect we lost a few members for that
reason.

If I had to repeat the first two months of my involvement
in the group I think now I would drop my doctrinaire attitude toward no leadership until the group picked up some
background from either reading or discussion. When men's
liberation has become a nationwide movement and at least a
few men in a given group have done careful thinking about

it, then the disadvantages of leadership probably outweigh the advantages again.

Ironically, the major resistance point of the group at this stage was also the area in which we were most improving. We were becoming more personal, but we were still defining "personal" as sexual. We were unable to talk about our personal involvement in housework (in women's liberation terms, "the shitwork").

"It's not one of my central concerns," John explained.

"Whose is it? Your wife's?" Dan chided.

We avoided discussing housework like a person with a Ph.D. asked to do a math problem by his eight-year-old child: It seemed so elementary, we had nothing to gain by getting involved and a lot of "face" to lose by failing. John illustrated the extent of our vulnerability in this area when I asked him to make the second round of coffee during a meeting at my apartment. He refilled the coffee pot with fresh water and left the old grounds in the pot. When we all choked over the resultant "hot water with coffee flavoring," he attempted to resurrect the situation by putting a few additional grounds on top of the old grounds to make the coffee stronger.

If this seems like trivia, it is. We were beginning to see how frequently that was what women's work was about, and how infrequently men get to discussing it. Our participation in these chores was forcing us to share this concern for the trivia and to spend part of our time talking about it. It was forcing us to recognize more than just intellectually the need for minimizing the amount of work of this nature which women do if we expect to live with women whose discussion of trivia is also minimized.

As we discussed these points Lewis objected, "Sometimes, if you do housework, women get threatened. For example, Ruth came up to the apartment the other day and I made this elaborate omelet for us. She thought it was great, and if I do say so myself, she was right! But a few minutes later, rather than acting happy, she seemed sort of sulky—disappointed. I asked her what was wrong and she said, 'You can do everything so well,' as if to say, 'What do you need me for?' "

"Of course, you can't expect her to give up her role before she has something to take its place. That's like creating a vacuum."

"Have you worked with her on developing *new* interests?" Hank asked.

"Yeah. I've been telling her she's got to be more well rounded—I've even shown her how I budget my time, how I do my graphics . . . "

"It sounds like you're making her more insecure. You're setting yourself up as God. It seems to me she's got to feel good about *herself* before she takes up new interests."

"Wait a minute. You guys are always saying 'be personal,' so I'm being personal. I'm showing her things from my personal life that she can learn from."

"How about *asking* her things about her personal life that *you* can learn from? Like how many drawings or omelets or sexual positions or whatever has she shown you?"

"You know something, Lewis, I've only heard you talk about your strong points and her weak points. From the way you've spoken she doesn't seem to have anything to offer you. If this is not true, man, maybe you'd better start finding out what's right with her; and if she really has nothing to offer, then what are you going with her for, your ego?"

"Underneath all this veneer it seems you really like women who kowtow to you, don't you?" Rod pressed. "Are you afraid to expose yourself to a woman who could teach you something?"

"No. I went with a woman who was very liberated when I lived in Europe, and I liked it a lot."

"It seems funny that in the final analysis you broke with

her and chose what seems to be an unliberated woman," Rod continued.

"Well, we moved away from each other and just didn't keep in touch that much—and when I got here I met just these unliberated types."

"How do you go about meeting women?"

"I don't know. Usually I guess there'll be a girl—woman—sitting next to me at a meeting or something, and she might lean over and start talking. Maybe we'll get into a conversation and that will lead to something. I don't go seeking women out, though. I just don't have the time and I don't like to do that. I like a woman to take an interest in me."

"Now you're putting your finger on it," Rod challenged. "You don't go seeking women out. Why? Because you can be refused and vulnerable? You wait for them to admire you and you get the type of woman who's going to seek out and kowtow to men rather than be interested in her own development first."

John interrupted our dialogue with Lewis and we did not return to this point with him until some meetings later. We repeated our tendency to stay with a person for just so long. (There is always at least one member who really wants to change the topic to himself.)

John made a few references to Wilhelm Reich and Marcuse; in disgust we consciously ignored him. (Dan felt John knew he was intellectualizing and was continuing it in hopes of obtaining the group's attention.) The conversation switched to Larry, whose experience with Maria was falling into a pattern. "Maria's mother is always encouraging her to value things which are expensive. Everything has to be the best for Maria and the only one who can afford the best is her mother. I think her mother is making her dependent on the values which reinforce her dependence on her mother. Every time I try to get her to think outside her mother's pattern I find myself having to buck this whole damned relationship.

Even I get dependent on how her mother thinks after a while. I become as much a slave to buying silver, a traditional wedding, a certain type of diamond and all that junk (to say nothing of 'fidelity') , as those two are. And yet Maria is really bright and compassionate in those areas where she hasn't been so well-programmed. I can't really break with her because she has so much to offer—but I feel like a sort of slave."

The emerging pattern was one of deep resentment on the part of a number of us toward what we perceived as unliberated women, and yet a tendency to contribute to that dependence on both conscious and unconscious levels. We were still focusing on ways in which the woman did not live up to the "broader perspectives" that we had established for them. While there was validity to many of our points, when we discussed women we never discussed problems which the women had in their relationships with the men in the group. We never suggested "things that most bother my attaché about me" as a topic.

We also still refused to become concrete about the sharing of roles. We still did almost no reading about women's liberation. (No books were written on men's liberation.) We had spent the evening concentrating more on the *history* of our relationships. My hope at this point was to spend evenings concentrating on how we could change the *future* of our relationships, and start examining some of the problems with our own masculine tendencies.

At our next meeting we discussed housework—and promised ourselves we would stay concrete. We decided to go around the group and ask ourselves basic questions such as, "Who does the wash?" and how the cooking, ironing, dusting, cleaning and other household chores are divided up.

John explained, "My mother does the wash, and she also cooks and waxes the floors—would you believe twice a week?

If my mother sees an undershirt which I have worn for even one day it automatically goes into the wash. As soon as the room gets dusty or something is a bit out of place my mother always straightens it out. She *wants* to do this. This is what makes her happy."

"If this is what you mother wants," Hank interjected, "it's ridiculous to try to change it."

Lewis agreed. "You should do what's comfortable; don't rock the boat. You'll only create a hostile situation."

"What can I do? My mother would have a fit if I did the wash. She would not know why I was doing it."

"Have you ever spoken with her about it? Have you even sat down and had a conversation about it?" Dan asked.

"I did once, but she didn't really listen. After a few moments she got up and walked away and started doing the dishes."

Someone in the group suggested, "Why don't you just take the wash out of your mother's hands and do it?"

A new member of the group objected. "I don't think John is exploiting the situation. After all, the woman is his mother. How can you exploit your mother?"

"Does it bother you to have your mother do the wash and cook the dinner?" Tim asked.

"Yes, I want to liberate myself and her."

"In what way would you be liberating yourself?"

"My mother always wants me to do so well, supposedly so I'll be happy, but her dependence on my doing well makes me afraid to go off even once in a while."

"Why, though," Tim pursued, "do you feel it's your duty to liberate your mother? Don't you think she's happy now? What do you think would make her most happy?"

"I think my finishing law school, receiving a degree and succeeding would make her the happiest."

"Yea, that's just the way my mother is," another man agreed, with nods of recognition.

"Maybe I'm wrong," Jonathan said quietly, "but saying your mother is happy—could this be a cop-out too? I can recall sitting back letting my mother handle chores like the dinners. When I first made an attempt to participate a big to-do was made of it. After a while this subsided and my mother began to use her time to do other things. Once she accepted that I didn't mind cooking she lost a lot of her guilt and she could really enjoy other things. It didn't change her life but I think she liked what time she had."

"I think you may be trying to draw up a policy statement, John, and be a William the Conqueror," I offered. "Just open your eyes for inconspicuous opportunities to iron a shirt, pick up after yourself, dust, sew on a button or do the wash. Don't make a big thing of it, or you'll just succeed in threatening your mother. It's too easy to fall into the 'Look at me, I'm a feminist' routine."

We decided to discuss specific *alternatives* John might pursue that might ease the transition.

Tim suggested, "Maybe you could do the wash or something on your mother's birthday and give her the tickets to a play to fill up the gap. Initially, the occasion would appear to be the reason, but your mother might say, 'Hey, this is great. I'd like this life all the time.' Once she reacts like that, doing the dishes more often seems like more of a defensible action on your part. Then, you know, *your mother isn't put in the position of having to defend her role.*"

Lewis added, "This is something like the vacuum effect that I got involved with when I cooked the omelet before Ruth had developed other interests."

"I don't think you can just *do* things, like give a ticket. I think it requires discussion too. Both work together, really."

After a number of alternatives were suggested, a few of the members—especially Hank and Lewis—protested that we were overemphasizing housework. Ralph disagreed. "This is the first time I have thought about why my mother should

have to do my wash." This was a contrast to the reason Ralph
gave for attending the group at the first meeting: so he could
learn how to help women in areas such as equal pay for equal
work. His initial attitude had indicated little understanding
of how he was directly involved in keeping women in their
place: he had thought that this was society's fault.

A new member of the group who described himself as a
politically "radical"* Socialist burst in frustration: "This
whole conversation is fruitless. This society is too corrupt to
do a thing. What do you think you can change here? The
whole society needs changing; it's rotten to the core. That's
what's wrong. You guys aren't going to change a thing. You're
wasting your time."

"Come off it. Sure society's at fault, but aren't you part of
this 'at fault' society? Just listen to *yourself,* Mr. Big Changes
—'only the Big Changes concern me.' Men are so used to
getting power or money or status for everything we do. No
wonder we can't discuss housework—to say nothing about
sharing the responsibility for it." I could feel myself getting
angry.

"How can you get so emotional about housework?" Tim
queried.

"I'm sure most of us are liberated enough to pitch in and
do about half."

"Half of what?" I asked.

"Well, the wash, and I do a lot of the chores around the
house. Like maybe they're typically men's—fixing cabinets,
painting, putting in light bulbs, taking out the garbage—but
they take time, and I pitch in on the others when I can."

"When you say you do half the wash, what does that mean
you do?" I pursued, trying to get the discussion as specific as

---

* The word "radical" is derived from the Latin *radicalis* or "root," and entails getting to the core or root of a problem. By putting quotes around
radical I am suggesting that blaming society for women's oppression is
often an escape from the root of the problem, which may be that individual
and others like tir self.

possible, and knowing how much I personally hated doing the wash.

"Well, like a few times I can remember helping Anna fold some sheets, and I've often transferred the stuff from the washing machine to the dryer. And I always put my socks and things back in the drawer. I consider that about half."

"Half!" I exploded. "Let me tell you what the wash means to me. It means like two days before, I've got to start saving quarters and nickels to put in the machines. Then if it looks like I'm the one who's going to do it, I've got to ask Ursie what clothes she wants done, then check through all my shirts, separating the clean from the dirty and smelly, then strip the beds of the sheets (which usually means I get saddled with putting new sheets on), then check out the hamper and separate the colored wash from the white and pack them into separate pillowcases and then drag out the cart from the closet to take the wash downstairs. Last week I did all that and then realized we were short on detergent. It was Sunday so I couldn't get any from the supermarket, so I checked with two of the neighbors and got involved in a half-hour discussion in exchange for a cup of detergent. I left the apartment in frustration, almost locking myself out, got downstairs and found two washers broken and two extra people waiting for the others. So I ran back upstairs to get a book, lost my place in line and twenty minutes later got my first washer, then waited another ten minutes for the next two to get free.

"I then debated whether to go upstairs where it wasn't so wretched hot and I could get some reading done (and maybe persuade Ursie to take over from there), but where I risked having some shirts stolen from the washer. I got upstairs, set the timer, sat down to read and the phone rang. When I got off the phone the timer had already rung, so I went downstairs. What greeted me, but my wash laid out all over the table and a few pieces laying on the dusty floor behind the table. Then—Oh, shit! I forgot to turn the water-temperature switch to warm for the colored wash and a brand-new twelve-dollar red-and-white shirt was now an integrated pink—Ursie will kill me! That was a birthday present! And all her colored nylon panties aren't supposed to be in hot water either! Ugh.

"I looked around only to see five faces who had been staring at me muttering to myself quickly glance back at their machines. Then I put everything into the dryers and stayed downstairs since I had experienced before that some of the dryers don't dry the elastic in my underwear or the heavy towels completely so that I have to juggle those things into an empty dryer to give them more heat toward the end of the cycle. And besides, if I let my wash-and-wear shirts settle in the bottom after they dry they become more like 'guaranteed iron and wrinkle.'

"So I stayed down there, and when the cycle was finished I unloaded and started the only job I absolutely despise—folding. Folding a king-size sheet by myself and getting the corners to match—I still don't know how Ursie does it and she's got smaller arms (I think). Then the socks. If it's two weeks' wash that's twenty-eight of my socks to separate out from the static electricity and then match up and then fold. After that and twenty-eight pieces of my underwear and I don't know how many of Ursie's—matching and folding, matching and folding—I'm getting all sorts of thoughts like 'Is *my* time worth this?' and 'How the hell did I ever get into this women's liberation stuff?'

"Finally I put everything into the cart, spanking clean and nicely folded, and so help me, if there's a kid on the elevator with gooey hands who even looks cross-eyed at that wash he's gonna feel my masculine-mystique wrath upon him—*or* her. Inevitably I get in at the back of the elevator and being on the third floor I have to fight my way through without dropping anything out of the cart, and then balance the cart on my knee while I dig up the key to open the door. So help me, Tim, if I get inside and Ursie were to just put the wash back in the drawers, refold a sheet and say 'You wanna make love? You shouldn't be tired, I did half the wash,' I think I'd start crying!"

"So that's why you get emotional about my oversimplifying housework," Tim said, somewhat cowed. "Just remind me to keep you off of that topic around Anna!"

Fourteen

Joint Consciousness-Raising: Where the Future Lies

Before we met again I received a phone call from a woman who was a member of women's consciousness-raising group associated with an East Village church. She expressed interest in a joint meeting with our group and explained, "We met previously with a group of men who asked us, in essence, 'What do you women want?' When we told them, they rebutted, and the hostility increased until the meeting assumed a totally adversary nature. We'd like to avoid that this time. We think we have a lot to gain from this."

When I broached the possibility of a joint meeting to the men, there was a generally defensive reaction, typified by Larry's statement that "we should get ourselves together first, man." Jonathan's concluding argument that we had learned a lot about ourselves from our last meeting with the women addressed Larry's complaint and prevailed.

We held one more men's meeting before our meeting with the women from the church, during which three or four references were made to our forthcoming meeting with the radical feminists. While the impression probably originated from periodic facetious remarks about the possibility of meeting with radical feminists, we did discuss on at least two occasions the fact that the women's very interest in meeting with a group of men probably meant they were not radical in the separatist, man-hating sense that a number of the men seemed to fear. As we got our fears out into the open, Ralph explained: "I feel like they might poke holes into everything I say, but then I figure I can always just keep quiet and sort of observe and then they couldn't do anything too drastic to me."

"Do you have an image of what they'll look like, Ralph?"

"Well, I sort of have this caricature of . . . of . . . a bitchy-type woman, ready to sort of jump on me (but not physically—ha!) and call me a chauvinist and say, 'Why are you *really* in a men's consciousness group?' You know what I mean?"

With these caricatures and fears compounded by another week of waiting we assembled with the women at the East Village Church: Audrey, Fran, Jan, Martha, Debbie, Grace, Lynn (the organizer) , and Sharon.

We began talking in a light tone which kept its lightness as the conversation focused on women's role as a sex object. A couple of women related experiences of walking down a street and having a man whistle at them. Lynn, who had contacted me about the meeting and who was acutely perceptive about women's liberation, asked, "How would you men react to being whistled at, like a sex object?" We acknowledged that "some men might object, but most would not."

(Note how we avoided saying, *"I* would not object.") Grace, an articulate architect with an ability to draw careful distinctions, explained there was an obvious distinction between a man and a woman being treated as a sex object: "A woman (with her consciousness raised) recognizes that sex objectification threatens to be the *total* representation of what she is to a man. She recognizes that it threatens to reestablish the image of herself as being worthy only in a sexual sense—an image she is doubtless still fighting to overcome. For a man, however, it is an addition to his life, not the totality of it. As an addition, it can be enjoyed."

Sharon, a relaxed woman with a sophisticated demeanor, asked, "Do any of you men ever try to pick women up on the street—you know, sort of whisper 'Hi-ya cunt,' or whistle, or use them as property in some way?"

We all patted ourselves on the back for not doing that. Then Hank spoiled it all. "Come on. I may be thinking 'what a piece of ass,' but my middle-class training tells me it's counterproductive to go up to some woman and say 'Hi-ya cunt,' so I try to strike up a conversation about the weather or something and hope it leads to what I had in mind to begin with."

Fran, a quiet woman who seemed always to be thinking as we talked, asked, "If men are always thinking of women as something they can use, I wonder if maybe a statement I've often heard is true: that men really don't like women." When Dan said he felt this was true, I can remember being somewhat bewildered ("What, men not like women? They spend their life chasing them").

"Men," Dan explained, "often feel women are petty and scheming and cannot always be trusted. The stereotypes of feminity are encouraged by men but become the basis for men's hatred of women." Dan was careful not to personalize his point until he explained that not only were women disliked by men, but that they were also often disliked by women. Dan continued, "When my wife was attending school she always liked to get into these intellectual discussions. We both noticed she was gravitating toward the men. When I asked her why she just seemed to have male friends she said, 'Women are so goddamned boring. They never want to think. It's really awful, but it's true, Dan.' "

"Women are not disliked by women," Fran retorted. A defensiveness masked as an offensiveness began to form, and for the first time tension permeated the room.

"Wait a minute, Fran. Women are disliked by women now. It doesn't help to deny what is presently true, as long as we try to overcome what makes it true. As long as we put women into a small world they'll continue talking about small things. Even if a woman is in college she is still aware that the essence of her future is living through a man, her home and her children—even today."

Lynn objected. "No, it's more than that. Many of us do make intelligent suggestions and they go unrecognized. We hear the same suggestion made by a man ten minutes later and everyone is relating to it. At work I make suggestions more softly than the guys I work with, but I've usually done my homework. Their suggestions are paid attention to because they present them more forcefully, and in a broad general outline. I've often followed through my ideas in great detail only to have my boss call me petty. You guys look at things the way that suits your image of us. What many of us are finding out right here is that we all have a lot of sides to us and those sides would come out if you gave us half a chance."

"Part of it is our fault," Audrey added. "When men used to ask me what I was involved with, I would only mention that I was a director of religious education to men I wanted to turn off, but I found it did more to interest men in me as a person. I think men will respond to women in the terms we present ourselves."

"Maybe our dislike for women on an intellectual level is part of a vicious cycle: We approach you on a sexual level and you keep appealing to us on that level," Larry said.

"But you never look beyond that level even when we do appeal on other levels. And besides that, we are dependent on you to choose us. At a party, for example, if we do not attract you on a sexual level, you invariably choose someone else."

"But being an interesting person is a less apparent characteristic than being physically beautiful," Rod added. "That's the problem with living in a capitalist society. We're taught to stress the tangible and ostentatious—the immediately apparent status symbol. Men use women as sex objects; women use men as security objects. Everyone responds to these pressures by making themselves just one more product."

Some of the other men pointed to the connection here between women's and men's liberation—that both sexes suffered by perpetuating this cycle and that men would really like it if women took the initiative sexually.

Grace, the architect, with short, blond hair and a determined personality, observed, "Everything we have talked about tonight in relation to women relates to sex. Granted we are attempting to criticize the role sex plays, but in our own way its very dominance is indicative of the dominance that it seems to have in men's minds all the time, and until now we, as women, have oriented our lives accordingly."

As I reflected on this comment two thoughts occurred. First, people criticize what concerns them most. A church group, for example, might criticize religion, but their critique of the subject does indicate the centrality in their life of that concern. Sex did seem to be our central point of concern about women. We asked the women what they usually discussed. They concluded their central concerns were competition and jealousy—although they were also trying to minimize competition and jealousy, as we were our focus on women predominantly as sex objects. It became apparent the women were also discussing that which most dominated their thinking. Grace felt that doing this perpetuated the problem. She asked rhetorically, "If you leave a meeting discussing sexual relations with women, don't you continue thinking of your sexual relationship with women, as opposed, say, to housework or careers? If you want to get away from focusing on women as sex objects shouldn't you start looking at something else we do, beside provide sex?"

At this point Dan interjected, "For the past forty-three minutes I did a timing of the conversation. The women spoke nine minutes and the men thirty-four. This is despite the fact that I remained quiet to keep track of the timing."

Although the men occupied thirty-four out of forty-three minutes, this was not as outrageous a figure as when we had met with the first group of women two months earlier. As with the first group, the dominance was not recognized by either sex, and in this case not even by women with high consciousness. However, while the first group of women, *who had met together only once before,* made excuses for our dominance ("the men know more about the subject"), the women with us now reinforced the observation by pointing out how even the participation which did take place by the women was often in the form of questions to the men and then responses to the general framework the men had established.

"You know," Lynn said in frustration, "all of this just reinforces my doubts that a man can really have what it takes to live with an independent woman. My experience is that men are great at theorizing but in the final analysis they always back down, especially when it gets to be a conflict between their independence and our independence."

"That's questionable," Tim defended. "You're assuming women know how to assert their independence. At our meeting with the NOW women, for example, all of us contributed to the problem. Besides, my wife is a damned successful stockbroker—making much more than I do, and I've spent many evenings that I could have spent on my career working with Anna on her confidence and strategies for succeeding. I think you're being unfair."

The women asked a few of us to review some of the stages through which we and our attachés had come as women's liberation became a relevant issue. Again both the women and the men were playing the respective roles of question-asker and question-answerer. This time I was the answerer. "My wife was brought up traditionally, with one of her main goals to please her husband. I guess that was one of the things I liked about her. When we were first married, Ursie took care of all the ironing, cooking and even preparing of lunches for me even if I was going to be home the next day while she was at work. Some of these things I was used to doing for myself, but Ursie felt it was her role; I can recall questioning this occasionally, but only in a token manner. It was only when we began to realize the conflict between her performance of all these chores and her developing herself in other ways that a greater amount of sharing began to take place. When she finished everything it was sometimes almost midnight and she was exhausted. We both began discussing this, you know, asking whether being a good wife necessarily meant being a good slave. However, because pleasing me was such a high value, Ursie found it hard to accept this on an emotional level until she thought I also accepted this on that level. What she really liked was my assuming responsibilities without being asked; if she had to ask she felt guilty."

At this point the woman sitting next to me, Debbie, almost exploded. She said she felt Tim and I were trying to make liberated women out of our wives, and that this was no good either. "You are talking about how Ursie became liberated, not how you developed a liberated relationship."

I missed Debbie's objection about developing a liberated relationship and continued to focus on Ursie's guilt. "I think

although my 'helping' Ursie sounds chauvinist, it was a necessary interval in our relationship. Ursie was trained to serve
her husband and for her a great amount of guilt occurred
when she didn't. It only required a normal sensitivity on my
part to participate in trying to help her overcome it. The
goal—to overcome this guilt—was the goal of both of us.
However, just as Ursie often has to help me discipline myself
to work to finish my dissertation—that is, to obtain a goal that
we both desire—I have to help her get rid of the guilt which
is in the way of her developing herself as an independent
person."

As I talked this out to Debbie and the group I felt on the
defensive. I began to understand my role in helping Ursie
better but still did not recognize how I was playing teacher
and Ursie student. Debbie and Lynn pressed me on this:
"Was there any way that Ursie helped you understand how
you were keeping her in her place?" It took me a while to
recall that I had hoped Ursie would use her newly found
time to develop a social conscience—by which I meant an
awareness of some of the social sciences and a liberal bias
toward political issues. This was on the top of my masculine
value system. As Ursie had more time, however, she began
developing areas of her interest.

I started to recollect this part of the process. "She began to
take up watercolor painting. Her proficiency (as a beginner)
gave her a lot of satisfaction. As she began painting and
reading fiction—another area for which I had no substantial
appreciation—she began actively to want more time to herself. I remember as she started going through books about
painting that I was constantly learning new things from her
in this area and still am.

"I can also remember that one night when Ursie was paint-
ing and I had to go out I hinted that I needed a shirt ironed.
She asked if I wouldn't mind doing it. I *can* see from that how
I was helping to contribute to her guilt. She would not have

asked me to iron her dress. The final stage came when I began to appreciate Ursie's values of art and fiction rather than pressuring her to use her new spare time to develop my values of a social conscience."

"Well," said Lynn, "that was an improvement in your social conscience! I'd like to hear more about what some of these changes meant to you guys as men."

Larry said, "I can recall being pretty pissed when my girl friend—or woman friend—started asking if I was still going to go off on weekends to play lacrosse after we were married. I'd like her to be more liberated so I'd have some freedom. I don't want to set a double standard. If I can do this type of thing, so can she—and do it when she wants to. But if her idea of a marriage is just to be stuck together without any freedom for herself or me, I just don't want that."

"I can understand that. I think my husband has liked it better for the most part, now that I'm more 'liberated,'" Debbie observed. "During the first year or two of our marriage, my standards for housekeeping were much higher than my husband's. When I began to want him to share the housework the conflict between our standards became a problem. Since I've joined women's liberation my standards are much less compulsive, although I have to admit that if my husband had not wanted me to be involved I do not know if I would have joined. He recognizes the need for me to be busy since he is so busy as a medical student. When he comes home late I am not as upset if I'm enjoying what I am doing. (And that doesn't mean doing more than my half of the shitwork!)

"You see, Warren," Debbie continued, "you think in terms of saving your wife from guilt. I feel I'm saving my husband from guilt. Medical doctors are always said to outgrow their wives and then feel guilty for divorcing them or having affairs after their wives have put them all through med school, internship and residency. If he's not oppressing me now he's a lot freer from guilt if we get divorced later.

Also, I don't fear divorce like I used to—I guess because I have my own life now, and may outgrow him, especially emotionally. What I'm finding also is the more interested I get in myself the more he seems interested in me. I'd say our relationship has improved for the most part even though he's not always crazy about my not being there to serve him."

Jonathan mentioned the way women's liberation affected him as a man. "In my case, I don't really enjoy making decisions, and if Nancy makes them it doesn't threaten me. What it does is give me the freedom to participate in those decisions I want to participate in and opt out of the decisions I don't want to make. I also don't like to do things like repair cabinets and all those mechanical 'man's chores.' "

Dan laughed. "Beth and I practiced men's and women's chores so subtly that I would make a telephone call about a car repair and she would make a telephone call about the laundry!"

Debbie and Martha remained skeptical of the practicability of the man participating appreciably in any attempt to "liberate his wife." I offered, "If women's liberation does mean my liberation, then it's natural I might want to start the liberating process. Different couples have to work this out in different ways, according to their personalities."

I looked around the room and saw Jan and Audrey. They had spoken barely a word during these two and a half hours and seemed good examples of women unlikely to initiate a liberating process that required conflict. I wasn't sure if I dared mention them as examples. I feared almost certain attack. But I could also see how it would be even more condescending if I kept from the group what I was thinking and thought of them in a way I was unwilling to express. It was a good fifteen minutes before I got up the nerve. "For example," I said, wiping the sweat off my brow, "Debbie and Lynn might very well speak up and provide the initiative for their own liberation, but I suspect Jan and Audrey, who barely spoke at all in this mixed group, may represent a lot of other women, including my wife, who would be quite hesitant to do that—especially with any consistency, so that the man would really see the relationship was at stake if he didn't shape up.

"I think for this kind of woman, a husband who is at least cooperative has an important role. It's unrealistic to expect a woman whose entire life is her husband to suddenly hop from the traditional role of a woman to a liberated woman without help and encouragement from her husband or mate. Besides, a husband's participation is going to make him aware of his responsibilities to participate in all of the little chores which keep a woman tied down."

I was too nervous to stop talking. "How can we claim a woman's guilt is so all-pervasive and then expect her to over-come it so easily? If Ursie's and other women's consciousness depends on attacking men, then the men who are responsive are just going to be a lot of guilt-tripping male masochists. I can't see the movement reaching millions of women on that basis."

As I ended my speech, Sharon replied with considerably greater patience than I expected, "That's a great idea, but it doesn't usually work. Unless women get together to liberate women we'll always see ourselves as dependent on men. Jan and Audrey may not be saying anything now, but wait a few months. As long as men like you keep telling women they should talk rather than asking things of them then they're not ever likely to see themselves as independent of you."

I was too defensive at the moment to do anything more than make a mental note of Sharon's reply, but taking the risk of saying what I thought did prove helpful in creating the tension that both forced the incident and caused Sharon's reply to spin around in my head for the next few days. It was a turning point for me in making me focus more on my own head and on other men as well as toward recognizing more clearly what women were doing for each other.

As the evening came to an end, we discussed whether each of us felt inhibited by the presence of members of the other sex. The general response was that the atmosphere was very uninhibiting and brought out many things we were not able to discuss in our three months of meeting as a men's group. The focus on the gray line between helping another and exerting control over another helped all of us become a bit more sensitive to when well-intentioned attempts at liberation undermined another's attempt to develop a sense of self.

THE EAST VILLAGE CHURCH: II

As we gathered to meet with the women from the East Village church for the second time we were all anxious to find out how the other group felt about our previous joint meeting. Tim put it most accurately in his quasi-facetious projection of all our feelings: "What did you say about *me* at your meeting?"

This anxiety set the stage for our formation into "security blocks" of alternating groups of men and women—blocks formed almost naturally as each new person entering the meeting sat next to someone with whom te felt most secure (always a person of the same sex and consciousness group). Lynn noticed this and asked one of the men to change seats with her, affecting a type of integration in two of the four segregated blocks. Before the meeting, we found ourselves exchanging the same blend of dangling conversation, falsely relaxed smiles and uneasiness which pervades a party at which the guests are unknown to each other.

Martha opened the meeting. "I think we would all benefit from talking about how we felt about our last meeting. I know I learned a lot about myself from the meeting." We asked Martha to elaborate. "I remember as I was sitting here I felt very competitive. I know I had a need to bring the men's attention to myself and to look physically attractive. I felt particularly competitive with Lynn. I thought she was possibly trying to take over the meeting and make herself look good in the eyes of the men. Actually, I'm annoyed with you this evening too, Lynn; you usually come dressed very casually to our meeting with all women. But no, not to-night—you come all neat and dressed up in your kilt and sweater and everything."

"Let me just explain one thing, Martha. I came to this meeting directly from work, and these are my normal office clothes. Usually I have a chance to change before our meetings."

Martha's expression of her own feelings of competitiveness was particularly important since after the last joint meeting she told some of us that she felt she ought to have come to the defense of Audrey and Jan (the two "quiet women") when I had used them as examples of women needing men's support. At that time she emphasized the need for unity among women. This dichotomous feeling of competitiveness with stronger persons combined with a simultaneous desire to protect weaker persons is a problem we noticed consistently among a number of men. Powerful countries (ruled by men) often practice the same dichotomy, a trap the liberated woman faces should liberation mean anything more to her than playing men's role of protector. Myrna Lamb calls this psychology of competitiveness "the inner capitalist ethic."

Sharon added, "I have one reservation about our joint meeting I think is important. A couple of us—the men especially, I think—were talking about people outside of the group. I really dislike it when the men talk about women when they are not here to defend themselves. Tim and Warren and Lewis did this a couple of times, talking about how they were trying to establish a more liberated relationship. How do I know what they're really trying with someone that's not here? I think we've got to work with what's here in the group—the ways we act with each other that are oppressive."

Tim objected. "I think you're being unrealistic; what I do during the week is important. That's my life, and I'm coming to these meetings to learn how I can improve that life."

"You can learn that by improving yourself right here in your interactions with us," Sharon replied. "How can you get insight into what you need improvement on if you're giving an account of how you helped liberate your wife and we don't get to see how you might be stopping her from liberating herself?"

"This turns into a therapy group, then," I objected. "I don't think anyone here has the training to lead that type of group. I agree with Tim. I'm trying to improve the life I lead outside this group—not just be a hero in the group who goes back to my old way of life during the week. The most relevant person in that life during the week is Ursie."

"Perhaps then you men should meet with your wives or women friends," Sharon suggested.

In the time since this meeting I have maintained the portion of my viewpoint that upholds the relevance of discussing relationships with our attachés. I have changed, though, in two ways. Sharon's suggestion motivated us to suggest joint meetings to our attachés. During the past two years these have turned out to be by far the most successful method of bringing about behavioral change, and convinced me that a most effective way of talking about the "relevant people outside of the group" is to meet *with these people.* Our projections of "their hangups" could be clarified a lot faster—especially if "their hangups" are really our hangups. We still find it useful to meet separately as an all-male group, as do the women in a parallel context. In these separate meet-

ings we alternate among discussions of our expectations to
perform as males, our relations to men within the group,
and our relations to women outside of the group.

The second change in my thinking concerns the value of
focusing on our conduct within the group. A number of our
masculine traits are with us wherever we go. Dominating,
interrupting, condescension, disrespect, aggression, obsession
with sex, egotistic behavior, intellectualization, put-downs,
and a lack of empathy, emotion, openness, warmth and
contact with persons as human beings rather than competi-
tors for power and position—all occur or fail to occur within
the group context. Pointing out one example while it is
occurring is worth ten discussions of it occurring in the past.
One does not need in-depth psychological training to recognize how these behaviors are annoying or limiting to another
group member.

"Let's try talking about our feelings toward members
within the group," Sharon suggested.

Ralph responded in an emotional, feeling and yet humorous way. "I've just been wanting to say something. I've been
thinking about a question from our last meeting—the question about whether men hate women. I asked myself, 'Do I
hate women?' I don't know. I have a fear of women, and
when I am around them I try to be funny, which is my
façade. Clowning is my façade. When I came here I was
nervous. I feel so awkward around women and I know I often
discriminate against them." Ralph explained this with a
series of anecdotes which evoked an understanding and almost hilarious laughter. A strong feeling of approval and
warmth ran through the group. However, none of us asked if
Ralph's anecdotes were not the continuation of the façade he
had just explained he used to cover his fear of speaking with
women. The group also avoided inquiring into the reasons
he felt he discriminated against women. We had made an
unconscious decision to reinforce Ralph for his style of hu-

morous emotionality without questioning his substance. In contrast, Lewis' and John's styles turned most persons off to the point where we may have been overly critical of their content. It was important for us as a group to make the distinction, and while recognizing the importance of expressing feelings, not just excuse everything prefaced by "I just feel this way," as being positive.

Larry's contribution of "feelings" was next. "I was thinking about dominating and listening in relation to the timings Dan did. I see the point and all, but I just can't listen artificially. If I play a role of being less dominant than I really am, I am going to find a woman who wants me that way. If the listening is artificial then I must either pretend in that role or count on changing my basic personality. Unless I live as the man I really want to be, I am not going to find the woman I want to find—who reacts to the *real* me."

Larry's thought struck us as being quite beautiful, particularly at the time. After some discussion, however, we noted that *the whole purpose of the group is reexamining what we want our true selves to be.* Sometimes that takes a temporary time period of experimenting with a new role, and sometimes experimenting can be artificial.

Audrey spoke up: "What is 'natural' for a person is so tricky. I've personally seen many women talk intelligently with other women, but become the inquiring know-nothing when men are around."

Lynn added, "I was somewhat uncomfortable last meeting about the two categories in which we spoke of women— 'brain' and 'body.' I am more than both brain and body." We asked her to explain. Lynn reached her arm into the air and said, "That!" as though her gesture were to reflect a unique part of her as a person. "I am everything I do—gestures, attitudes, the way I feel, the vibrations I offer, the way I act, the way I interact . . ."

Sharon interjected, "Women have so much to offer that

this society—and we here—haven't even touched upon: a concern for people, a humanity, an ability to sympathize and empathize—values that are not inferior or irrelevant, but that no one gives us credit for. People aren't taking courses on how to be humans—just how to be managers or leaders. That's what's valued, and even here we've been discussing ourselves as either body or brain but not person. You understand?"

We understood.

"I also want to say something about this dominance–submissive talk of Larry's," Lynn continued. "Everything men do reinforces their dominance. Even sexual intercourse is a power game. The man's penetration comes only when his penis is hard, when he is ready to do it, whereas the woman must be always ready to accept it, whether she's really ready or not. This makes it a power game almost by definition—unless we broaden the definition of making love. Then society adds to this by idealizing the woman as one who must be ready to give in to the man's desire 'if she really loves him.'" None of us commented on this, but I remember thinking that I had never considered that perspective, and that although I did not think it was always true, it would make me be more aware of the possibility of a woman not being ready the next time I felt I was prepared—a perspective I never received from the men's group.

Martha started to speak a few times, only to be met with unintentional but consistent interruptions. "I really feel—" she started three or four times. Finally someone got wind that Martha might want to say something. "Hey, we've been ignoring Martha. She's been wanting to speak for the past ten minutes."

"I've been wanting to say something I've really felt deeply, but I don't want to be isolated in doing it."

"What?"

Slowly she unraveled an occasion which she and her attaché Bob had shared.

"Bob and I were at the beach together, just sort of roaming around, each wandering our separate ways and then getting back together again. Every time I got away from Bob I would start gathering some driftwood. I'm really fascinated by driftwood and love to look at a piece and think how I can use it to decorate my room. Eventually I collected a whole armful, but when I was walking toward Bob I remembered I had stacks of driftwood in my closet at home and had not done anything with it. I just knew Bob would put me down for it and ask, 'Why are you bringing back more driftwood when you haven't done anything with all that junk in your closet?' I resented this and it was really getting to me inside. I felt he would be judging me as a complete failure for never finishing anything I started. This has always been one of my problems; I guess it's a problem of a lot of women. But I hated that he was always in the position to judge me. He always seems to have the upper hand—men always seem to have the upper hand.

"Then I remembered that last time Bob had carried the driftwood back and that I was assuming in my mind that he would do it again. It suddenly dawned on me that then he would be taking part of the responsibility for the driftwood and that would put him in an even stronger position to say what happened to it. I decided I would tell him immediately that I would carry it. It was mine and my responsibility in all ways."

"That's beautiful," Rod said. "It's so symbolic—how taking the load on one's back gives a person not only a responsibility but a freedom from being judged by a superior. I think I can appreciate it from Bob's point of view, too. He had the physical load of driftwood and the mental load of judging taken off his back."

One of the ironies of Martha's story was that for all its meaning, it was an incident which involved someone outside the group. The group gave immense support to Martha for speaking as she felt about this outside incident, but it also gave support to the concept of not speaking of outside incidents.

After the meeting Jonathan said, "I kept feeling the women were trying to teach us and make us their students. I didn't feel we were being treated as equals. I was quite uncomfortable."

I shared Jonathan's observation, but as we were talking we recalled the bedroom scene in the movie *Joe* in which Joe says to the woman, "Let's get together again sometime in the near future," and the woman, sitting on top of him, says, "I don't think so." He retorts, "But that's a one-night stand." She smiles. "I am sure you have had one-night stands before." Joe stares back. "Yeah, but *I* decided when they would be one-night stands." Perhaps part of what we resented was the power being in the hands of the woman, as well as the attitude of superiority. However, since I objected to Lewis' attitude of "bringing women up to his level," it seems justifiable to resent it from the women as well.

In evaluating the meeting, I believe we allowed ourselves to be too uncritical of statements prefaced with "I just feel this way" and not empathetic enough to the possible emotional involvement behind statements which did not carry this more humble preface. The first stages of expressing feelings are bound to be somewhat artificial, and yet it is important that we not compete to "outfeed" each other—to become "the biggest jock in the sensitivity group."

I also began to see that many of the therapy and encounter portions of the group were quite instructive. Toward the end of the meeting Grace mentioned that sometimes when I spoke I seemed to be compelled to have thought through my statement rather than being willing to say something about which I was uncertain and risk being wrong. She felt this was my unconscious way of not forfeiting the group leadership and that it was hurting me. When I thought about it, I felt I could benefit by loosening up my style and being willing to be more vulnerable, that I was in fact holding in some things to which I felt the group would have a negative reaction.

At our next men's meeting we spent an hour "analyzing" the meeting with the women from the East Village church. I am afraid the "analyzing," though, was little more than gossip, and the gossip little more than an escape mechanism from dealing with ourselves.

Finally, Tim dealt with our present and unresolved problems. "Lewis, your girl friend told my wife that she felt you did not really want her to get involved in women's liberation too seriously. You've been telling us that you've been trying to get Ruth involved."

Lewis was taken aback. "Well, I do want her to get involved, but I don't want to be in the position of 'taking Ruth to task' for not becoming involved. That's putting myself in a position of power vis-à-vis Ruth and that same old trap of making my own little liberated woman. You have to understand, Ruth is a nice and fine person but she just isn't the type who wants to develop her own independent self. I wish she did. Then we'd get along a lot better."

This apparent contradiction fostered a barrage of questions forcing Lewis to respond defensively.

"Who drives when the two of you go out?" Dan challenged.

"Well, we have a stick shift, and Ruth didn't know how to drive a stick shift until recently. She doesn't feel really comfortable with it, so I drive. I'm not going to go around forcing Ruth to drive half the time. That's ridiculous."

"Do you think Ruth would like to drive a stick shift?"

"In theory, sure, but she feels uncomfortable doing it."

"How long have you spent discussing it?"

"We've talked about it some—I can't force these things on her."

A discussion slowly evolved on the importance of extensive discussions with our attachés and how this usually leads to agreeing upon certain *goals*. Once the goals are agreed to, it takes still more effort for each partner to achieve them. Sometimes that does mean a constructive taking the other person to task for slipping back into the old way—again, once both agree on the goal. A careful line must be drawn here between the responsibility for making the effort that the change requires and the danger area of the man becoming the director or controller of the change. We were later to find that danger minimized in a joint group, when both partners usually desired some change and the relationship was balanced.

"When you go out, Lewis, who plans the evening?" Tim pursued.

"We both do, of course."

"How do you both go about doing it?"

"That's a silly question. How do you think?"

"I'm serious. For example, does she ever initiate a suggestion that you haven't dropped a hint about?"

"Well, not usually."

"So you're assuming that her agreement with your idea means both of you planning an evening!"

Lewis objected, "You're making Ruth into something she's not. She doesn't initiate. When we go to movies or plays she doesn't even want to discuss the meaning of them afterwards. I don't know if she's really dumb because she doesn't have stupid reactions, just no reactions at all."

The more we heard from Lewis, the more we realized we were playing the game of the *Ladies' Home Journal* which features a column entitled "Can This Marriage Be Saved?" The question we should have been asking was "*Should* This

Marriage Be Saved?" or in this case, "For what reason did the relationship between Ruth and Lewis even exist?"

Dan asked the crucial question: "If Ruth were a man, would you be friends with her?"

Lewis answered no without hesitation.

Lewis was relating a classic example of the sex-object trap and yet it had taken us all this time to discover it. He was spending large amounts of time with Ruth which he was not enjoying purely to get a few hours of sex in the end. On the other hand, if Ruth sensed Lewis did not have the self-confidence to handle an independent woman, then she was likely to fall back on just developing her sexuality. The sex-object trap, in which Lewis as well as Ruth were caught, is another example of the need for interaction between attempts at women's liberation and men's liberation.

Lewis and Ruth were also feeding off of their common lack of self-confidence. Lewis did not have the self-confidence to seek out and maintain a liberated relationship; Ruth did not have the self-confidence to seek out new areas of self-development independent of what Lewis could handle.

As the dialogue reached this point, John intervened with a long explanation allegedly related to Ruth and Lewis, in terms of power, security and the family. We all grew impatient and edgy, but just at the point of explosion, John caught himself. "Wow, there I go, intellectualizing again!" Dan almost fell off his chair. Lewis began a new topic and I fell back into my leadership role and asked, "Ralph, we've had little chance to discuss your relationships. You've started to speak twice tonight."

Ralph immediately perked up, "I'm going with this girl . . . er, woman, named Judy, now. She's really liberated—assertive and aggressive and everything like that. I have a real good relationship with her and I haven't always had successful relationships in the past. I guess my three hundred pounds keeps 'em at a distance! But Judy—Judy seems to like everything I like—even W. C. Fields movies. I always get suspicious about that—I just cannot seem to get over the fact that someone really seems to like the same things I do."

"What does Judy do, Ralph?" Rod queried.

"She works for the city, in city planning. We met when we were working on Bella Abzug's campaign."

"Oh! That's fascinating," said Rod, who had just joined a city-planning organization himself. "What area is she in?"

"Well, we haven't talked much about city planning," Ralph informed us. "I don't really know anything about what she does besides that. You've gotta understand, Judy is pretty timid and shy about her work. She doesn't like to talk much about that."

"Wait a minute. A minute ago you told us she was 'assertive and aggressive,' " I contradicted.

"You see," Ralph clarified, "she's assertive and aggressive at work but timid and shy otherwise."

"But Ralph, doesn't the 'otherwise' mean the times you are able to observe her—in other words, when she's around you, she's shy. Isn't Judy doing the classic feminine thing—expressing the dual type of personality that women who are competent but have been taught to make men feel good learn to express? It seems the only way she is liberated is to the extent she does not carry this shyness into her work atmosphere. Her work atmosphere is apparently doing something to bring out her assertiveness which you aren't doing. Maybe, Ralph, it's respecting her opinion or depending on her?"

"Who pays for the dates, Ralph?"

"I do. I don't believe in following 'the fifty-two rules of women's liberation' and telling Judy that she must pay for half the dates just because women's liberation says that is the right thing to do."

"Don't you think her economic independence might give her a psychological independence to plan her equivalent of W. C. Fields movies?" Tim asked.

"Have you really sat down and discussed with Judy the possibility of her planning completely on her own the dates for two or three nights?"

"No, she'd probably plan what she knows I'd like anyway."

"Wait a minute. If she has so many interests at work, don't you think once she senses a real interest on your part she'll have interests?"

Ralph admitted, "Sometimes she does mention a desire to do something and I do pay attention to it, but I usually make a suggestion too, and she always says, 'Let's do that.' I guess she's feeding my ego."

"Taking a *real* interest takes a hell of a lot of work."

I recalled, "When Ursie and I sit down to discuss a new area it is always awkward at first. If I don't know the personalities of her colleagues at work or anything about her work (computers), then she has to explain all of this background before she even gets to the first point that she wants to make. Of course, she won't want to talk about it. The only way we could overcome this was to have discussions with her about the specific names of the persons with whom she worked and to attend parties with her whenever I could, as well as to encourage her to invite her colleagues over for dinner. The combination of all of this meant that she could come home and tell me something that occurred at work, mentioning five or six personalities and a few semitechnical things about computers, and I would understand with a relatively minimal effort. She would be able to receive some real empathy and involvement from me because I had met some of the persons she was talking about at a party and could imagine them reacting in a given way in the office. Therefore, now when she comes home exhausted, she doesn't have to go through a long explanation which she is too tired to give, but can get to the point fairly quickly and have me appreciate in sincerity all the little things that make the story meaningful to her."

What I was saying, in essence, was that in order to learn something from someone else it took more than asking a question of "Do you like W. C. Fields movies?" with the answer being yes or no. That was us asking the questions from our area of interest, rather than involving ourselves in the other person's area of interest.

"I don't know if I know where to start." Ralph mumbled.

"Bullshit, Ralph. Start anywhere," Rod replied. "Keep your eye out for news about city planning. Take a look at the new book projecting plans for New York City during the next ten years. Spend a few evenings meeting some of her friends from the city-planning area. Ask her to bring some literature from her office that discusses some of the areas in which she's involved. Maybe you'll learn something, man."

"Yeah, I guess city planning could be fascinating."

"No, you'd be learning a lot more about *Judy*—and your-self—how you interact with a woman who has her own inter-ests, how she interacts with colleagues, and so on. To say Judy is assertive at work and then express no interest in her work is like saying 'I like a liberated woman as long as she doesn't show it around me.' " This was, in turn, exactly the dual sense in which Judy was operating.

The group's handling of Ralph was, in my opinion, an improvement in a number of ways. We stayed with Ralph rather than jumping around, we asked him to be more and more specific, we suggested concrete alternatives oriented toward developing or liberating both Ralph and Judy, and we tried to imagine some of the events from Judy's per-spective. However, Judy was not there, and when we followed through some weeks later, asking Ralph how things had changed with Judy, we found he had only really broached the topic to her in a brief conversation and he had never personally followed through with assuming an active interest in her work, except to attend a few of her functions.

This minimal change was in stark contrast to a similar

situation between Hank and his attaché Dorothy. A key difference appeared to be that *Dorothy was present.*

Hank had told the group on several occasions that he had never had a woman friend who enjoyed sex as much as Dorothy; he frequently mentioned how she liked to do all the things he liked. To the group, the relationship seemed quite compatible and stable.

One evening, Lewis, Ursie and I coincidentally ran into Dorothy and Hank in the Village; we decided to stop in one of the Village cafés. In the course of the conversation Dorothy mentioned that she played the guitar, and she referred several times to close friends of hers who were apparently unknown to Hank.

As the discussion became more personal and Dorothy and Hank drifted into separate conversations, Dorothy admitted that she had wanted to get Hank interested in the guitar and have him meet some of her friends who shared her musical interests. "Sometimes I'd prefer an evening over the guitar to . . . to sex even . . . but I feel forced to make love to Hank or lose him."

Hank jolted out of his conversation. "Christ, I never realized that!" With a slightly false sense of conviction, he added, "But now that I'm aware of it, and more sensitive to your needs, things'll work out."

With cautious determination, Dorothy pressed on. "Will they work out, Hank? Will I always have the courage to bring them up and insist on doing things my way? You weren't even paying attention to my conversation until you heard me mention sex."

"Well, from now on we'll plan dates together; you should have said this before."

"Hank, I've mentioned my interest in the guitar before, but you've always just nodded and postponed doing it. You always had a better suggestion. You must know that 'together' has never meant together."

"Suppose," Ursie suggested, "you actually had total responsibility for planning two nights a week, Dorothy?" (of the four to five she said they usually spent together) .

Dorothy lit up and started ticking off all they could do.

"Okay, and I won't even suggest ideas on your nights, Dorothy, so you won't feel any pressure," Hank offered.

"I'm afraid if we don't write down my nights this will all be so much theory," Dorothy said with a look of grim realism.

We eventually grabbed a napkin and drew a calendar of the nights for which Hank and Dorothy would make the plans and which nights would be left open. We concluded by discussing specific alternatives for a lot of the barriers they felt prevented their carrying this out, such as how they could alternate driving and paying, and whether Dorothy felt pressured into always ending the evening with sex. It was understood that the structure of the calendar would remain only until the sharing of planning became natural.

This café conversation was the beginning of a major change in Hank's and Dorothy's relationship. Hank started missing meetings; we discussed whether to call him or not, and whether by calling we were betraying the spirit of voluntarism. We decided that a call in a time of turmoil only showed human consideration. Hank returned and some major changes followed—although not unmitigated by turmoil. It is obvious, however, that little of this would have transpired if Hank's impressions of Dorothy hadn't been challenged by Dorothy herself. This reinforced for many of us the importance of meeting with our attachés.

EXPERIENCES OF LATER MEETINGS

The above were relatively detailed accounts of a few of our early meetings. A summary of some of the insights and events evolving from this background can now be appreciated. I am limiting myself to events which I have found to present problems common to a number of groups.

The account of the meetings only gave a hint of the antagonism that was building toward John. The group felt he was talking *at* us rather than with us—and that his contributions involved an inordinate amount of condescension, self-involvement, intellectualization and assumptions that what he was saying was the definitive answer. In a sense it was a good experience for *men* to be so consistently talked at, but the "good experience" did not dispel the antagonism. Now we were facing a problem encountered by almost every therapy group and many consciousness-raising groups—whether the group has the right to ask such a member to leave, and if it does, have we been using the member as a scapegoat, and if we have not, how do we proceed?

We finally called a special meeting to talk with John about our feelings. We gave example after example, but by the end of the evening it became apparent that John was concerned only with reducing each example to some type of misunderstanding or intellectual difference rather than trying to see the underlying personality conflict. He seemed to need the group for therapy, and while it was tempting to respond, we had to remind ourselves we were not equipped to be a therapy group. We discussed this with John without asking him directly to leave.

A few weeks later the antagonism increased when Dan discovered John had been talking about him outside the group. "You've broken the strongest ethic this group has, John—confidentiality. How can any of us be expected to reveal ourselves to the group if it is going to be distorted outside the group? I'm really pissed at you. As long as you're in this group I'm not going to feel free to open my mouth about anything that matters."

A second series of indiscretions occurred when a woman

(Ann) who had been unsuccessfully trying for months to get
her husband to join a consciousness-raising group called a few
of us in desperation, asking if we would speak with her to see
what motivated us to change—hoping she could apply this to
her husband. We were somewhat surprised, but since her
husband would not discuss it directly, agreed. The meeting
revealed that Ann had a very serious problem, was immensely
upset and emotionally torn, and was constantly analyzing her
own worth and unable to feel any freedom at all to be herself.
The meeting brought tears to her eyes three or four times.
She had explained to us that her husband, a truckdriver of
strict Eastern European background, felt her involvement in
women's liberation was a sickness. Now he was on the road;
she had come without his knowledge. After the meeting John
offered to take her home. Two days later I received a call.
Ann's voice was trembling. "Warren, a terrible thing has
happened. Remember the other night when John took me
home? When we got to the house . . . well, we did some
things together, I mean, made love. Oh, I guess it was my
doing as much as his, but I couldn't face my husband—I just
couldn't face him without telling him. My husband just does
not know how to take it. He's in a state of shock. He's mad at
me but it's not just madness—and he wants to see John.
Warren, could the four of us get together quickly before
something drastic happens? This is really an emergency."

John pointed out that Ann had "led him on" in many
ways, but his insensitivity to the problems such a relationship
might create and the group's responsibility not to add to
those problems was apparent from his constant transferral of
the incident to the level of "but we both wanted it and
enjoyed it—isn't that enough?" He had contributed to an
incident which would make her husband view the entire
situation as "her problem, her affair, her immaturity, her
sin." For her husband this was a moral sin of unforgivable
proportions. John reduced the whole problem to the stupid-

ity of her telling her husband and to the group's inability to
see how he was really helping her.

I am not so certain the group had the right to condemn
John for something that was essentially his business—our
purpose is to suggest alternatives, offer support through
recognizing common problems, not to impose "morality"—
but the combination of circumstances precipitated our finally
asking John to leave the group. The decision was particularly
difficult because John obviously needed the group more than
any of us; he was intensely lonely and had deep family problems about which he almost never talked. Yet it had reached
the point where the group was spending huge chunks of time
dealing with the antagonisms John seemed to stimulate, and
the rest of us were finding our own development reaching a
plateau. I believe it is the latter criterion a group must use to
determine whether to ask a member to leave. However, it
must do this only after it faces the question of whether it is
using this member as a scapegoat and an excuse for not
developing. We probably should have faced that more carefully.

A crisis within a group almost always brings a new awareness. John's behavior forced us to recognize how many of our
problems of masculinity could be discovered right within the
group. Our discussions now showed more concern for the
individual speaking, but we still had a long way to go. We
still started with phrases like "the point is" (as if we had the
only possible point). We were still manipulating others into
respecting us but not getting ourselves to respect and draw
out the best in others. We now had some empathy for the
feelings of others as we destroyed their arguments, but de-
stroying still seemed more important than the feelings or the
constructive alternative-seeking. As we readied for the phase
of meeting with our attachés, a masculine self-centeredness
was still our habit.

Perhaps Steven, a new member of the group who was a fifty-two-year-old plumber and former president of a union local, recognized this more than any of us. "I used to view everyone in terms of power, how much they had—that is, how much they might threaten my power base. I never gave others a chance, never showed them real respect. We've got to keep after ourselves to overcome that as much as possible. Otherwise we won't really get anywhere."

The group did make some substantial changes, though, even on the behavioral level. Lewis saw the narrow basis for his relationship with Ruth and the two of them parted ways in a friendly manner. "I must admit that if I had not been in the group I would have tried to manipulate Ruth into continuing the relationship until I was able to develop a dependable sexual relationship with other women."

The problem for Lewis was not over, though. "Now that Ruth and I have split, where do I find a liberated woman? The only women's liberation group open to men is NOW, and no men's liberation organization exists which is open to women, so what do I do?" Lewis had a point. Unless this situation is modified, the claim that women cannot find a liberated man, as well as men's counter-claim, will be a self-fulfilling prophecy.

Other behavioral changes developed in the group as I learned to forfeit some of my responsibilities for leadership. For example, I was asked to speak on "men's attitudes toward women's liberation" at a local university. I decided instead to recommend Dan. Dan hesitated, uncertain of "how it would go" and whether he could really do it well. Finally, to give himself a security base, he sat down and wrote out a speech. He found himself developing and clarifying many of his thoughts. His presentation was reportedly well received, and reading his speech contributed a lot to my own thinking. The progression in his thinking from when he first entered the group was also apparent. He was now concentrating much more on his own insecurities, becoming highly personal, and focusing on his own problems of masculinity rather than viewing liberation mainly as his attaché's problem.

The struggles involved in giving up leadership—especially unofficial leadership—are not easy. When the conversation was wandering from one man to the next, the pressure to reassert control returned from some members (or was that "pressure" my projection, in my imagination?) But other members pointed out that now it was no longer the blind leading the blind and the responsibility for that type of control must come from the group at large; otherwise it would never be able to be applied outside the group. We agreed that unless each man reached the point where he was sensitized to his own ego trips and power plays and *wanted* to trade them in for a new openness and sensitivity he would eventually return to his previous behavior. Most importantly, I found that my personal growth and openness was much greater when I had totally withdrawn from that role and could spend time examining myself.

As our behavior did start to change we had to ask whether it was changing merely as part of a show we were putting on. Was our new consciousness like a new stereo to which we wanted everyone to listen? Were we becoming missionaries just to support our own egos, or was "the word" spreading from the examples we set as persons able to respect others through the new respect we had found for ourselves?

While we needed to keep in touch with our motives in the process of changing our behavior, we also had an obligation not to allow the accusation of "showing off" to provide an excuse to keep our behavior changes confined to the group. In the final analysis, a little false pride is probably a necessary compromise to compensate for the periods of insecurity inevitable in becoming a liberated man, or at least in becoming more than a "closet human."

Our first joint meetings with our attachés were tense, filled with undoing of distortions we each held about the other—both as individuals and as a sex. But the meetings were more open and honest than any of us had expected, and usually more interesting than our men's meetings. During these first two meetings Beth had been particularly helpful in encouraging assertiveness and confidence on the women's part. She was president of an important volunteer organization where she had a reputation for being able to help others. It was somewhat ironic, then, that when our topic for the third joint meeting was "What would we like to be doing five years from now?" Beth opened the conversation with "I'd really like to be a free-lance interior decorator."

Dorothy asked, "Well, what's preventing you from becoming an interior decorator, Beth?"

"Oh, there are lots of hassles—first getting industry connections and then building up a clientele. I just don't have the time to go through all that. We have two children and that's draining enough."

Ursie intervened, "What about all your activities? Somehow you've made the time for them. If you really want to go into it, what's preventing you? Especially now that Dan has said he would take care of the children half the time."

"Do you think the fact that Dan is already a successfully independent artist has anything to do with your hesitation?" Dorothy asked.

"What do you mean?"

Dorothy answered sharply. "I can see in your face that you know what I mean, Beth. I mean that you're afraid you'll fail in an area in which Dan is already successful, and your failure will seem even greater. So instead, you've taken the volunteer-organization route. What a cop-out."

Beth was obviously uptight, but she answered quietly. "I think maybe you're right. I think maybe my new sense of self-confidence is not ready for the blow of failing where Dan has been so successful—especially in a similar field. I'm beginning to feel I can never be anything but 'Dan's wife.' Also, I feel so out of it; I've been away from the decorating scene for over eight years."

"I can help you make contacts," Dan offered, "and I am willing to share the child care."

"I don't want your help, Dan, hear? I don't want it! If I set up a clientele I'll do it myself!" Beth shouted, almost in tears.

Marion leaned over to Beth. "Remember how you told me I shouldn't let Steven define me? Now you're doing the same thing. Others will still care for you whether you set up a successful clientele or not. I can remember when I was your age [Marion is 51], I was afraid to try a new style egg because I might mess it up. We can't let other people's expectations define us so much, Beth. You of all people have helped me see that."

Beth was sweating, with a nervous, anxious look in her eyes, trying on one hand to find an out, on the other hand aware that she wanted this—that it could be a turning point. We could see her reaching a precipice, and then "the savior" spoke—called "the savior" because inevitably when crises occur someone either takes off on an ideological sidetrack or defends the person with whom the group is working by interjecting a "stop it, leave her alone," or a "this is not getting anywhere." The savior problem is a common but difficult one, since at times the savior's sensitivity to someone being hurt is valuable, but in general if a tension is resulting from a constructive attempt to help a group member gain confidence it is one of the most important contributions the group can make to the person's growth.

As a result of the savior, we never returned to Beth. A few of us called her during the week, though, and this "follow-through" did precipitate extensive talks between her and Dan. Dan viewed Beth's change as a challenge for both of them. They started immediately to work out arrangements for him to completely share the child care. (During the course of his involvement in the men's group Dan put artistic success increasingly into perspective. He used to spend twelve to thirteen hours a day at the studio.) Beth eventually dropped her voluntary organization and slowly started calling professional contacts. "Their encouragement," she explained, "encouraged me. I find myself beaming with my old self-confidence—that I am worth enough to demand something in return for my services. I wasn't getting that return with voluntarism." Within two months Dan and Beth had changed their living arrangements totally: they had moved into a commune where Beth had an office and was soon to obtain her first free-lance projects.

The conversation transferred to Tim and Anna (a successful stockbroker), who became involved in what at first appeared to be a simple argument about why they did not share driving. It seemed to reach a fair settlement when Tim agreed "Okay, anytime you want to drive, just ask me. I'll give you the keys."

Anna sat back. "That sounds fair, but there's something wrong with that arrangement. In order for me to drive, I have to be doubly assertive. I have to go out of my way to ask you for the keys. It's assumed you'll drive unless I ask. Just like it's assumed men will hold management positions unless women protest. So the women who make it have to overcome all these barriers that men don't have to. Then the men wonder why the women who do make it are even more aggressive than men. 'Bitches.' We have to be. You make us make a choice between femininity and being aggressive. That's it. That's the whole fallacy of 'equal opportunity' the way men practice it."

"Maybe. But we're both locked into a habit. It doesn't seem like it's so difficult for you to ask if you want to drive. In fact, it would be nice if you could get more experience and learn how to drive well. It would be good for you."

"It would be good for you, too!" Anna responded furiously. "Lots of times you and I leave a party and you're tired when I'm not. And you still feel you have to drive. You can't admit even a bit of weakness, so you're caught in your own trap. You'll drive until you drive us both off the road. Damn it. You've got to realize that you need to change, too. You always think of changes as if I'm being brought up to your level. That's why I don't think you men really feel you have any stake in this movement."

Some concrete changes were evolving from the joint meetings. Almost everyone altered tes outlook and life style to a certain extent, but the biggest single change in living patterns was the creation of a communal household. Dan and Beth decided it would be easier for them to build Beth's clientele if they were only caring for children one-quarter of the time. They decided to share a house with another couple, Curt and Joan, who then joined the consciousness-raising group since Dan and Beth's changes in their own life style were so interrelated with those of their new living friends.

Both couples had two children. When they combined resources they were able to rent a large house in northeast New Jersey, which provided more space for the children and separate workrooms for the adults; it also provided relief from the omnipresent burden of child care, cooking, shopping and cleaning.

The communal arrangement provided an incentive to do more than just save time and maximize space; it forced everyone to completely rethink the "marriage contract." At first, they each planned to assume the responsibilities which came easiest to tir. "I hate cooking," Dan complained, and Curt added, "That's all right, I hate getting up early in the morning." As they talked it out they began to divide themselves into new roles. They also began to see a pattern: Joan observed that the members who "hated" things usually had only an image of what was involved but almost no experience with it. Dan seldom cooked and Curt almost never got up with the children. Joan suggested, "We have four people, so why don't we rotate, each trying everything one-quarter of the time for a full year. At the end of the year we can decide what we like and dislike. Right now I'm afraid of doing repairs, but maybe if I have to do them for a while I'll lose my fear and end up liking it."

The rotating of all responsibilities seemed to have unmitigated positive results. Dan wrapped himself up in cookbooks and was soon talking about his new dishes with the kind of pride Richard Nixon normally reserves for a description of his newest Cabinet member. Toward the end of the week Dan found that cooking was becoming routine, but at that point his responsibility ended for three weeks. Everyone involved found they were eating better (fortunately they are all thin!) , and their cooking improved. Rotation alleviated the boredom of routine.

Curt obtained similar reinforcement from the job he expected to hate—getting up early to take care of the children. "Everyone treats me with sympathy when I get up early. I always get asked if I want some juice, or extra bacon. It's like everyone knows what I've been through and is appreciative of having slept late, and like I'm the hero, you know. Also, I really get to know the kids then. I have them all to myself at a time when they're not cranky or tired."

Curt continued, "I like it now that we each have definite assignments rather than being expected to always be helpful. Before, if I sat down while Joan was cooking I felt guilty for not helping with the meal, but now when we each have a definite responsibility, we each can enjoy our free time."

Dan pointed out that it also helped him understand how much each person needed appreciation, especially when te was trying something new. "Before, if Beth would try a new recipe I concentrated on 'advising' her what was wrong with it. Now I tell her what is right with it."

Beth agreed. "You're a lot less condescending now. Also, since we've been rotating, you don't use your expertise in areas like mechanics as a source of power over me. When I couldn't repair the car (which I still can't too much—but I'm learning!), I'd do three hours worth of child care to 'equal' your one hour of car repair. It sort of seemed that your stuff should be valued more, because I attached a mystique to it."

"You lose, Dan," Tim kidded.

Joan continued, "When Lisa first saw Curt cooking, she said to me, 'Daddy can't cook a *whole* dinner, can he?' She had seen the reality—that Curt was just 'helping' me—while we fooled ourselves into thinking we both shared the cooking. Rotating has helped that a lot."

Children were often a topic of discussion in our joint group. Of eight couples, five were married with children, one married without children (Ursie and me), and two unmarried and childless. During one of our first discussions Ursie and I asked the couples with children why they decided to have them.

Joan jumped in. "Decide to have them?! We didn't really decide . . . I mean not consciously—did we, Curt? We just knew we were going to—or maybe it's knew we were supposed to—have them."

Before Curt could give his viewpoint, Beth supported Joan. "Yeah. We didn't decide either. We didn't ever once, I don't think, really ask ourselves whether or not we should have them."

Dan added, "That's true. I guess children were sort of programmed into our life. We decided when to have them and how to have them, but not whether to have them."

Steve and Marion, whose children were twenty-six and twenty-four, were more enthusiastic. "It's a real experience," Steve explained. "I learned a lot about myself. I could see my kids going through the same patterns I went through. You never understand the whole cycle until you're a parent." Marion added, "And it's made me much more human, in touch with young people."

"Well," Dan mused, "child-raising may be great, but did you ever consider what we might have done had we not had children?"

"Frankly," Marion responded, "I had nothing else I really planned to do with my life. I didn't think of myself in any other way. I don't know if I even would have had the confidence to do anything else if I didn't have the children."

A number of us just sat in contemplative silence; Marion's frankness could not help but get us to examine our own motivations.

Dan offered, "A lot of things motivate a person to have children. I think if I'm honest, I have to admit that I always had an underlying curiosity or fear about whether I was sterile. When I had children I found I wasn't."

"That's a pretty big price you paid for some pretty meaningless information," Steve chided. "Confidence is an amazing thing. We drive ourselves all our life to prove we're worth something. We have children to prove we're fertile. We raise them totally by ourselves because we need the assurance they are totally our possessions."

"Don't get me wrong," Dan retracted, "children are a great experience. Sometimes they're so cute it makes up for everything, and then it's an indescribable experience. But increasingly I've been resenting the lack of freedom I have—especially since I've been spending the eleven hours per week caring for them. Whenever I leave the house I feel, well, guilty. The kids are in a phase now where every time I start to leave they shout, 'I love you, Daddy! I love you, Daddy!' That makes it hard. Recently I've had little free time."

"Imagine if you had to raise them full time like I did before we lived on the commune. If I wasn't paying attention to them every moment I felt guilty," Beth recalled. "Sure I love the kids—I really love them, but when they're hanging onto my feet . . . that's 'adorable,' but try walking two hours a day with an 'adorable' thirty pounds wrapped around your feet and then having enough energy to do all the other 'exciting' chores . . . and then feel sexy at night. Ugh."

Lenore and Myron, a new couple who had been living together for a while were whispering together in apparent disagreement. "I think a certain amount of discipline is often necessary," Myron broke out. "They have to understand that some time must be your time, just for you."

"Oh God, Myron," Beth shouted, "it's obvious you've never had children. You're talking about being rational. I can't be rational because they aren't rational. Last night, for example, I had just finished all my chores and I gave Lisa some juice. Before I put the juice away I asked if anyone else wanted juice. 'Peter, Sue, Jimmy—would you like any juice? Say so now because I'm putting it away and I'm going to sit down and read for a while.' They all said no. So I sat down to read. I located the book, turned on the light, found where I had left off—and wouldn't you know it, Sue comes bouncing over. 'Where's my juice? I want some juice.'

"You'd think it's a clear-cut case—you've told her no, right? Well, I repeated the no. She tells me, 'I want some, Mommy, I want some, why won't you get me some?' I explain the whole thing and reaffirm the no. She keeps it up, pleading. I know she's really just asking for attention, not juice, so I begin to feel guilty. I say to myself, 'Even if I have an obligation to be strict about the juice, don't I also have an obligation to be attentive to her? Suppose she grows up always missing that love?' Well, it's a big fat gray area, Myron. And you can never decide for sure when you're doing the right thing. And when you go through all the turmoil to come to the proper decision, you've blasted a goddamned big hole in your so-called free time."

"At least now, since the commune, Beth and I have been

going out since we don't have to go through that baby-sitter hassle. If Joan or Curt are home, they'll take care of the children pretty much on the spur of the moment."

Dan continued, "It does give us more freedom, but the other day I thought how great it will be in fifteen years to get a small little apartment in the Village somewhere and have no responsibilities and lots of time together, do whatever we want together. What freedom! It would be like being lovers! And then came the horrible thought—fifteen years! God! we'll be getting into our late forties—almost fifty years of our life gone."

Kay and Cliff, another couple new to the group, were looking perplexed. Cliff asked, "What choices does all this boil down to? Do we have to choose between having children and having freedom? I'm finding our newborn baby just takes loads of time. Is it children *or* freedom? What are you two planning? [to Ursie and me]."

Ursie thought aloud. "I don't know. Since I've gotten over feeling that I have to be a mother, the whole thought is becoming less and less enticing—especially since I like my job so much. I think another thing bothers me. I know Warren really loves children a lot, and I think underneath it all, it bothers me that he might show me up as a parent. He's willing to stay home with them half the time but I'm not sure I want to stay home the other half."

I asked if the group would sort of brainstorm for some alternatives we might consider should we have children. The ideas included my teaching in the evenings, and the need for us to be willing to make money for child care a priority item if we wanted really professional help. We estimated we would need child-care assistance twenty to thirty hours per week. I'm sure we won't adopt more than a few of the alternatives, but it has stimulated us to plan much more carefully.

OPENING OUR MARRIAGES: SECURITY AND FREEDOM

A number of us thought our discussions of alternatives were particularly constructive, and at our next meeting we tossed around the possibility of discussing alternatives to monogamous sexual relations in marriage. For the first fifteen minutes there was far more cautiousness-raising than consciousness-raising.

Cliff, a young and highly logical internist who had contributed quietly during his first months in the group and looked more like a bright fifties college student who still slicked his hair with Wildroot than an intern, broke the cautiousness-raising trend. He observed, "It seems that whenever groups talk about extramarital sex no one is ever personal. We may talk about what we personally *think,* but not what we personally do."

A moment of nervous silence responded. Extramarital sex was still enough of a taboo area to make us nervous about discussing our own activities, especially in front of our spouses. Suddenly Kay, an articulate advocate of women's liberation and a former social worker, volunteered to discuss Cliff's and her extramarital relations. "Okay, I'll speak personally about extramarital sex. But I don't want to be the only one."

Others agreed, and Kay began in the increasingly conducive atmosphere. "You see, when we were married for a short period of time I had a brief, quick—hardly even a relationship with, but technically a physical relationship with, this guy. I didn't really even like him that much, but, well, it wasn't the high point with Cliff and me in our marriage and the situation at the moment was conducive to it—you know.

"Then I had to decide whether to tell Cliff. Cliff had said he could handle it if something like that happened. We had sort of discussed this before, so I told him during an 'understanding' mood—you know, one of those times when you're both feeling so close to each other you feel you can understand anything about the other person. Well, the response was, let me tell you, catastrophic. He blew up, started to call me a slut and everything. He just couldn't handle it at all. And it didn't wear off. The whole thing was terrible from beginning to end. The guy I had the relationship with felt guilty right after we finished; the sexual experience was mediocre—in and out, that was it—and then Cliff went into this tirade followed by his famous silences. Ugh.

"Well, I think we've both changed a lot since then. Our marriage is much better and we've discussed this a lot and I think Cliff could handle this now. I know I could handle it from him."

Cliff concurred. "Yes, I know I could handle it now."

Kay hesitated, then looked at Cliff, paused again, and continued, "As a matter of fact, I've had extramarital relations in the last few months, and I think our relationship has been better than ever."

The group sat in embarrassed silence. We were not quite certain whether Cliff had been told about this relationship or whether it was coming as news at this time.

Cliff finally reacted. "Wow, that's something. I'm really glad you said that. I just have this sudden feeling of closeness to you . . . Like, I don't know if I should admit this, but I think I respect you more. I mean I can hear myself thinking, 'Yeah, she has needs, too.' Usually I'm just thinking of my desires. The other thing is I think you're right about our relationship improving in the past few months. It's better than it has ever been. That's really amazing."

"Yeah," added Tim. "Outside relations haven't changed our marriage either. Like I haven't gone out and had outside relationships but Anna and I did have an experience which was similar . . ."

Tim paused. Then Anna laughingly finished, ". . . called group sex!"

Growing more serious, she continued, "It wasn't really all that much. We were at a party with some really good friends. Everyone was high. There were a number of couples there, but a few went home when it got later. The couple whose house we were at had this water bed and we all went in to test it out. We started rolling around and kidding and pretty soon we were making love with just about anyone. I don't remember that much of it, but we kept touching and feeling each other and the next thing we were having sex. Then it seemed we were waking up the next morning."

"All I could remember the next morning," said Tim, "was reaching for my underwear, looking at the first pair I picked up and saying . . . 'Ugh—this isn't my underwear! Where am I? What happened?' The whole thing seemed unreal."

Anna made a pointed observation. "You know, Tim, this is the first time we've brought this topic up since then. We never said a word about it to each other since then—until just now. I thought it was weird that Kay would talk to the group about what she hadn't discussed with Cliff. But we sort of did the same thing."

Steve, coming out of deep thought, began his story. "I had an experience a number of years ago, which I've never discussed either. I had a group of writer and artist friends I was real good friends with. I saw them like almost every week for years. But one night . . ." Steve hesitated but was encouraged to continue. "We got to feeling especially good, and a few of the guys started getting physical with each other. Pretty soon it sort of turned into touching and feeling each other everywhere. Everyone was beginning to do it and I found myself—well, I just became part of it. It seemed awkward not to be doing it. But it was great. I lost all my inhibitions. I felt much freer once I had had the relationship.

"Until that time I could never even picture myself having a relationship with another man. Mostly the thought didn't occur to me—like I had no desire for that, you know. If I thought of it for a second it repulsed me. They were the first men I could even come close to mentally without being afraid of something. I thought men who had these relationships were, well, queer. I didn't think I would ever be able to get over something like that. I'll tell you, I honestly thought it would leave a lasting effect on me psychologically, that I would feel like a pervert or guilty or maladjusted or something. I could never really have understood that a person who had a homosexual experience could be completely normal. I would always have been somewhat suspicious of him.

"Now I feel differently than even then. I don't think I could really be free until I had experienced that. But I don't only mean free in a sexual sense, but in a political sense too. I would still be imprisoning others with my own beliefs of how they should act. This is repression. That's what it is. Repression. People imposing their views on someone else all the time. Setting up all these norms and making people feel like deviants if they do what they think they might want to try."

Myron challenged Steve's purported freedom. "If you felt so good about it then and feel it's brought you all this freedom, why haven't you talked about it in the group before? You've been in the group for the last six months, right?"

"Mmm. I guess you're right. It's been years since I had relations with these guys, and I haven't mentioned it to anyone—ever, since then. Until Tim and Anna mentioned their group-sex experience I didn't feel free enough to bring it up here either. If it wasn't for this group coming closer and closer I would have brought this to my grave without saying a thing.

Our discussions of sex led us to questioning why we always thought of the other partner as "ours."

Kay was discussing what she thought about when she masturbated: "Sometimes I think of Cliff, maybe 'cause I want him there and he's off working at the hospital. Once when I was using a vibrator, I remember fantasizing that the vibrator was all sorts of different people—like I could see five fingers all blending into one, all working on me, just on me. Once I even imagined a cartoon character—"

"Oh, come on, Kay," Cliff interrupted, "don't act so silly."

"Kay is talking about herself, Cliff. Why do you feel so responsible for her?"

"I don't feel responsible for her . . . Well, maybe I do. I don't know, I guess I feel if she acts silly it reflects on me. You know, talking about cartoon characters in her masturbation."

"Wow! Don't you see how you're limiting Kay; she doesn't just have to worry about expressing herself. She has to worry about all the possible worries you might have when she's expressing herself. That's the problem with marriage: There's an ownership implied, a possessiveness. We treat each other like property: 'I own your body—it can only be used with me, when I want it. You can't even use it by yourself for your own pleasure, and if you do, don't tell anybody, and if you tell someone, don't say anything silly—it might embarrass me!' "

"I understand what you're saying, Beth," Cliff admitted, "but it's still hard for me to accept it when it actually happens. And I've seen Kay do the same thing to me."

Kay agreed. "That's true, it's hard for me to imagine Cliff using his body freely too. I'm afraid his freedom's going to spoil our relationship. I'd like to keep the stability, but we'd both like more freedom, I think. We're afraid that if we start allowing ourselves freedom, we're going to lose the stability. I know it's kind of uncool to talk about stability, but I think I really value that."

"Well," Ursie added, "it seems you almost lost your stability when you first told Cliff about your outside relationship—but didn't you say your marriage was at a down point then? Everyone seems to have affairs when their marriage is getting worse . . . But wait a minute, wasn't your marriage better when you had your second affair, and didn't you say that improved your relationship?"

"Yes, that's true," Cliff agreed. "I think underneath we've always been thinking that outside sex has to come out of negative reasons, when things are getting worse, when maybe we should be working on having outside sex out of positive reasons. I think that is the difference. The first time I felt negative about myself (and our relationship), and I associated her affair with a threat. The second time I felt better, and I didn't have to possess Kay every minute to feel secure with her. The second time I eventually thought about sex as adding to our relationship, rather than taking away from it. I saw that Kay was happier when other people were offering her reinforcement about her sexuality, and I guess that's why our sex life improved. (She felt better about herself.) But I still feel worried about Kay having certain needs fulfilled by someone other than me."

"That's what makes it great," Beth added. "I don't always want to have to fulfill all of Dan's needs all the time. That puts too much pressure on me. It forces me to have sex when I may not want to. Last week, for example: My period was heavy on Tuesday and Wednesday, and I just felt too uncomfortable to make love. Also, when Dan or I are traveling separately, why should we castrate ourselves? What I do want is to know that Dan is my primary relationship, that he's with me most all the time when he can be rather than with someone else."

"What do you mean by 'primary relationship'?"

"I mean that Dan doesn't go off with someone else at a time when I would like him to be with me. So this way I'm not sitting at home thinking about him with another woman."

"Doesn't that limit Dan?"

"Yes. But I'm willing to limit myself that way too, and it's the only way we assure ourselves of having time with each other. And it forces us to plan ahead, to check out the baby-sitter situation and generally try to schedule our affairs on nights which are not going to leave the other person lonely. It's our arrangement for combining stability with freedom. That's what I mean by primary relationship. To us, that's the difference between being married and being, well, just room-mates."

During the next few months a number of our conversations revolved around experimenting, honesty, possessiveness and developing ways of having outside relationships that would help each person grow. At one meeting Cliff and Kay summarized some of their developments.

Cliff started. "I think we've discovered something in the past few months. For a while we were keeping our affairs secret—thinking that wouldn't hurt the other person as much. We'd sort of protect each other. But whenever I'd go to the hospital to work overtime, Kay thought for sure I was having an affair. Then she felt left out, like 'Why is he leaving me when he could be home with me?' And I was mad because usually I wasn't having an affair and I was creating tension and not getting any benefits."

"That was why we brought up the topic of 'honesty' in the group a few weeks ago," Kay explained. "Since then we've been telling each other when we're going to have a relationship, and we try to make it on a night that the other person is busy. Like I take a class on Wednesday night, so Cliff tries to arrange his dates for then, and I try to arrange mine for Monday or Tuesday since those are the days he usually stays late at the hospital."

"But a problem we still have," Kay continued, "is that

neither of us gets jealous if we're both involved at a given time, but if one of us isn't involved, then jealousy creeps back in. We seem to need a certain amount of . . . I guess you could call it *evenness.*"

"That's true with us, too," Lenore added. "But it was usually Myron who was uninvolved. I was always getting guys asking me out, because not being married guys assume you're available; but for Myron, he had to *initiate* an interest in another woman—he says women never do that—and he felt funny about initiating because it was a clearer indication that he desired outside relationships. With me, I could just respond to 'someone else's interest.' "

"I guess that's the difference," Kay continued. "Men know I'm married, and I can't easily advertise 'I'm available,' whereas Cliff can approach one woman and quietly explain his arrangement to her without having the whole hospital know."

"Wait a minute," Lenore interjected. "You and I are still playing the old 'feminine' game of expecting to be asked. I'm still into the bag of throwing out hints, but almost never overtly taking a risk by asking a guy I'm not pretty certain will respond with enthusiasm."

"Yeah. I know you're right. But how am I going to get over that? I'm really scared to go around asking guys to go to bed with me. Especially if I'm really interested—then it would hurt even more if I got rejected."

"Don't worry." Tim laughed. "No guy is gonna reject an offer like that!"

"Maybe it would be fun to do some role-playing," Myron suggested. "Why don't you tell me what a typical situation is at your office, Kay?"

After a few suggestions that "role-playing wouldn't be helpful," someone finally reminded us that we had found in the past that the worst thing an experiment could do was fail.

"Okay, I work in a social-work agency, and I'll usually meet a fellow if we're both in the office between cases, or if he's one of the directors, since most of the other caseworkers are women."

"All right, then, you play yourself, Kay, and I'll play a guy you'd like to go to bed with who has a mild interest in you sexually. You try to be aggressive."

Myron and Kay started their role-playing with a serious conversation about social work for the first few minutes. Finally Myron said, "You really look happy today." Kay answered, "Thanks," and continued on the topic of social work. After a few minutes, Myron stopped.

"Kay, I tried moving the conversation to the personal level twice and you didn't pick it up. Besides, you should be the one moving it to the personal level if you have the interest in me. You could have said something about the way I look, or that you enjoy being with me, or *some*thing! Let's try it again."

On the second round Kay did move the conversation to the personal level. The group then critiqued the role-playing to get Kay to suggest overtly that she and the man get together for dinner, rather than manipulating him into asking her out. The role-playing was embarrassing at points, filled with jokes which threatened to destroy its value, but eventually brought substantial dividends.

"I think I feel a lot better about being aggressive. It's really demeaning to have to depend on someone else to express an interest in me. I think if Cliff and I can have a . . . a . . . maybe you can call it a '*balanced involvement*' in outside relationships I'll lose my jealousy. Once I have that I can deal with him as an equal and be honest—and I can rationally plan it on nights convenient to both of us. Those seem to be the main problems."

After a few seconds of silence, Myron looked at Kay with

sheepish curiosity. "Kay, do you really have an interest in me, I mean the me me? Ha! I'm only joking."

"Ha! Sounds like you're manipulating me into asking you out! Mmm. I just realized something. I did think of you sexually for the first time as we were role-playing. It was during the second round, when I had to be aggressive—I found myself getting sexually turned on to you. I had never even allowed myself to think of you in those terms before. Not that I repressed it, but . . . but, well, maybe I did repress it."

"That's fascinating, Kay," Anna noted. "Because my whole objection to your arrangement was that it seemed like you had to keep up with Cliff, that 'balanced involvement' stuff. I was thinking, 'Suppose I just want to stay home and read during a week when he's going out.' "

"Well, that's all right too. The point is that I have the freedom. I don't always have to have sex. I can stay home, just rest, do anything."

"No," Anna started. "What you just said to Myron meant even more to me. *You became more interested sexually as you took the initiative.* I always think of myself as less interested in men than Tim is in women, but I also never take the initiative, like never. I think one of the reasons men get turned on is that they're always supposed to have their minds in high gear."

"It's called the sex drive!" Tim joked.

"This is serious, Tim. I feel like I've hit on a whole new insight to myself. Before I was thinking it's my *choice* if I want to be home when you're out, but it's only a theoretical choice until I develop my sexual side to the point that I feel comfortable choosing sex. And what Kay is saying is that her sexual appetite increased as she took the initiative. There's hope for *me* then!"

In the few months we spent discussing sexual attitudes we did a lot of thinking about topics that have turned out to be

crucial in the lives of many group members: feeling responsible for our partner; overcoming jealousy and possessiveness
while maintaining stability; working out a "primary relationship"; masturbating; vibrators; extramarital relations
out of positive reasons; honesty; "balanced involvement" in
extramarital relations, and becoming sexually assertive.

A few weeks later our topic for the evening was emotions.
Cliff cited medical and psychological literature and some
experiments undertaken by a colleague of his on emotions.
We were soon barraging Cliff with questions about the validity of the experiments. Kay got furious.

"Look, everyone—just stop one damned second and look at
what's happening. Look at what he's doing. How can you
men stand yourselves? How can you sit there and take this
crap? How can you let yourselves talk like that—about emotions! If I were like that I couldn't stand myself.

"Really. You wonder why women are turning to women.
I'll tell you why. For emotional support. For understanding.
For conversation. For human contact. Love. Even physical
contact and physical love. How can you get warm physical
love out of a book—out of an intellectual boor? This is why
women are going to turn to women. And once they do it,
they aren't going to come back. There's nothing to come
back to. You have nothing to offer to anyone—least of all
yourself. Women's liberation, shit. It's the men who need
liberating!"

There was no response to Kay, but it marked the end of
our intellectual debates about the science of emotions.

During the summer Jonathan and Nancy "temporarily"
broke their relationship and both left the group. During an
evening walk with Jonathan he explained why he was leaving. "I'd feel funny without a partner in the mixed group,
but mostly I want to let things settle and see where I'm at

with Nancy before I come back to the group. I like to think things through before I say them."

We discussed how Jonathan's tendency to "think things through before I say them" paralleled his contribution to the group. He would often sit for over an hour without saying a word; we could almost feel the presence of his silence, as if in judgment of the rest of us. When he did speak, his soft voice, his modesty, and our almost unconscious need for his approval drew a silent attention to him. He then quietly offered his carefully thought through assessment of our discussion.

"Why do you feel unable to discuss some of your problems with us, rather than just analyzing our problems?" I asked.

"I get all nervous in my stomach when I'm sitting in the group talking about something like Nancy and me if I think maybe somebody's going to find a big hole in something I'm saying."

"You can always reject what we say, but if you don't expose yourself what are you getting out of the group? Don't you sort of become like a guest lecturer? It's great for the group . . . Well, maybe it isn't even as great for the group as I've been thinking, because it's harder for us to express fears if you're always a fountain of strength. That's the whole masculinity trip—avoiding vulnerability, always having to have the answer. Isn't it?"

I felt disappointed we were not sensitive enough to draw Jonathan out more (in a supportive way), rather than doing him the injustice of touting him as the ideal member. Jonathan left the group and did not return.

Another quiet member of the group, Curt, did undergo a number of changes during the year which seem to have resulted from what might be called "the osmosis effect," a type of power which the consciousness-raising group has over all its members to some extent but over a few in particular. While most of us seemed to change most when directly confronted, Curt seemed to absorb the atmosphere of the group and slowly transfer it to his own life. In Curt's and Joan's case, one of Joan's major complaints was Curt's unwillingness to discuss anything that was depressing him. In the group I had also tried to "bring Curt out," only to be told that he would speak if and when he wanted to. For this reason Joan's discussion of the way Curt had changed since he joined the consciousness-raising group came as a surprise to me. "Curt had changed so much in the past few months—all the changes are more than I ever believed possible a year ago, like his sharing of absolutely everything around the house. But I don't think that's even what I care about most. A year ago I couldn't get any emotion—any enthusiasm or warmth out of Curt. I always wanted—needed—someone else to talk to. Now for the first time, since he's been with the men's group, he is communicating and talking with me. It's almost like a different person. I feel so much closer to him." Curt smiled, but didn't say a word.

Curt's change taught me that developing principles which benefit the group at large should be stressed, but not without carefully considering the personality of each group member. Most of us did change most effectively when drawn out, but apparently Curt absorbed what the group was doing and benefited without verbal communication. Whether we could have used techniques to draw him out which would have provided even greater benefit or whether they would have turned him off is an unresolved question. Perhaps the best guideline is that groups can experiment with new techniques unless an individual member feels it will have a negative effect on tir, but should not use "the group's welfare" as an excuse to avoid such experiments. The following problems, topics and techniques are presented with that caution in mind.

Fifteen

Additional Problems, Topics
and Techniques in Running
Consciousness-Raising Groups

Many of the problems common to consciousness-raising
groups are discussed in the introduction to Chapter 13 on
men's consciousness-raising, and others are given enough attention throughout the preceding chapters as to need no
attention here. However, some important problems, techniques and topics can be best summarized here now that
some feel for the practical experiences of groups has been
gained. I will discuss them in the context of *men's groups,* although much of this section is also applicable to joint groups.

PROBLEMS

Lateness. Most groups are casual to the point of annoyance.
One group reported: "People drifting in an hour late sort of

undermines the morale of the rest of us. It seems to say the group isn't important enough to be worth their making it on time. We found the best way to handle it was to confront the members with our annoyance."

Lateness is an indicator that the group's meeting is being treated as a social engagement, where an hour's lateness is acceptable. The only guideline which seems to help the lateness problem is starting exactly fifteen minutes after the set meeting time, plus the guidelines covering dropping out and attendance.

Dropping out of the group. "One ground rule," a man from a group in Chicago explained, "concerned dropping out of the group. We all agreed no one would drop out without telling one of us." This ground rule has been helpful in a number of groups since the greatest temptation to drop out often comes at a crisis point, when a man is moving past the "plateau effect" and starting to change behavior, but is also hurting from the pain of reexamination. A little human encouragement at this down point is usually enough to provide the base of security needed by most of us to change. Becoming sensitive to the points at which encouragement is needed is a way of implementing our theories on the importance of being sensitive. The rugged individualist approach— "if he wants to come, he'll come"—is a way of avoiding the process of extending ourselves in order to avoid rejection.

Attendance. Since fluctuating attendance breaks down trust and continuity, many groups have established basic ground rules about attendance. An example from a New Jersey group: "If one of us must miss a meeting he calls at least the man at whose home we are holding the meeting. This also helps the rest of us know whether we should wait for him or start the meeting." It also tends to encourage attendance.

New members and contacts outside the group. It usually helps to keep the group somewhat large (ten to thirteen) for the first four or five weeks so that it can slowly close itself off to new members and still allow for attrition. A 50 percent attrition in men's groups and a 20 to 30 percent attrition in couples or joint groups is about average. New members should be brought in with considerable caution after the first few months since the need for repetition provides an excuse for the group not to break new ground.

Should the group be made up of colleagues or friends? It is difficult for most persons to open up to colleagues whom they know they will see at work the next day. (It is ironic that the persons who know us best in one context—such as family and colleagues—know us least in another.) However, since a goal of consciousness-raising is to lead a liberated existence even among colleagues (and ultimately in the family), the answer to the question is that it depends on whether the new member feels he has developed to the point that he is able to handle it. This problem is especially acute in groups started in small towns. In a university community in Ohio one man explained, "I think it's going to be very difficult for us to be open. For example, I've got Al here in a class of mine, and Bill is on the personnel committee responsible for my tenure." This group developed an extremely strict ethic of confidentiality. This man later wrote that he had found the group "the most liberating force in my life. For the first time I'm seeing Al as a person rather than a student, and for some reason, although my contact with Bill has grown incredibly close, probably assuring tenure, I no longer care that much about it."

Confidentiality. As the case with John illustrates, absolute confidentiality is essential. Progress reports (e.g., "John is really changing") are among the most inhibiting betrayals of confidentiality since they tend to discourage persons from broaching areas where they have failed to change. *Outside gossip is like a group report card which restores the performance ethic.* Discussions of the overall value of the group which do not reveal identities must be the limit of outside discussion.

"We've covered everything." An almost universal phenomenon among the men's groups is the tendency to reach a point at which all the stories are told and the basic rationale for a man's relationship with his wife is understood. A tension is reached. Each man knows the other man's standard response to a challenge, but he is afraid to question this too deeply; he knows that if a precedent for challenging basics is established, his own basic stories are open to challenge. Nothing makes him more vulnerable than this. Often a group escapes by moving totally into therapy mode, where it can avoid questioning sex roles in the home, or by just ceasing to function.

At this point meeting with women can be especially helpful. If the group has only been functioning for a month or so, it helps to meet with a group of women unrelated to the men—a group separate from the group with which the men may eventually alternate meetings. At the very least, when the group senses a plateau is reached, an outside person (woman or man, preferably with group experience) might be asked to come to one or two meetings and offer observations.

Press. With any new movement some groups face requests for a reporter to sit in on a session to "get a feel for the dynamics." Since men's consciousness-raising will only reach a handful of men without the press, the idea should not be met with total negativism. I have found the following precautions helpful to our group:

a. All meetings with reporters are held *in addition to* regular meetings, so the continuity of regular meetings is not interrupted.
b. Attendance at reporter-attended meetings is obviously volun-

tary; each member makes it clear whether he wants his real name mentioned; every member is invited.

c. The reporter agrees ahead of time to interview each man individually since no reporter can be expected to understand the purposes of the group from one session, which can provide only a snapshot. This prevents one man from becoming a star and assures the reporter's seriousness of purpose.

If these precautions are taken it is generally unnecessary to require approval of the story—a type of Agnewism-of-the-left. I have found it more important to check out the individual reporter's past stories than to worry about the newspaper or magazine's reputation. Also, the papers with the worst reputation usually reach the people who most need exposure to breaking down sex roles.

The haphazard problem-solver. Men's groups will often pay attention to a man for a few moments, make a suggestion, move on to someone else and never return the next week to ask whether the suggestion was helpful. This typifies men's tendency to be more concerned with the ego enhancement involved in quick solutions rather than the drudgery of long-term empathy. A method of avoiding the haphazard problem-solver trap is discussed in the section on techniques called "follow-through hour."

TOPICS

Four topics that can serve as starters for the first meetings of men's groups are "Becoming a man"; "How my attaché and I share or divide the breadwinning, children, or housekeeping role"; "Things that most bother my wife or attaché about me"; and "The meaning women's liberation has to me." These get the man to focus on himself but also do not ignore his relationship to women.

A beginning approach for a group of strangers meeting at a conference is answering such questions as "What does 'masculinity' mean?" "What is femininity?" and "What combination of these do we want ourselves (or our attaché) to be?" (Some joint groups also use this approach to begin with.) Some ideas on topics follow:

Becoming a man. Experiences at camp, in school and in locker rooms; penis measuring; sex books; fears of rejection by girls.

A Wisconsin group had each man bring in a picture of himself as a child along with one or two important childhood mementos (e.g., a trophy). This stimulated the men to plow through memories in their past which they forgot had any bearing on their present attitudes.

Rejection. Times I have felt rejected (by groups, by individuals, by men or women) ; things I do in the group to prevent rejection (e.g., do I speak more to try to get attention or less to avoid being rejected?) .

From the discussion of some of these feelings, a new topic emerges: "Why have we not discussed feelings of rejection before?" The psychologist Jerome Kagan finds it a typically male trait to suppress anxiety over social rejection.[1] The male is supposed to be able to slide in and out of social relationships with grace and control and without a hint of being rejected.

Vulnerability. What do I presently feel most vulnerable about this group discovering about me?

Attitudes toward women. My first views of women. Viewing her as a sex object; learning to be "superior"; developing contempt for women.

Child care. Do I spend as much time with our children as my attaché? What alternative might make that a possibility? How could I complement them?

Abortion, vasectomies. Would I consider getting a vasectomy? Do we know anyone who has had a vasectomy? An abortion? How did they feel about it later? How do we think we would feel?

Putting children through college (or sending them to a private school, or paying for private lessons). Am I motivated by a need to have my children succeed as a reflection of my own success?

Listening. Who talks most in serious conversations in front of company, me or my woman friend? What I've *learned* from listening.

Learning to be a leader. How did school teach me to value leadership? What pressures to be a leader do I receive from peer group, wife, parents? What pressures do I still put on myself?

Competing. Do I feel competitive at work; in the group; with my attaché or living friend?

Breadwinner role. Do I view my career as more important than my attaché's? How much time do we spend discussing her career? Am I free to pursue interests that would force me to take a substantial drop in income? Does my attaché do things for me (typing, cooking) more often than I for her? If so, does this pressure me in the long run to have to keep producing on my job?

To put one's job into perspective, a useful technique is to list one's specific values or priorities. "How important is my job in relation to time with my wife; my children; travel?" Weigh these values, and then compare the time spent devoted to fulfilling each. Ask whether the preoccupation with the job and status values blots out a practical consideration of the other values.

A good entrée into discussions of ambitions and jobs is a discussion of fantasies. For example, "What would I like to be doing if I could do *anything* I wished, now and ten years from now?"

Expressing emotions versus thinking emotionally. Must a person who expresses emotions think without logic or does it ultimately free one to think logically? When are emotions helpful? Expressing emotions within the group. Fears of expressing emotions.

Crying. When did I last cry? Would I like to be able to cry more? What are the purposes of crying?

Recent progress. What changes did I successfully make last week? What changes did I consider but not follow through with in practice?

Other topics, such as sexual readiness, specialization, fears of being effeminate, sports, the sharing of housework, jealousy and dominance, can be culled from the entire section on consciousness-raising and throughout the book.

TECHNIQUES PARTICULARLY USEFUL FOR MEN'S CONSCIOUSNESS-RAISING

Some of these techniques are designed to help solve some of the problems we've been discussing as common to many groups, such as the haphazard problem-solver. Others hopefully create new insights into the behavior of the men in the group, such as the technique of drawing pictures together. Still others are consciousness-raisers, such as the men's beauty contest.

- A *"follow-through hour"* at the beginning of a group meeting is a good method for countering the problem of men's groups offering solutions to a problem without ever expressing continued interest in whether the problem was resolved or whether our alternatives were helpful. We found that a follow-through hour offers considerable insight to the complications involved in even our simplest suggestions. For example, we suggested to a man in our group that he assume the bulk of responsibility for making and serving the dinner when his boss comes, since the boss was his friend. When he was subject to four or five sarcastic comments from his boss (who was threatened by his wife's suggestions that he should do the same thing) and when we analyzed how most of the comments were poking fun at his masculinity, we could see the importance of follow-through hours for gaining new insights into our fears and into social pressures discouraging us from changing. In this case the follow-through hour led to the man questioning whether his job was creating a pressure for him to resist adopting some of the alternative life styles he discussed enthusiastically in the group.

- Silence among some members (e.g., Jonathan) and dominance by others is the perfect situation for the *distribution of either toothpicks or pieces of paper* to each man with instructions to forfeit one item each time he speaks. (Asking a brief question of someone who is talking does not require forfeiting a toothpick.) Once a man has thrown his three or four toothpicks into the center of the circle he waits for the other men to finish using theirs. This helps the dominant men to listen and the silent ones to speak. Joint groups have also found this technique useful as a method of illustrating male dominance and simultaneously discouraging it.

- The simple method of *rotating discussion* of a topic also helps to balance talkers with nontalkers. This method is most effective when the rotation starts with a member who generally speaks very little.

- *Brainstorming* or *alternative-seeking* can be used to solve a problem a member brings to the group. After the problem is explained, everyone randomly tosses out alternatives. There is *no discussion* of the alternatives until the group has exhausted its supply. When the alternatives are discussed at the end, only the ones that appear most appropriate are analyzed further, rather than criticizing each one as it is mentioned. Therefore the least applicable alternatives are not subjected to criticism. This method takes the pressure off of any given man to have *the* solution readily available (the mystique of "man the problem-solver"); in joint groups it encourages women to have the confidence to make suggestions since they know their ideas will not be torn apart.

- *Role-playing* can be one of the most important techniques in a men's consciousness group because it stimulates a much-needed empathy and understanding. I have observed two effective methods: one is to have the man play the role of himself while another man plays his attaché. The other is for the man to play the part of his attaché while another man takes his role. With this method it helps to change seats physically prior to changing roles since the possibility of role-playing is usually first suggested as a half-joke and the switching of seats encourages a seriousness and attentiveness which surrounds an upcoming "event." In joint groups role reversal is usually most helpful.

- As a men's group becomes more stable, if it contemplates turning activist, a *beauty contest* might be an excellent consciousness-raiser and even a fund-raiser. Every man attending the contest is carefully surveyed by the women in the audience as a possible nominee. Nominations are made from the floor, only by women. A man waiting through a half-hour of nominating without his name mentioned will begin to feel the pressure of being a sex object—especially an unsuccessful one. After nominations, men are paraded in bathing suits, and a group of women judges comment on the shape of their legs, their buttocks, their chest span (or lack of one), the way they walk, their posture, arm muscles, hair thickness; the women make guesses at their penis size, read waist and chest measurements, and then ask them a few simple questions to see if they are "talented."

- During a discussion of competition and dominance, group together in twos, distribute Magic Markers and crayons, and *draw a picture together*. Analyze how the picture developed, who created the basic design, what decisions were made as the picture was created, who dominated and what feelings of jealousy and competition were evoked.
- *Alternating apartments* is a method our group used to help ease the tendency for the men to look toward me for leadership. When we met at my apartment I naturally felt more in control and that control was what we all wanted to break.
- A group in Iowa used the alternating of apartments as a basis for a game. The men guessed what type of bedroom the man had whose home they were going to be at the following week. The game did help the men communicate with each other about how uptight or relaxed they thought the other man was. The accuracy of the guesses also made the men aware that others could see through their façades.
- If the group is having problems with turnover, the establishment of a *steady meeting date* is helpful.
- Discussions on the development of masculinity were accompanied during a Berkeley group meeting with each man *undressing* in turn while the other men remained dressed. Each man described the inadequacies he felt about his body. The group reported that of the nine men undressing only one was completely positive about his body. Many of the men were only conscious of their own inadequacies; the discovery that other men who they thought had no problems also felt inadequate made them much more secure with themselves.
- A group-therapy technique which assists introspection is to have each man do a simple *drawing on a paper bag* of two of the people he felt he was as he walked into the room that evening—two sides of his personality. The

group can then discuss to which sides they were sensitive and how their own preoccupation with self may have clouded over any sensitivity.

- Getting men to express emotions and feelings can be stimulated by having each man write a *poem* and reading it first to one or two other men and then to the group.
- As mentioned above, if the group is bogging down or is in conflict, the bringing in of a *trained observer* from the outside or of a person who has been involved in other consciousness-raising groups has helped some groups break out of a downward spiral.
- Some groups have gained a perspective on their discussions by *taking notes* at one or two sessions, writing up the notes and going over each person's observations at a subsequent meeting. A similar technique is to *tape a session* once every two months and observe whether the content and tone of the conversations have changed.
- A discussion of vulnerability can be stimulated by writing on a piece of paper the response to a question such as *"What would a woman have to do to make me vulnerable?"* (For example, "criticize me in a group," "ignore me," and so on.) Then shuffle the papers, redistribute them and have each member read another's paper to the group (keeping the paper anonymous). The responses can be used as a basis for discussion.
- A method to overcome "self-listening" is to open the meeting with the question "What's been happening with you this week?" Ask the question of each person separately, with no one allowed to interrupt. The *rotation* without interruption helps every person to completely listen to the person speaking, and thereby minimizes self-listening. It also sparks a number of possible topics, avoiding reliance on one or two leader types to guide the group into a topic.
- One group used a technique which it said was an old Indian custom that is still practiced at Quaker meetings.

After each person's contribution they allowed *one minute of silence*. It used this method as a way of thinking carefully about what each person said, but it also indirectly encouraged each man to speak more thoughtfully since he knew his comments would be thoroughly considered.

EXPERIMENTS IN NONVERBAL COMMUNICATIONS

- Many groups meet in informal settings, sit on the floor, remove their shoes and occasionally experiment with touching or massaging other members. "We usually keep our eyes closed," one member described, "and I found I often wasn't sure who I was touching. When we tried it in a joint group, I found a woman's toe and a man's toe felt identical! It was the fastest way to get me over my worst hangups about homosexuality. I was getting myself turned on thinking I was touching a woman only to discover the person had too much hair on her legs and had to be a man. I'd then get appropriately turned off until I finally realized the game I was playing with myself. I'm a compulsive heterosexual!"
- A Chicago group met for two hours, during which period they allowed themselves to do anything they wished except engage in conversation. This sensitized the group to the value of nonverbal communication and made any return to intellectualizing appear even more noncommunicative.
- Groups in the Boston and Berkeley areas have experimented with touching exercises which gradually led to touching of the genitals. A number of the straight men reported they recognized for the first time what it felt like to be exploited and trespassed when they were touched before they felt comfortable about it.

TECHNIQUES USEFUL ESPECIALLY FOR JOINT
CONSCIOUSNESS-RAISING

- *Countings and timings.* One of the purposes of the men's
  and women's groups meeting together is to avoid distortions about who is preventing whom from developing. The
  mixed group serves as a laboratory in which interrupting,
  dominance, condescension and automatic role assumptions
  can be caught and stopped while they are happening. Nothing raises consciousness as quickly as catching our stereotyped behavior in progress, but the group is often unaware
  of it occurring. Before the group even starts, as people are
  coming in the door, greeting each other and taking off
  coats, some fascinating counts can be taken (the person
  who does the counting should make sure others are unaware of tes activity) :

1. If there are exchanges of kisses or hugs, who does the initiating? Among persons of the same sex, do the women hug or
   kiss other women more frequently than the men hug or kiss
   other men?
2. After the greeting, count the number of times each man
   initiates touching a woman (e.g., putting an arm around her
   shoulder or momentarily taking her hand or wrist) as opposed
   to each woman initiating the touching of a man. Do the
   women feel comfortable enough to even respond? How does a
   man feel by seldom having someone initiate touching him?

Once the group session has started, try the experiments
listed in Chapter 1 (self-listening, etc.) , along with the following:

1. How often do the women apologize before speaking (as opposed to the men) ? For example, do they preface their statements with "I don't really know about this, but maybe, do
   you think that . . . ?"

2. How often do the men (as opposed to the women) cite authorities to give their own assertion more authority?
3. Watch eye movements. Do the women lower their eyes as they
   speak, and the men use their eyes, as with a direct and confident
   stare, to exert control?
4. Count the number of interruptions made by the men as
   opposed to the women.

The timings or counts have been helpful to many groups
in understanding the unconscious direct power exerted by
men and the indirect power exerted by women. It can also
be observed between consciousness-raising sessions outside
of the weekly meetings. Do business*men* (bosses) put their
arms around their secretaries more frequently than the
secretaries put their arms around bosses? Would the owner of
a house be more likely to put his arms around a servant than
vice-versa? Does the foreman touch the worker more frequently? The teacher the student? *When touching is not
reciprocal it is an indicator of status or power.* It is only when
it is reciprocal that it is a sign of intimacy, according to
extensive studies of touching by Nancy Henley.[2]

The use of first names is the verbal equivalent of nonverbal
touching. When used reciprocally it indicates intimacy; when
used nonreciprocally it indicates the superior status of the
user.

- *Reversing roles* can be employed in a different manner by
  a couples group than in an all-male group. The role reversal can become an actual experiment in which the
  couple reverses roles during a week's period, with the in-
  tention of discussing its success with the group at a subsequent meeting (the follow-through method).

In one couples group the reversal evolved from the woman
admitting that "deep down I don't think my husband can
care for the children as well as I can. I don't think he knows

all the things he has to do to take care of them—like how they look when they're tired and how to feed them properly. He considers me overprotective; I think he'd be completely permissive and let them run wild."

The woman and her attaché did agree, though, to reverse roles during two weeks of the summer vacation. She reported back to the group that although some of her fears were well founded, he acted differently once he had the *responsibility* for the children, including having to live with the results of any neglect. Her husband explained: "I started out by planning to prove that all a woman had to do was carefully organize her day and she would have considerable amounts of free time. I found that my master plan just didn't organize the children, that the phone would ring at unorganized moments, that friends would call once they knew I was home, that I became responsible for staying home while the telephone repairman was supposed to show up but never did, or staying home three days in a row waiting for new drapes to be delivered. I've also become a lot more aware of the importance of doing little things. For example, I was making dinner one evening after a pretty hassled day. I came out to set the table and found it already set. Jona had turned the lights low and lit just two candles. She had wine on the table and a couple of flowers in a small vase. A lump came to my throat. I never thought those little romantic things that I did once in a while 'to please her' could be so important. I'll never forget the way I felt when I first saw that."

- A fascinating method of reversing roles in a mixed group which need not be couples is to have a meeting in which the men attempt to learn something from the women, such as knitting. This process—the men making mistakes, the women trying to correct them, the men saying, "Oh, this casting on or purling is easy" and then messing it up —places the man in a student position. This is in contrast to the man's relationship with a woman as primarily her teacher—the most common situation. Then he will also tend to view the traditional woman's values with a greater appreciation.

- A technique for illustrating the masculine value system in a beginning session of a mixed consciousness-raising group was tried by Dr. Mary Calderone. The women gathered in the center of a circle and discussed the characteristics they would like to see men develop, while the men sat in the back and did not participate in the conversation. She describes the discussion afterwards: "At first, the men were defensive about adjectives they termed predominantly 'feminine,' such as tender, gentle, empathetic, nurturing, artistic. But the women convinced them that these were desirable qualities that would enhance men's own evolution as individuals." She explained the men felt they were "not permitted by society" to develop these qualities, but that they would, now that they thought about it, like to work on developing them.[3]

- A marriage contract is a good method of encouraging a couples group to rethink every aspect of marriage. The general principles for a contract can be discussed profitably by the entire group. The details, though, are probably best worked out in smaller groups of one or two couples. "Bogging down in the details" of a contract is not so bad if the details reflect specific experiences in the past that are likely to arise again. However, when the contract starts to include penalties or is consistently hypothetical projections into the future, then the discussion usually becomes unnecessarily acrimonious. Penalties should not be a necessary part of the contract.[4]

BECOMING A LIBERATED MAN, THEN . . .

Becoming a liberated man, then, is achieving new freedoms—freedom beyond proving oneself; beyond worrying about appearances, on the playing field or in the office; in earned degrees or in job titles; in clothes, status or swagger. It is getting beyond condescension and contempt toward women, needing to be in control and have an answer to all problems at all times; beyond specializing, needing to become the expert, being the sole breadwinner, the victim of male bribes—ultimately a security object. It is learning how to listen rather than dominate or self-listen; to be personal as well as intellectual; to be vulnerable rather than construct façades of infallibility; to be emotional rather than emotionally constipated; to be dependent as well as independent; to value internal, human rewards as well as external rewards. It is recognizing the trap involved in treating women as a sex object while at the same time not becoming a success object. It is being happy at the success of others rather than comparing it to our own success. It is working toward new dimensions of self while not rebelling against the best of the old self. It is being mature enough not to have to always appear mature. It is getting in touch with the childlike parts of our personality—rejoicing at little happinesses as well as big events. It is getting in touch with the feminine parts of our personality—without worrying who's looking. It is being willing to spend hours asking "How do each of these areas apply to me?" rather than searching for the areas where they don't apply. It is always working on the process of liberation rather than thinking one has reached it. Becoming a liberated man, then, is never underestimating the complexity, the joy or the pain of getting in touch with one's humanity.

Notes

1. WOMEN'S LIBERATION AND THE MASCULINE MYSTIQUE: THE NEGLECTED CONNECTION

1. *The New York Times,* August 24, 1970.
2. For example, see Roxanne Dunbar and Lisa Leghorn, "The Man's Problem" in *No More Fun and Games, A Journal of Female Liberation,* Issue Three, pp. 25–28.
3. Evelyn W. Goodenough, "Interest in Persons as an Aspect of Sex Differences in Early Years," *Genetic Psychology Monograph,* Vol. 55 (1957), pp. 287–323.
4. Morris J. Paulson, "Psychological Concomitants of Premenstrual Tension," *American Journal of Obstetrics and Gynecology,* Vol. 81 (1961), pp. 734ff. Paulson relates six environmental and attitudinal factors to premenstrual tension.
5. This example is cited in Charles D. Orth and Frederic Jacobs, "Women in Management: Pattern for Change," *Harvard Business Review,* July–August 1971, p. 141.

2. THE MASCULINE VALUE SYSTEM: MEN DEFINING REALITY

1. Robert S. Wyer, Donald Weatherly, and Glenn Terrell, "Social Role, Aggression, and Academic Achievement," *Journal of Personality and Social Psychology,* Vol. 1, No. 6 (June 1965), pp. 645–648.
2. Charles D. Orth and Frederic Jacobs, "Women in Management: Pattern for Change," *Harvard Business Review,* July–August 1971, p. 141.

3. Credit for this idea to Mimi Lobell, co-author of *John and Mimi*
   (New York: Bantam paperback, 1972).
4. Elizabeth Pochoda, "Even the Sympathetic Ones Are Maddeningly
   Patronizing—It's Separatism or Complete Re-education, Says a Radical in Women's Lib—So Where Do Men Fit In?" *Glamour*, July
   1970, p. 142.
5. *Chronicle of Higher Education*, May 17, 1971.

3. THE DEVELOPMENT OF MASCULINITY

1. Dan Wakefield, *Going All the Way* (New York: Delacorte Press,
   1970), p. 195.
2. Susan Goldberg and Michael Lewis, "Play Behavior in the Year-Old
   Infant: Early Sex Differences," *Child Development*, Vol. 40, No. 1
   (March 1969), p. 29. See also Sylvia Brody, *Patterns of Mothering*
   (New York: International Universities Press, Inc., 1956), p. 356.
   The data for the article by Goldberg and Lewis is drawn from
   children of parents from all classes but limited to Caucasian
   families.
3. Goldberg and Lewis, *op. cit.*, p. 29.
4. *Ibid.*
5. *Ibid.*
6. See J. Money, "Sex Hormones and Other Variables in Human
   Eroticism," and J. L. Hampson and Joan G. Hampson, "The
   Ontogenies of Sexual Behavior in Man," in W. C. Young (ed.),
   Sex and Internal Secretions, Vol. II (Baltimore: Williams and
   Wilkins, 1961); J. Money and Joan G. Hampson, "Idiopathic
   Sexual Precocity in the Male: Management Report of a Case,"
   Psychological Medicine, Vol. 17 (1955), pp. 1–15; and Joan G.
   Hampson, "Hermaphroditic Appearance, Acting and Eroticism in
   Hyperadrenocorticism," *Bulletin of the Johns Hopkins Hospital*,
   Vol. 96 (1955), pp. 265–73. Information on California Gender
   Identity Center cited in Lucy Komisar, "Violence and the Mas-
   culine Mystique," *Washington Monthly*, July 1970.
7. Jerome Kagan and Howard Moss, *Birth to Maturity* (New York:
   John Wiley, 1962) is the source for the high achievers; the source
   for the highly creative is E. P. Torrance, "Sex Role Identification
   and Creative Thinking," *Research Memo* BER–59–10 (Minneap-
   olis, Minnesota: Bureau of Educational Research, University of
   Minnesota, 1959).
8. Cited in Patricia Cayo Sexton, *The Feminized Male* (New York:
   Random House, 1969), p. 93, citing Kagan and Moss, *op. cit.*
9. P. H. Mussen, "Some Antecedents and Consequents of Masculine
   Sex-Typing in Adolescent Boys," *Psychological Monographs*, 1961,
   Vol. 75, No. 2 (Whole No. 506); and P. H. Mussen, "Long-term
   Consequences of Masculinity of Interests in Adolescence," *Journal*

of Consulting Psychology, Vol. 26 (1962), pp. 435–440. Both are cited in Jerome Kagan, "Acquisition and Significance of Sex Typing and Sex Role Identity," in Martin L. Hoffman and Lois Wladis Hoffman, eds., *Review of Child Development Research* (New York: Russell Sage Foundation, 1964).

10. NOW's study is by Women on Words and Images (Central New Jersey NOW), *Dick and Jane as Victims: Sex Stereotyping in Children's Readers* (Princeton, N.J.: Women on Words and Images, 1972). Earlier studies even found females portrayed as being *morally* inferior to males. See I. L. Child, E. H. Potter, and E. M. Levine, "Children's Textbooks and Personality Development," *Psychological Monographs,* 1946, Vol. 60, No. 3 (Whole No. 279), p. 32.

11. Women on Words and Images, *op. cit.,* p. 33.

12. Lorrie McLaughlin, "Out of Her Shell," in Helen M. Robinson, *et al.* (eds.), *More Roads to Follow* (Chicago: Scott, Foresman and Co., 1965), p. 24, as cited in *Ibid.,* p. 24.

13. Story regarding Girl Scout dinner, S.R.A. Comprehensive Reading Series, Level K (1966), as cited in *Ibid.,* p. 68.

14. Irma Simonton Black, ed., "After School," in *Around the City,* The Bank Street Readers (New York: Macmillan, 1965), p. 29, as cited in *Ibid.,* p. 65.

15. Lippincott's Basic Reading Teacher's Edition, H Book (New York: Lippincott, 1970), p. 191, cited in *Ibid.,* p. 64.

16. Sophia Lyon Faho and Dorothy T. Spoerl, "A Boy Full of Troubles" in *Beginnings: Earth, Sky, Life, Death,* in Helen M. Robinson *et al.* (eds.), *Cavalcades: Book 6* (Chicago: Scott, Foresman and Co., 1965), p. 363, cited in *Ibid.,* p. 65.

17. Lippincott's Basic Reading, *op. cit.,* p. 273, cited in *Ibid.,* p. 64.

18. Sexton, *op. cit.,* p. 93, citing Kagan and Moss, *op. cit.*

19. Ruth E. Hattley, "Children's Concepts of Male and Female Roles," *Merrill-Palmer Quarterly,* Winter 1959, p. 85.

20. Kagan, *op. cit.,* p. 162.

21. Brown, *op. cit.,* pp. 197–202, cited in Sexton, *op. cit.,* p. 100.

22. Susan W. Gray, "Perceived Similarity to Parents and Adjustment," *Child Development,* Vol. 30 (1959), pp. 91–107, cited in Sexton, *op. cit.*

23. Fortune Survey, *Fortune,* August 1946, cited in Sexton, *op. cit.*

24. M. Raban, "Sex-Role Identification in Young Children in Two Diverse Social Groups," *Genetic Psychological Monograph* 42 (1950), pp. 81–158, cited in Kagan, *op. cit.,* p. 153.

25. Lippincott's Basic Reading, *op. cit.,* p. 42 in Women on Words and Images (Central New Jersey NOW), *op. cit.,* p. 64.

26. Irma Simonton Black (ed.), "Jack and the Beanstalk" in *My City,* The Bank Street Readers, *op. cit.,* p. 103, cited in *Ibid.*

27. Eldonna Everts and Byron H. Van Roeke (eds.), *Seven Seas,* Basic Reading Program, Book 6 (Evanston, Illinois: Harper and Row, 1966), p. 406, cited in *Ibid.,* p. 66.

28. Susan W. Gray, "Masculinity-Femininity in Relation to Anxiety and Social Acceptance," *Child Development,* Vol. 28, No. 2 (June 1957), pp. 203–214.

29. Another difference between the physical and student strivers is the physical striver's preference for contact sports such as boxing at about a four-to-one ratio to student strivers, or academically high achieving boys. Many noncontact sports such as tennis are preferred by the student strivers. See, for example, Sexton, *op. cit.,* p. 69.

30. Psychotherapist Jeanne Knakal, during a conversation with Myron Brenton cited in Myron Brenton, *The American Male* (London: Unwin Brothers Ltd., 1967), p. 13.

31. John Canaday, "A Wasp's Progress," *The New York Times Magazine,* March 19, 1972, p. 88.

32. Richard Hale, *Brother: A Forum for Racism and Sexism,* No. 4, April 1972.

33. *Ibid.*

34. Robert M. Liebert, "Television and Social Learning: Some Relationships between Viewing Violence and Behaving Aggressively" (Overview) in *Television and Social Behavior:* A Report to the Surgeon General from the Surgeon General's Scientific Advisory Committee on Television and Social Behavior, Volumes 1–5 (Washington, D.C.: National Institute of Mental Health, U.S. Government Printing Office, 1972).

35. M. L. Kohn, "Social Class and Parental Values," *American Journal of Sociology,* 1959, Volume 64, pp. 337–351; and R. R. Sears, E. E. Maccoby and H. Levin, *Patterns of Child Rearing* (Evanston, Illinois: Row, Peterson, 1957).

36. Jerome Kagan, *op. cit.*

37. Germaine Greer, *The Female Eunuch* (New York: McGraw-Hill, 1971), p. 30.

38. *Ibid.,* p. 258.

39. Myron Brenton, *op. cit.,* pp. 142–143.

40. Jhan and June Robbins, "Why Young Husbands Feel Trapped," *Redbook* (March 1962), cited in *ibid.,* p. 142.

41. Garry Wills, *Nixon Agonistes* (New York: New American Library, Signet Books, 1971), p. 541.

42. See Wakefield, *op. cit.,* p. 176.

4. THE CONFINES OF MASCULINITY

1. Interview reported in Sunday Newark *Star-Ledger,* October 31, 1971, p. 64.

2. Reported in Sunday Newark *Star-Ledger,* October 31, 1971, Health

and Medicine section.

3. Ruth Free, "Cross-Cultural Sex Roles: An Anthropological View," paper delivered at Seton Hall University Symposium on Sex Roles and Social Change, March 22, 1972.

4. Greer, *op. cit.*, p. 305.

5. *Ibid.*, pp. 34.

6. Brenton, *op. cit.*, pp. 22–23.

7. Erving Goffman, *Asylums: Essays on the Social Situation of Mental Patients and Other Inmates* (Garden City: Doubleday Anchor Books, 1961), p. 386.

8. *The New York Times*, March 9, 1972, p. 32.

9. T. W. Adorno, Else Frenkel-Brunswik, Daniel J. Levinson and R. Nevitt Sandford, *The Authoritarian Personality* (New York: Harper and Brothers, 1950), p. 235.

10. See Jerome P. Skolnick, *Justice Without Trial: Law Enforcement in Democratic Society* (New York: John Wiley and Sons, Inc., 1966), p. 61, cited in Arthur Niederhoffer, *Behind the Shield: The Police in Urban Society* (Garden City, N.Y.: Doubleday, 1967), p. 117.

11. See Niederhoffer, *op. cit.*, pp. 116–117.

12. See Chapter 11, "Highlights of Experiments on Changing Men's Attitudes."

13. Max Weber, *Essays in Sociology*, translated by H. H. Gerth and C. W. Mills (New York: Oxford University Press, 1946), p. 214.

14. See Louis J. Cutrona, Jr., "What Goes on Inside a Men's Liberation Rap Group," *Glamour*, August 1971.

15. Nicholas von Hoffman, "Misogyny in Everyday Life," Washington *Post*, August 14, 1970.

16. Anne Steinmann and David J. Fox, *The Male Dilemma* (New York: Jason Aronson, 1973).

17. E. M. Bennet and L. R. Cohen, "Men and Women: Personality Patterns and Contrasts," *Genetic Psychology Monograph* 59 (1959), pp. 101–155; and Pauline S. Sear, "Doll Play Aggression in Normal Young Children: Influence of Sex, Age, Sibling Status, Father's Absence," *Psychological Monograph*, 1951, Vol. 65, No. 6 (Whole No. 323), p. 42.

18. *The New York Times*, March 8, 1973. The Police Department actually posts *Wanted* ads to actively censure or dismiss violators of these rules.

19. See Robert Luce, "From Hero to Robot: Masculinity in America— Stereotype and Reality," *Psychoanalytic Review*, Vol. 54, No. 4 (1967), pp. 53–74.

20. John P. Kee and Alex C. Sherriffs, "Men's and Women's Beliefs, Ideals, and Self-Concepts" in Jerome Seidman, *The Adolescent: A Book of Readings* (New York: Holt, Rinehart & Winston, 1960).

21. *Ibid.*

5. SUPER BOWL: SEXISM, PATRIOTISM, RELIGION, GANGS AND WARFARE

1. *The New York Times,* January 15, 1972, estimated this number of Americans as the number watching the Super Bowl on January 15, 1972.
2. *Ibid.*
3. Most of whom are males.
4. *The New York Times,* March 4, 1972.
5. *Ibid.*
6. "The Wedge Meets the Headhunters," *Life,* December 3, 1971, p. 34.
7. *Ibid.,* p. 39.
8. *Ibid.,* p. 34.
9. Dave Meggyesy, *Out of Their League* (Berkeley, Calif.: Ramparts Press, 1970) , p. 24.
10. The telephone inquiry was made of an ABC-TV general producer on February 9, 1971.
11. Interview in Dayton, Ohio, on March 9, 1972. Phil Donahue is the host of *The Phil Donahue Show.*
12. This entire experience can also be applied to Little League baseball. However, the girl in the town with Little League baseball often has no source of rewards—not even the equivalent of figure skating.
13. Meggyesy, *op. cit.,* p. 20.
14. *Ibid.,* p. 181.
15. *Ibid.,* p. 50.
16. *Ibid.,* p. 182.
17. *Ibid.,* p. 75.
18. *Ibid.,* pp. 182–183.
19. The way lower-class values are adopted by the middle class for national and international (e.g., foreign policy) purposes is discussed by William Kvaraceus and Walter B. Miller, *Delinquent Behavior: Culture and the Individual* (Washington, D.C.: National Education Association, 1959) , p. 65.
20. Marvin E. Wolfgang, *Patterns in Criminal Homicide* (New York: Wiley, 1966) , pp. 269–283.
21. Gene Weingarten, "East Bronx Story—Return of the Street Gangs," *New York,* Vol. 5, No. 13, March 27, 1972, p. 33.
22. *Ibid.,* p. 34.
23. Talcott Parsons, *Essays in Sociological Theory,* rev. ed. (Glencoe, Ill.: Free Press, 1954) , A. K. Cohen, *Delinquent Boys: The Culture of the Gang* (Glencoe, Ill.: Free Press, 1955) , W. B. Miller, "Lower Class Culture as a Generating Milieu of Gang Delinquency,"

Journal of Social Issues, Vol. 14, No. 3 (1958). From Richard Cloward, *Delinquency and Opportunity* (Glencoe, Ill.: Free Press, 1960), pp. 48–51.

24. Walter B. Miller, "Violent Crimes in City Gangs," in Thomas Dye, *Politics in the Metropolis* (Columbus: Charles E. Merrill Books, Inc., 1967), p. 141.

25. Yablonsky, Lewis, *The Violent Gang* (New York: Macmillan Co., 1963), p. vi.

26. *Ibid.*, p. x.

27. *Ibid.*, p. 16.

28. *Ibid.*, p. 8.

29. Walter B. Miller, "Violent Crimes," p. 133.

30. Robert K. Merton, *Social Theory and Social Structures* (New York: The Free Press, 1957), pp. 227–236.

31. R. R. Sears, Eleanor E. Maccoby, and H. Levin. *Patterns of Child Rearing* (New York: Harper, 1957). Cited in Walter Mischel, "A Social Learning View of Sex Differences in Behavior" in Eleanor Maccoby, ed., *The Development of Sex Differences* (Stanford: Stanford University Press, 1966), p. 73.

32. Miller, *op. cit.*, "Violent Crimes," p. 141.

33. Lucy Komisar, "Violence and the Masculine Mystique," *Washington Monthly*, July 1970.

34. Neil Sheehan *et al.*, *The Pentagon Papers* (New York: Bantam, 1971), pp. 630–637.

35. "The Wedge . . . ," *op. cit.*, p. 34.

36. D. B. Leventhal and K. M. Shember, "Sex Role Adjustment and Nonsanctioned Aggression," *Journal of Experimental Research in Personality*, Vol. 3, 1969, pp. 283–286. The authors used the Guilford-Zimmerman Index of Masculine Interests to determine masculine values.

37. Sexton, *op. cit.*, p. 130.

38. See Peter Corning, "An Evolutionary-Adaptive Theory of Aggression," American Political Science Association meeting, Chicago, September 1971, for a review of this literature. Corning is at Stanford University, as of 1974.

39. A. Bandura, "Relationship of Family Patterns to Child Behavior Disorders," Progress Report, 1960, U.S.P.H. Research Grant M1734, Stanford University.

40. Theodore N. Ferdinand, "Psychological Femininity and Political Liberalism," *Sociometry*, Vol. 27, No. 1, March 1964, p. 75.

41. Leventhal and Shemberg, *op. cit.*

42. Jerome Kagan, "Acquisition and Significance of Sex Typing and Sex Role Identity," in Martin L. Hoffman and Lois Wladis Hoffman, *Review of Child Development Research* (Russell Sage Foundation, 1964).

6. MASCULINE IMAGES IN ADVERTISING

1. Pierre Martineau, *Motivation in Advertising* (New York: McGraw-Hill, 1957), p. 141.
2. Leslie Gill, *Advertising and Psychology* (London; New York: Hutchinson, 1954), p. 169.
3. Ralph Glasser, *The New High Priesthood* (London: Macmillan, 1967), p. 30.
4. Martineau, *op. cit.*, p. 141.
5. *Ibid.*, p. 141.
6. *Ibid.*, p. 142.
7. Ernest Dichter, *Handbook of Consumer Motivations* (New York: McGraw-Hill, 1964), p. 443.
8. Martineau, *op. cit.*, p. 65.
9. *Esquire Magazine*, June 1971, p. 6.
10. For example, see *Esquire Magazine*, January 1971, inside front cover.
11. *Business Week*, May 15, 1971, p. 88.
12. *Business Week*, June 26, 1971, pp. 22–23.
13. *The New Yorker*, April 22, 1972, p. 135.
14. *Business Week*, May 22, 1971, p. 110.
15. *Esquire Magazine*, June 1971, p. 81.
16. *The New Yorker*, April 22, 1972, p. 16.
17. Glasser, *op. cit.*, p. 21.
18. Dichter, *op. cit.*, pp. 113–114.
19. *Esquire Magazine*, February 1971, p. 121.
20. *New York Magazine*, April 17, 1972.
21. NOW, "How WABC-TV Projects a Biased Portrayal of Women's Role in Society," p. 13.
22. American Cancer Society, "'72 Cancer Facts and Figures," p. 5 (projected 1972 deaths).
23. Dr. William Asher, "Young Drivers Who Die," *Concepts* Spring–Summer 1972.
24. Advertisement appeared in *The New York Times Magazine*, October 10, 1971, p. 4. The poem was taken from a collection of poems by fifth-graders published by the Creativity Center of Fordham University, under the sponsorship of the Center for Urban Education.
25. *Life*, June 12, 1970.
26. *Business Week*, October 25, 1969, p. 22.
27. *Business Week*, November 15, 1969.

7. THE FAMILY: REDEFINING MOTHERHOOD AND FATHERHOOD

1. See as examples David Graham Cooper, *The Death of the Family* (New York: Pantheon Books, 1971) and R. D. Laing, *The Politics*

of the Family and Other Essays (New York: Pantheon Books, 1971).

2. Robert Lane, *Political Thinking and Consciousness* (Chicago: Markham Publishing Co., 1969), pp. 262–263.

3. David J. Levy, "Anti-Nazis: Criteria of Differentiation," in Alfred H. Stanton and Stewart E. Perry (eds.), *Personality and Political Crisis* (Glencoe, Ill.: Free Press, 1951), p. 155.

4. Russell Middleton and Snell Putney, "Political Expression of Adolescent Rebellion," *American Journal of Sociology*, Vol. 68 (1954), pp. 527–535.

5. See Nena O'Neill and George O'Neill, *Open Marriage* (New York: M. Evans & Co., 1972) and Carl R. Rogers, *Becoming Partners: Marriage and Its Alternatives* (New York: Delacorte Press, 1972). The family and marriage may appear to be on the way out, since it is now an unusual marriage that lasts more than ten years. But it is just as unusual a commune that lasts more than one year. The family and marriage cannot be easily dismissed as an option if we are to avoid imposing new dogmas in the name of liberation.

6. Evelyn W. Goodenough, "Interest in Persons as an Aspect of Sex Differences in the Early Years," *Genetic Psychological Monograph*, Vol. 55, 1957, pp. 287–323, cited in Patricia Cayo Sexton, *The Feminized Male* (New York: Random House, 1969), p. 100.

7. Betty Friedan, *The Feminine Mystique* (New York: Norton, 1963). See especially Chapter 2.

8. B. Seay, B. K. Alexander and H. F. Harlow, "Maternal Behavior of Socially Deprived Rhesus Monkeys," *Journal of Abnormal and Social Psychology*, Vol. 69, No. 4 (1964), pp. 347.

9. *Ibid.*

10. M. I. Heinstein, "Behavioral Correlates of Breast-Bottle Regimes under Varying Parent-Infant Relationships," Monograph of Society for Research in Child Development, Vol. 28, No. 4 (1963), cited in John Nash, "The Father in Contemporary Culture and Current Psychological Literature," in *Child Development*, Vol. 36, No. 1 (1965), pp. 261–297.

11. See Joan Curlee, "Alcoholism and the 'Empty Nest,'" *Bulletin of the Menninger Clinic*, Vol. 33 (1968), pp. 165–171.

12. See Pauline Bart, "Depression in Middle-Aged Women: Some Sociocultural Factors," *Dissertation Abstracts*, Vol. 28 (1968), p. 4752.

13. Norman L. Farberow and Edwin F. Schneidman, "Statistical Comparisons Between Attempted and Committed Suicides" in *The Cry for Help* (New York: McGraw-Hill, 1965).

14. Otto Pollak, *The Criminality of Women* (Philadelphia: The University of Pennsylvania Press, 1950), p. 84 and pp. 20–21.

15. See, for examples, Edmund Dahlstrom, *The Changing Roles of Men and Women* (London: Duckworth, 1967) and John Nash,

op. cit.; and E. Mavis Hetherington, "A Developmental Study of the Effects of Sex of the Dominant Parent on Sex-Role Preference Identification and Imitations in Children," *Journal of Personality and Social Psychology,* Vol. 2, No. 2 (August 1965).

16. Joseph Veroff and Sheila Feld, *Marriage and Work in America: A Study of Motives and Roles* (New York: Van Nostrand Reinhold Co., 1970), p. 335.

17. Maccoby, *op. cit., The Development of Sex Differences,* pp. 36–37, cited in Greer, *op. cit.,* p. 95. Again, if a father were kept at home to take care of children only, his dominance would also inhibit the child's creativity and development.

18. David Levy, *Maternal Overprotection* (New York: Columbia University Press, 1943).

19. L. M. Terman and C. C. Miles, *Sex and Personality: Studies in Masculinity and Femininity* (New York: McGraw-Hill, 1936); see also I. Bieber, *et al., Homosexuality, A Psychoanalytic Study* (New York: Basic Books, 1962), the source of the .001 statistic, Robert Stoller, *Sex and Gender* (New York: Science House, 1968), and G. Gorer, *The American People* (New York: W. W. Norton, 1964).

20. *Ibid.*

21. F. Nye, "Employment of Mothers and Adjustment of Adolescent Children," *Marriage and Family Living,* Vol. 21, No. 3 (1959).

22. W. L. Chinn, "A Brief Survey of Nearly 1,000 Juvenile Delinquents, *British Journal of Educational Psychology,* Vol. 8 (1938), pp. 78–85.

23. R. G. Andry, "Faulty Paternal and Maternal Child-Relationship, Affection and Delinquency," *British Journal of Delinquency,* Vol. 97, 1960, pp. 329–340.

24. L. Eisenberg, "The Fathers of Autistic Children," *American Journal of Orthopsychiatry,* 1957, pp. 715–725. For similar results with maladjusted children see W. Warren and K. Cameron, "Reactive Psychosis in Adolescence," *Journal of Mental Science,* Vol. 96 (1950), pp. 448–457, and Portia Holman, "The Etiology of Maladjustment in Children," *Journal of Mental Science,* Vol. 99 (1959), pp. 654–688.

25. See Per Olav Tiller, "Parental Role Division and the Child's Personality Development," in Dahlstrom, *op. cit.,* p. 88, and Leon J. Yarrow, "Separation from Parents during Early Childhood," in Martin Hoffman and Lois W. Hoffman, *Review of Child Development Research* (New York: Russell Sage Foundation, 1964).

26. T. Ferguson and J. Cunnison, *The Young Wage-Earner* (London: Oxford University Press, 1951). The authors' implicit definition of delinquency—convictions for breaking the law—may disregard inadequacies of the law, but data which attempts to take such in-

adequacies into account is not available in statistical form to this writer's knowledge.

27. Eleanor E. Maccoby, "Effects Upon Children of Their Mothers' Outside Employment," in Norman W. Bell and Ezra F. Vogel, eds., *A Modern Introduction to the Family* (New York: The Free Press, 1960), p. 524.

28. Charlotte Perkins Gilman, *The Man-Made World, Our Androcentric Culture* (New York: Charton Co., 1911), reprinted by Source Book Press, p. 45.

29. Raphael Patai, *Women in the Modern World* (New York: The Free Press, 1967), p. 457.

30. Artie Gianopulous and Howard Mitchell, "Marital Disagreement in Working Wife Marriages as a Function of Husband's Attitude toward Wife's Employment," *Marriage and Family Living*, XIX (November 1957), pp. 373–378.

31. *Ibid.*

32. F. Ivan Nye and Lois W. Hoffman, *The Employed Mother in America* (Chicago: Rand McNally & Co., 1963), p. 272.

33. David Levy, *Maternal Overprotection* (New York: Columbia University Press, 1943).

34. Brenton, *op. cit.,* p. 22.

35. Reported by *The New York Times* (September 4, 1963).

36. Vance Packard, *The Pyramid Climbers* (New York: McGraw-Hill Book Co., 1962), Chapter 20.

37. Brenton, *op. cit.,* p. 19.

38. See A. R. Crane, "A Note on Pre-Adolescent Gangs," *Australasian Journal of Psychology and Philosophy*, Vol. 3 (1951), pp. 36–43, and F. M. Thrasher, *The Gang* (Chicago: University of Chicago Press, 1927).

39. Tiller, *op. cit.*

40. E. S. Ostrovsky, *Father to the Child* (New York: G. P. Putnam, 1959).

41. H. L. Kohn and J. A. Clauson, "Parental Authority Behavior and Schizophrenic Patient," *American Journal of Psychiatry*, Vol. 106 (1949), pp. 332–345, cited in Nash, *op. cit.,* p. 275.

42. W. N. Stephens, "Judgments by Social Workers on Boys and Mothers in Fatherless Families," *Journal of Genetic Psychology*, Vol. 99 (1961), pp. 59–64.

43. M. M. Johnson, "Sex Role Learning in the Nuclear Family," *Child Development*, Vol. 34 (1963), pp. 319–333.

44. James K. Skipper and Charles McCaghy, paper delivered at American Sociological Association, September 1969, reported in New York *Post*, September 3, 1969.

45. Tiller, *op. cit.,* pp. 79–105, based on Tiller's study, "Father Absence and Personality Development of Children in Sailor Families,"

Nordisk psykologi's monografiserie, No. 9, Einar Munksgaards forlag, Kobehavn 1958. See also E. Gronsetti, "The Impact of Father-Absence in Sailor Families Upon the Personality Structure and Social Adjustment of Adult Sailor Sons," Part I. N. Anderson, ed., *Studies of the Family,* Vol. 2. Gottingen: Bandenoeck and Ruprecht, 1957, pp. 97–114.

46. *Ibid.*
47. Patai, *op. cit.,* p. 119.
48. Lane, in *Political Thinking and Consciousness,* defines attachment through specific comments in his interviews which indicated that the boy would rather be home than away from home, that his family tolerated dissent and was supportive. See Robert Lane, *Political Thinking and Consciousness* (Chicago: Markham Publishing Co., 1969), p. 298.
49. Parsons and Bales, *op. cit.,* pp. 13–15.
50. *Ibid.,* p. 21.
51. Veroff and Feld, *op. cit.,* p. 330.
52. Lane, *op. cit.,* p. 297.
53. Donald E. Payne and Paul H. Mussen, "Parent Child Relations and Father Identification Among Adolescent Boys," *The Journal of Abnormal and Social Psychology,* Vol. 52 (May 1956). Also, Paul Mussen and Luther Distler, "Masculinity Identification and Father-Son Relationships," *The Journal of Abnormal and Social Psychology,* Vol. 59 (November 1959). Also, Charlotte Himber, "So He Hates Baseball," *The New York Times Magazine* (August 29, 1965).
54. Torrance, *Guiding Creative Talent* (Englewood Cliffs, N.J.: Prentice-Hall, 1962), p. 78.
55. D. W. MacKinnon, "What Do We Mean by Talent and How Do We Test for It?" *The Search for Talent* (New York: College Entrance Examination Board, 1960), pp. 20–29, cited in Torrance, *ibid.,* p. 68.

8. CONCRETE ALTERNATIVES: TOWARD A MEN'S LIBERATION MOVEMENT

1. Edith H. Grotberg (ed.), *Day Care: Resources for Decisions* (Washington, D.C.: Office of Economic Opportunity, Office of Planning, Research, and Evaluation, June 1971), p. 121.
2. R. E. Hartley, "Children's Concepts of Male and Female Roles," *Merrill-Palmer Quarterly,* Vol. 6 (1966), pp. 83–91.
3. Mott, 1954, cited in Grotberg, p. 121.
4. See Grotberg, *op. cit.,* p. 436.
5. *Ibid.,* pp. 78–79.
6. See citation in "Bibliography for Starting a Child-care Center" about Ford Foundation.

7. Grotberg, *op. cit.*, p. 122.

8. *Ibid.*, p. 64.

9. *Ibid.*, p. 122.

10. Ingrid Frederiksson, "Sex Roles and Education in Sweden," *N.Y.U. Education Quarterly*, Vol. 3, No. 2, Winter 1972, p. 20.

11. Birger Wiklund, Mya slöjden bra för vänskapen mellan pojkar och flickor, "PM Pedagogiska meddelanden froån Skolöverstyrelsen" (Stockholm 0, 7, 1970) cited in Frederiksson, *ibid.*, p. 21.

12. *The New York Times*, April 6, 1972, which found from an interview with Riva Poor of Cambridge (a specialist on the short workweek) that 1,000 companies were transferring to the plan and from a survey by the Conference Board (a citizens' organization that studies corporations) that 700 are already using it.

13. Keneth Wheeler, *et al.*, *The Four Day Work Week* (New York: The American Management Association, 1972) pp. 4–5.

14. Reported in *The New York Times*, March 25, 1971. Survey taken from February 19–21, 1971.

15. See *The New York Times*, April 6, 1972.

16. Grotberg, *op. cit.*, p. 85.

17. Reported by the Port of New York Authority and the Downtown-Lower Manhattan Association in April, 1972, after a two-year study, reported in *The New York Times*, April 4, 1972, p. 1.

18. Telephone interview with Mr. Midttun, lawyer for Norwegian Embassy in the United States, September 28, 1973.

19. Robert O. Blood and D. M. Wolfe, *Husbands and Wives: The Dynamics of Modern Living* (Glencoe: The Free Press, 1960), p. 60.

20. *Ibid.*, pp. 54–57.

21. The task force is an official part of NOW. Although the author is its present coordinator, current information may always be obtained by writing the national headquarters at 5 South Wabash, Suite 1615, Chicago, Illinois 60603.

22. Under Executive Order 11246, as amended by 11375; enforced by Office òf Federal Contract Compliance.

23. Lgr 69. Läroplan för grundskolan. Stockholm: Svenska Utbildningsförlaget Liber AB, 1969, cited in Frederiksson, *op. cit.*, p. 22.

24. Birger Wiklund, Mya slöjden bra för vänskapen mellan pojkar och flickor, *loc. cit.*

9. FACTUAL AND SELF-FULFILLING MYTHS

1. The Women's Bureau, U.S. Department of Labor, telephone interview with Mary Kramer for latest figure as of October 1, 1973.

2. Bernice Sandler, "Patterns of Discrimination and Discouragement in Higher Education," in New York City Commission on Human Rights, *Women's Role in Contemporary Society* (New York: Avon

Books, 1972), p. 568, and telephone interview with Ms. Sandler on October 1, 1973, for 1973 data.

3. Datagram, *Journal of Medical Education,* February 1972 (figure for 1973 from Association of Medical Colleges).

4. The Division of Legislation and Standards, Women's Bureau, U.S. Dept. of Labor, interviews with Pearl Spindler and Bea Rosenberg, September 28 and October 1, 1973. See also *Congressional Quarterly,* July 10, 1970, p. 1745.

5. Judith Nies, "The Abzug Campaign: A Lesson in Politics," *Ms.,* February 1973, p. 78.

6. See G. Rattray Taylor, *Sex in History* (London: Thames and Hudson, 1953).

7. Patai, *op. cit.,* p. 110.

8. Taylor, *op. cit.,* p. 65.

9. Brenton, *op. cit.,* p. 148.

10. *Handbook on Women Workers, op. cit.,* p. 76.

11. Caroline Bird, *Born Female* (New York: David McKay and Co., 1968), p. 67.

12. A survey conducted by Prentice-Hall editors of companies' hiring policies of college graduates, reported in Prentice-Hall, "Why Doesn't Business Hire More College-Trained Women?" Report Bulletin 4, Volume XVI, April 15, 1969, p. 296.

13. *Ibid.*

14. Dr. Bernice Sandler, *op. cit.,* pp. 570–571.

15. Sandler, *op. cit.,* p. 568.

16. *Ibid.*

17. See "Why So Few Women Doctors? The U.S. Lags," *The New York Sunday News,* February 15, 1970, pp. 5–8.

18. *Ibid.*

19. Patai, *op. cit.,* p. 447.

20. Dr. R. D. Gillespie, *Psychological Effects of War on Citizens and Soldiers* (1942), study cited in Montagu, *The Natural Superiority of Women* (New York: Macmillan, 1968), pp. 95–96.

21. Drs. Thomas F. Pugh and Brian MacMahon, study cited in Montagu, *op. cit.,* p. 86. Also Sexton, *op. cit.,* p. 7.

22. Department of Transportation, *Motor Vehicles Assigned Risk Plans,* August 1970, pp. 26–27.

23. *1970 Statistical Abstracts of the United States,* pp. 145–147.

24. For levels of stability, see Morroe Berger, *The Arab World Today* (Garden City: Doubleday Anchor Books, 1962) and Manfred Halpern, *The Politics of Social Change in the Middle East and North Africa* (Princeton, New Jersey: Princeton University Press, 1963); for Arab sex role differentiation see Patai, *op. cit.,* pp. 106–129.

25. "Man Has No 'Killer' Instinct," in Ashley Montagu, ed., *Man and Aggression* (New York: Oxford University Press, 1968), pp. 27–37.

26. See "Most Men Try to Tease Women 'To Death' at Work," Salisbury *Evening Post* (North Carolina), August 3, 1970 for elaboration on the next paragraph.

27. Montagu, *op. cit.*, p. 58.

28. Sexton, *op. cit.*, p. 9.

29. *Ibid.*

30. F. J. Kelly and C. S. Berry, *Special Education: The Handicapped and Gifted*, White House Conference on Child Health and Protection (N.Y.: Appleton-Century-Crofts, 1931) cited in *ibid.*, p. 10.

31. H. Schuell, *Differences Which Matter: A Study of Boys and Girls* (Austin, Texas: Von-Boeckman-Jones, 1945).

32. Frances Bentzen, "Sex Ratios in Learning and Behavior Disorders" *The National Elementary Principal*, Vol. 46, No. 2 (November 1966), pp. 13–17.

33. Montagu, *op. cit.*, pp. 74–77.

34. *Ibid.*, p. 78.

35. Andrew Sinclair, *The Emancipation of the American Woman* (N.Y.: Harper and Rowe, 1966), p. 179.

36. A. C. Kinsey, *et al.*, and the staff of the Institute for Sex Research, Indiana University, *Sexual Behavior in the Human Female* (Philadelphia: W. B. Saunders Co., 1953). More recently, see Jessie Bernard, *The Future of Marriage* (New York: World Publishing Co., 1972).

37. *The New York Times*, August 24, 1970.

38. The Rumania and Czechoslovakia figures are both from "Political Activity of Women in Eastern Europe," in *Annals, op. cit.*, pp. 67–71.

39. *The Village Voice*, November 27, 1969 (italics hers).

40. *Ibid.*

41. Montagu, *op. cit.*, p. 59.

42. *Ibid.*

43. D. Wechsler, *The Measurement of Adult Intelligence* (Baltimore: Williams and Wilkins, 1941), cited in Sexton, *op. cit.*, p. 109.

44. Montagu, *op. cit.*, p. 126.

45. *Ibid.*, p. 125. See also I. H. Anderson, B. O. Hughes, and W. R. Dixon, "The Rate of Reading Development and Its Relation to Age of Learning to Read, Sex and Intelligence," *Journal of Educational Research*, Vol. 50, 1957, pp. 481–89, and Mildred C. Hughes, "Sex Differences in Reading Achievement in the Elementary Grades," *Supplementary Educational Monograph* cited in Robert D. Hess and Judith V. Torney, *The Development of Political Attitudes in Children* (Garden City: Anchor Books, 1967), p. 201.

46. Sexton, *op. cit.*, p. 10.

47. Frances Bentzen, *op. cit.*

48. Montagu, *op. cit.*, p. 126.

49. Findings by J. W. Everett indicate that certain environmental variables, such as handling, illumination, exposure to cold, and mechanical stimulation of the cervix will influence the timing of puberty in rats and guinea pigs. Maccoby points out this possibility of environmental influence with application to human beings has not been adequately explored. See J. W. E. Everett, "Central Neural Control of Reproductive Functions of the Adrenohyphysis," *Physiological Reviews*, Vol. 44, 1964, pp. 373–431.

50. J. M. Tanner, *Growth at Adolescence* (2d ed.) (Oxford: Blackwell Scientific Publications, 1962), cited in *ibid.*

51. Philip Goldberg, "Are Women Prejudiced Against Women?" *Trans-Action*, April 1968, pp. 28–30.

10. WOMEN'S LIBERATION AS MEN'S LIBERATION: TWENTY-ONE EXAMPLES

1. Marya Mannes, "Women's Lib: Can Men Gain?", Sunday Newark *Star-Ledger*, December 13, 1970, Section 3, p. 1.

2. The use of "marriage" and "husband and wife" is done for the sake of brevity, but application of all these points applies to any man and woman living together, and usually under most alternate life styles as well.

3. See Alfred C. Kinsey, *et al.*, and the Staff of the Institute for Sex Research, Indiana University, *Sexual Behavior in the Human Female* (Philadelphia: W. B. Saunders, 1953), pp. 355ff., and Vance Packard, *The Sexual Wilderness* (New York: David McKay Co., Inc., 1968), p. 507.

4. Abraham H. Maslow, *Motivation and Personality* (New York: Harper, 1954), p. 257, cited in Betty Friedan, *op. cit.*, p. 312.

5. *Ibid.*, p. 245.

6. Greer, *op. cit.*, p. 242.

7. Reported in *The New York Times*, March 25, 1971. Poll conducted from February 19–21, 1971.

8. This point called to my attention by Lenore Saari.

9. Evidence of this figure was presented to me by the man who washes our windows, who explained he was faster and therefore made slightly more than most.

10. See, for additional information, Seth Low and Pearl Spindler, "Child Care Arrangements of Working Mothers in the United States," Children's Bureau, U.S. Department of Health, Education and Welfare and Women's Bureau, U.S. Department of Labor, 1968. Also see "Federal Funds for Daycare Projects," Women's Bureau, U.S. Department of Labor, February, 1969.

11. As Simone de Beauvoir, who until recently identified herself as a socialist and not a feminist, recently admitted, socialism is no pre-

requisite to women's liberation—that, in practice, it has never brought about the equality of women. She now believes feminism must come prior to and independent of socialism. Simone de Beauvoir is the author of *The Second Sex* (New York: Alfred A. Knopf, 1952), one of the most influential books behind the feminist movement. However, she only moved recently from identifying primarily as a socialist to identifying primarily as a feminist, as reported in an interview in "The Radicalization of Simone de Beauvoir," *Ms.* Magazine, July 1972. This is not to deny, of course, that capitalism may fight long and hard against that which will ultimately be to its benefit. The American Medical Association did this with Medicaid and men are presently doing this with women's liberation.

12. Reprinted in *The Militant,* August 7, 1970, as an example of women's advertising image. The italics ("*un*balanced") are mine.

13. Kagan, *op. cit.,* p. 163.

14. *Ibid.,* p. 161.

15. The Family Law Act which went into effect in 1970 in California, for example, provides for 50–50 division of community family property and alimony payments based to such an extent on need rather than sex that it is called "spousal support."

16. As late as 1961, eighteen states permitted women to be automatically exempted from service on jury duty. In 1970, in the state of New York, the decision for the case of *Leighton v. Goodman,* upheld the exemption. However, it did note that "the times may very well be ripe" for a change in the statutes. See John D. Johnston, Jr., and Charles L. Knapp, "Sex Discrimination by Law: a Study in Judicial Perspective," *New York University Law Review,* Vol. 46, No. 4 (October 1971), pp. 717–719.

17. The 1972 amendment to H.R. 1 provides for the equalization of these benefits as of 1975.

18. Dr. Effie Ellis, Special Assistant to the Vice President, American Medical Association.

11. HIGHLIGHTS OF EXPERIMENTS ON CHANGING MEN'S ATTITUDES

1. References to high, medium, or low knowledge or to agreement or disagreement (opposition) to women's liberation are based on the Knowledge Scale and on the Women's Liberation Agree-Disagree Scale, respectively. Each scale is divided into three categories to indicate degree of knowledge or agreement.

2. The conservative end of this continuum might be described as that segment of the population consistently opposed to change in the status quo. At the other end are men who maintain that alternative

standards of attitudes and behavior are superior. Somewhat in between is the "liberal," who often upholds attitudes of change, but
frequently maintains the status quo when it comes to behavior (as
do some radicals) .

13. MEN'S CONSCIOUSNESS-RAISING: TOOLS FOR BEYOND MASCULINITY

1. Albert Ellis and Robert Harper, *A Guide to Rational Living in an
   Irrational World* (Englewood Cliffs, N.J.: Prentice-Hall, 1961) .
2. *Ibid.,* p. 5.
3. *Ibid.,* p. 6.
4. See, for example: Alfred Adler, *Superiority and Social Interest*
   (New York: Viking Press, 1973) ; Erich Fromm, *Escape from Freedom* (New York: Farrar and Rinehart, 1941) ; Karen Horney,
   Feminine Psychology (New York: Norton, 1967) ; Otto Rank, *Truth
   and Reality* (New York: A. A. Knopf, 1936) ; and Harry Stack
   Sullivan, *The Interpersonal Theory of Psychiatry,* ed. by H. S.
   Perry and M. L. Gawel (New York: Norton, 1953) .
5. Gail Sheehy, "A City Kind of Love," *New York* Magazine, February
   16, 1970.
6. Vivian Gornick, "The Next Great Moment in History Is Theirs,"
   in *The Village Voice,* November 1969.

15. ADDITIONAL PROBLEMS, TOPICS AND TECHNIQUES IN
RUNNING CONSCIOUSNESS-RAISING GROUPS

1. Jerome Kagan, in Hoffman, *op. cit.,* p. 152.
2. Nancy M. Henley, "The Politics of Touch," paper presented at the
   1970 meeting of the American Psychological Association, available
   from Dr. Henley at 5401 Wilkens Avenue, Baltimore, Maryland.
3. Dr. Mary Calderone is director of the Sex Information and Educational Council of the U.S. The quote is from "It's Really the Men
   Who Need Liberating," in *Life,* September 4, 1970.
4. For more details on marriage contracts see "A Marriage Agreement," by Alix Shulman, in Sookie Stambler, ed., *Women's Liberation* (New York: Ace Books, 1970) .

Bibliography of Resources*

SOCIALIZATION

Leon F. Fannin and Marshall B. Clinard. "Difference in the Conception of Self as a Male among Lower and Middle Class Delinquents." *Social Problems* 13:205–214 (1966).

Ruth E. Hartley. "Sex-Role Pressures and the Socialization of the Male Child." *Psychological Research* 5:457–468 (1959).

Miriam M. Johnson. "Sex Role Learning in the Nuclear Family." *Child Development* 34:319–334 (1963). Good references.

William E. Know and Harriet J. Kupferer. "A Discontinuity in the Socialization of Males in the United States." *Merrill-Palmer Quarterly* 17:251–261 (1971).

Paul H. Mussen. "Long-Term Consequences of Masculinity of Interest in Adolescence." *Journal of Consulting Psychology* 26 (5):435–440 (1962).

Joe Pleck, "Is Brotherhood Possible?" In N. Glazer Malbin, ed., *Old Family/New Family: Interpersonal Relationships.* (New York: Van Nostrand Reinhold, in press).

UNESCO, "The Embattled Human Male," *Impact of Science on Society* 21 (1):55–62 (1971).

MEN AND CHILDREN

Joan Aldous. "Occupational Characteristics and Male Role Performance in the Family." *Journal of Marriage and the Family* 31:707–712 (November 1969).

* Bibliography compiled with the assistance of Joe Pleck, 1974.

Jerry J. Bigner. "Fathering: Research and Practical Implications." *The Family Coordinator,* October 1969, pp. 357–362.

Erik Gronseth. "The Breadwinner Trap," in L. Howe, ed., *The Future of the Family* (New York: Simon and Schuster, 1972), pp. 175–191.

Elizabeth Herzog and Cecilia E. Sudia. "Families Without Fathers," *Childhood Education,* January 1972, pp. 175–181.

J. G. Howells. "Fallacies in Child Care—That Fathering Is Unimportant." *Acta Paedopsychiatrica* 37 (2-3):46–55 (1970).

P. Lee and A. Wolinsky. "Male Teachers of Young Children: A Preliminary Empirical Study." *Young Children,* August 1973, pp. 342–353.

David L. Levi, Helm Stierlin and Robert J. Savard. "Fathers and Sons: The Interlocking Crises of Integrity and Identity." *Psychiatry* 35:48–56 (February 1972).

P. H. Mussen. "The Influence of Father-Son Relationships on Adolescent Personality and Attitudes." *Journal of Child Psychoanalytic Psychiatry* 4:3–16 (1963).

John Nash. "The Father in Contemporary Culture and Current Psychological Literature." *Child Development* 36:261–297 (1965).

Joe Pleck. "New Concepts of Sex Role Identity," *Merrill-Palmer Quarterly,* in press.

Norma Radin. "Father-Child Interaction and the Intellectual Functioning of Four-Year-Old Boys." *Developmental Psychology* 6 (2):353–361 (1972).

K. Seifert. "Some Problems of Men in Child Care Center Work." *Child Welfare* 102:167–171 (1973).

RELATIONSHIPS AND ATTITUDES TOWARDS WOMEN

Nicholas Babchuk and Alan P. Bates. "The Primary Relations of Middle-Class Couples: A Study in Male Dominance." *American Sociological Review* 28:377–384 (June 1963).

Leslie H. Farber. "He Said, She Said." *Commentary,* March 1972, pp. 53–59.

T. N. Garland. "The Better Half? The Male in the Dual Profession Family." In C. Safilios-Rothschild, ed., *Toward a Sociology of Women* (Lexington, Maine: Xerox College Publishing Co., 1972), pp. 199–215.

Nancy M. Henley. "Power, Sex and Non-Verbal Communication." *Berkeley Journal of Sociology,* Vol. 18 (1973–74), pp. 1ff.

Eugene Nadler and William R. Morrow. "Authoritarian Attitudes Toward Women, and Their Correlates." *The Journal of Social Psychology* 49:113–123 (1959).

Ruth Hill Useem, et al. "The Function of Neighboring for the Middle-Class Male." *Human Organization* 19:68–76 (1960).

MEN'S LIBERATION, CONSCIOUSNESS-RAISING

Warren Farrell. "Guidelines for Consciousness-Raising." *Ms.*, February 1973.

Warren Farrell. "Male Consciousness and the Anti-Power Culture," *Sociological Focus*, Winter 1971.

Warren Farrell. "Women's and Men's Liberation Groups: Political Power Within the System and Outside the System." In Jane Jaquette, ed., *Women in Politics*. (N.Y.: John Wiley and Sons, 1974).

Jack Sawyer. "On Male Liberation." *Liberation* 15 (6,7,8), August–October 1970.

Jack Sawyer. "On the Politics of Male Liberation." *Win* 8 (13):20–21 (September 1, 1971).

Unbecoming Men. Pamphlet available from Time Changes Press, Pennwell Rd., Washington, N.J. 07882, $1.35 + $0.35 handling. This is a collection of personal experiences, written by a group.

EMPLOYMENT

Fernando Bartolome. "Executives as Human Beings." *Harvard Business Review*, November–December 1972, pp. 62–69. (See also article by Richard Walton in this issue.)

Carol S. Greenwald. "Part-Time Workers Can Bring Higher Productivity." *Harvard Business Review*, September–October 1973, p. 20ff.

Michael Silverstein. "Power and Sex Roles in Academia." *Journal of Applied Behavioral Science* 8 (5):536–563 (1972). Also in *Insurgent Sociologist*, Fall 1972, pp. 4–19.

Ruth and John Useem. "Social Stresses and Resources among Middle Management Men." From E. Gartley Jaco, Ed., *Patients, Physicians and Illness* (New York: Free Press, 1958).

SEXUALITY

Dennis Altman. *Homosexual* (New York: Avon paperback, 1973).

Don Clark. "Homosexual Encounter in All-Male Groups." From L. Solomon and B. Berzon, *New Perspectives on Encounter Groups* (San Francisco: Jossey-Bass, Inc., 1972).

Steven G. Cole and David Bryon. "A Review of Information Relevant to Vasectomy Counselors." *The Family Coordinator*, April 1973, pp. 215–221.

Paul Gillette. *The Vasectomy Information Manual.* (New York: Outerbridge and Lazard, Inc., a subsidiary of Dutton Publishing, 1972).

Paul Gillette. *Vasectomy: The Male Sterilization Operation* (New York: Paperback Library, 1972).

Philip Roen. *Male Sexual Health, Illustrated* (New York: William Morrow & Co., 1974).

Roberta Steiner. "The Sacred Bull: A Bibliography on Male Birth Control." *Synergy* #40 (Spring 1973). Hard to find, but available from San Francisco Public Library.

George Weinberg. *Society and the Healthy Homosexual* (New York: St. Martin's Press, 1972).

MENTAL AND PHYSICAL HEALTH

Jack O. Balswick and Charles W. Peek. "The Inexpressive Male: a Tragedy of American Society." *The Family Coordinator* 20:363–368 (October 1971).

Sidney Jourard. "Some Lethal Aspects of the Male Role." Chapter 6 of *The Transparent Self* (Princeton: Van Nostrand, 1964), pp. 46–55.

Martha Weinman Lear. "Is There a Male Menopause?" *The New York Times Magazine,* January 28, 1973.

Daniel Levinson. "The Male Mid-Life Decade," in *Life History Research in Psychopathology*, Vol. II, ed. David Ricks (Minneapolis: University of Minnesota Press, 1974).

Estelle Ramey. "Men's Cycles." *Ms.,* Spring 1972. 8ff.

Arthur B. Shostak. "Middle-Aged Working Class Americans at Home." *Occupational Mental Health* 2 (3):2–7 (February 1972).

THE BLACK MALE

Jean Carey Bond and Pat Peery. "Has the Black Man Been Castrated?" From Robert Staples, *The Black Family: Essays and Studies* (Belmont, Calif.: Wadsworth, 1971), pp. 140–144.

Nathan Hare. "The Frustrated Masculinity of the Negro Male." From Robert Staples, ed., *The Black Family: Essays and Studies* (Belmont, Calif.: Wadsworth, 1971), pp. 131–134.

RESOURCES

Brother: A Forum for Men against Sexism (magazine and collective). Write to P.O. Box 4387, Berkeley, California 94704. $5.00 supporting subscription.

Brothers: A Men's Liberation Newsletter. C/O Rising Free, 197 King's Cross Road, London WC1, England.

Human Studies Bibliography. Includes large men's studies bibliography. Write to David Ferriero, M.I.T. Humanities Library, Cambridge, Massachusetts 02139.

KNOW, INC. Packet of articles on men's liberation. P.O. Box 86031, Pittsburgh, Pennsylvania 15221.

Masculine Mystique Task Force (NOW) packet: literature, bibliography and information on starting men's groups. Send $3.00 to NOW ($2.00 if member of NOW) at 5 South Wabash St., Suite 1615, Chicago, Illinois 60603.

Men's Anthology Collective. Soliciting manuscripts on masculinity for an anthology to be published in 1976. Write Amherst Men's Center, Jones Library, Amherst, Massachusetts 01002.

Ms. Magazine. Column on men almost every month—usually excellent.

Vocations for Social Change, *Workforce.* Has men's liberation section with current conferences, organizations and publications. Updated every two months. Write 4911 Telegraph Ave., Oakland, California 94609.

WIN Magazine, special issue on men's liberation, April 1974. Write Box 547, Rifton, New York 12471. Send $0.20 plus postage.

FILMS

Antioch Documentary Films, "A Male Condition" (1974). Antioch College, Yellow Springs, Ohio 45387.

"The American Male, Exploring Male Consciousness," a slide/music presentation by Rolphe Buzzell and Perry Kaufman. Write to Buzzell, 7510 Northeast Mason St., Portland, Oregon 97218.

"Masculinity" (1974), a four-part filmstrip series, available from Schloat Productions, 150 White Plains Rd., Tarrytown, New York.

"Sticky My Fingers, Fleet My Feet" (Time-Life, 1970) and "A Day Off" (1973) —two films available through University of Michigan Audio-Visual Education Center, 416 Fourth St., Ann Arbor, Michigan 48103.

GENERAL BOOKS

Robert Brannon and Deborah David., eds. *The 49% Majority* (New York: Addison-Wesley, forthcoming).

Myron Brenton. *The American Male* (New York: Fawcett Premier paperback, 1966).

Beverly Cassara. *Changing Male Roles,* forthcoming.

Edmund Dahlstrom, ed. *The Changing Roles of Men and Women* (London: Duckworth, 1967).

Marc Fasteau. *The Male Machine* (New York: McGraw-Hill, 1974).

Michael Korda. *Male Chauvinism: How It Works* (New York: Random House, 1973).

Eleanor Maccoby, ed. *The Development of Sex Differences* (Stanford, Calif.: Stanford University Press, 1966) . Contains an extensive bibliography, annotated.

Gene Marine. *Male Guide to Women's Liberation* (New York: Holt, Rinehart, and Winston, 1973) .

Joe Pleck and Jack Sawyer, eds. *Men and Masculinity* (New York: Prentice-Hall Spectrum Books, forthcoming) .

Anne Steinmann and David J. Fox. *The Male Dilemma* (New York: Jason Aronson, 1973) .

Bibliography for Starting
a Child-Care Center

1. *How to Start and Operate a Day Care Center.* E. Belle Evans, Vivian Shub, and Marlene Weinstein. (Boston: Beacon Press, 1971; $6.95 hardcover; $3.95 paper).

• Probably the best book to start with, including advice on forming a parent coop day-care center as well as a center with professional staff.

2. *Manual on Organization, Financing, and Administration of Day Care Centers in New York City.* For community groups, their lawyers, and other consultants, revised 2nd ed., 1971.

• Although it focuses on New York City, this book has wide applicability and includes sections on curriculum, materials, bookkeeping, health care, and so forth. ($5.00 from Bookstore, Bank Street College, 610 W. 12th St., New York City 10025.)

3. *Day Care Manual Series* will have two new publications ready by the publication date of this book. *Family Day Care* (about 100 pages), written to help parents start home-based centers, and *Preschool-Age Children* ($1.00 for each should cover publication cost). The series includes seven additional booklets, for a total of $5.00. Write to the Superintendent of Government Documents, U.S. Government Printing Office, Washington, D.C. 20402.

4. A report outlining 38 child-care centers' methods for cutting costs is available from the Ford Foundation-sponsored Educational Facilities Laboratory, 477 Madison Ave., New York City 10022.

5. *Hustling Resources for Day Care* by James A. Levine—available from Day Care Consultation Service, Bank Street College (address below).
• Strategies for getting government, foundation, industry, and volunteer support.

6. For practical ideas to help family day-care parents have fun and teach children simultaneously, write for the "Recipes for Fun" series and their bibliography at Parents as Resource, 464 Central St., Northfield, Virginia.

7. *Day Care for Administrators, Teachers, and Parents.* Richard Ruopp et al. (M.I.T. Press, 1973; $10.00).
• Offers a series of alternative ways for arranging day care. Creative and excellent.

Other important resources which provide consultation and materials on geting a child-care program together and developing curriculum:

1. Day Care and Child Development Council
   1401 K St., N.W.
   Washington, D.C. 20003
   (Ask for their *Resources for Day Care* and resource center closest to you.)

2. Black Child Development Institute, Inc.
   1028 Connecticut Ave., N.W.
   Washington, D.C.

3. James Levine
   Day Care Consultation Service
   Bank Street College of Education
   610 W. 112th St.
   New York City 10025
   • Working actively to help people organize not only day-care centers, but information and referral services, coops, and other informal or underground arrangements.

4. Information Referral Service
   Child Care Resource Center
   123 Mt. Auburn St.
   Cambridge, Massachusetts 02138
   (617) 547-9861

Appendix: Scoring Mechanism and Interpretation for Questionnaire

1) No score
2) 3, 2, 1, 0
3) 0, 1, 2, 3
4) 0, 1, 2, 3
5) 3, 1, 0
6) 0, 1, 2, 3, 4
7) Self-evaluate
8) a) 2, 0, 1
   b) 2, 0, 1
9) 3, $2\frac{1}{2}$, 2, $1\frac{1}{2}$ 1, 0
10) 3, $2\frac{1}{2}$, 2, $1\frac{1}{2}$, 1, 0
11) 3, $2\frac{1}{2}$ 2, $1\frac{1}{2}$, 1, 0
12) 2, $1\frac{1}{2}$, 1, $\frac{1}{2}$, 0, 0
13) 3, $2\frac{1}{2}$, 2, $1\frac{1}{2}$, 1, 0
14) 4, 3, 2, 1, $\frac{1}{2}$, 0
15) 0, 2, 1
16) 0, 1, 2

17) a.) 3, 2, 1, 0, 0
    b.) 2, 0, 1
    c.) 1, 0, 0, 0, 3, 0, 2
    d.) Intellectual: 3, 1, 0
        Gut: 4, 2, 0
18) a.) 1, 0
    b.) 2, 0
    c.) 3, 0
    d.) 1, 0
    e.) 2, 0
    f.) 3, 0
19) 0, 3, 2, 1
20) 1) 0, 2
    2) 0, 2
21) 2, 0, 4, 3, 3
22) 0, 0, 0, 3, 1, 1

PART II. ATTITUDES TOWARD MEN AND MASCULINITY

1) No score
2) 0, 1, 2, 3, 0

3) 3 for first reversal, 5 additional for second reversal

4) 5, 3, 1, 0
5) 3 if you can write it out, 0, 0, 0 for other responses
6) a) 0, 1, 2
   b) 0, 1, 2
   c) 0, 1, 2
   d) 0, 1, 2
7) 0, 1, 3, 4
8) 0, 4, 1
9) 0, 1, 3
10) 0, 1, 3, 6, 10
11) 3, 2, 1, 0
12) 3, 2, 1, 0
13) 3, 2, 1, 0

14) 0, 2, 4
15) 3, 0
16) Intellectual: 2, 1, 0
    Gut: 3, 1, 0
17) 0, 1, 3, 1, 0
18) 0, 3
19) 4, 3, 2, 1, 0, 6
20) No scoring—see Chapter 6.
21) 0, 1, 2, 3
22) 3, 2, 1, 0
23) 4, 3, 2, 0
24) 0, 1, 3, 8
25) 3, 0
26) 2, 0, 1

After you've scored yourself, review the questionnaire with an attaché;* see if te has the same view of you as you do. The scoring interpretation, like becoming liberated, has few pat, automatic answers. Here are a few possible interpretations:

160–184   You are beyond masculinity, or you are fooling yourself, or you are a woman.

140–159   You've Come a Long Way, Baby, or you weren't brought up like a "natural man," or you're fooling yourself, or the men's liberation movement needs you.

120–139   You're open enough to benefit from a consciousness-raising group, and you're closed enough to benefit from a consciousness-raising group.

100–119   An average man—insecure enough to want the security of rigid roles, secure enough not to overtly desire the oppressiveness of sex roles; uninformed enough not to think sex roles are that oppressive.

80–99   A threatened man; was probably persuaded to read this book by a woman.

60–79   An honest, unliberated man.

below 60   If you answered the whole questionnaire, you are probably more open than you are giving yourself credit for.

* See "Introducing Human Vocabulary."

Index

About the Author

DR. WARREN FARRELL ran a successful bookstore in New Jersey, was selected by President Johnson as one of the country's outstanding young educators in 1965, and has taught at Rutgers, American and Georgetown Universities. He is presently teaching the Sociology of Sex Roles at Brooklyn College and a course on consciousness-raising at Columbia University. He received his Ph.D. from N.Y.U. in 1974, having completed (with distinction) a dissertation on changing men's attitudes toward women's liberation.

Elected three times to the Board of Directors of the National Organization for Women (NOW) in New York City, and coordinator of the Task Force on the Masculine Mystique for NOW, he has started over one hundred men's and mixed consciousness-raising groups throughout the country. (Warren organized the First National Conference on the Masculine Mystique, which provided an organizational base for a men's liberation movement. In 1973 he left his full-time teaching post at Rutgers to move for his wife's career opportunities while he taught part time.)